AI and Learning Analytics in Distance Learning

Henrique S. Mamede
INESC TEC, Universidade Aberta, Portugal

Arnaldo Santos
INESC TEC, Universidade Aberta, Portugal

IGI Global
Scientific Publishing
Publishing Tomorrow's Research Today

Vice President of Editorial	Melissa Wagner
Managing Editor of Acquisitions	Mikaela Felty
Managing Editor of Book Development	Jocelynn Hessler
Production Manager	Mike Brehm
Cover Design	Phillip Shickler

Published in the United States of America by
IGI Global Scientific Publishing
701 East Chocolate Avenue
Hershey, PA, 17033, USA
Tel: 717-533-8845
Fax: 717-533-8661
Website: https://www.igi-global.com E-mail: cust@igi-global.com

Library of Congress Cataloging-in-Publication Data

Names: Mamede, Henrique Pereira São, 1965- editor. | Santos, Arnaldo, 1965- editor.
Title: AI and learning analytics in distance learning / edited by: Henrique Sao Mamede, Arnaldo Manuel Pinto dos Santos.
Other titles: Artificial intelligence and learning analytics in distance learning
Description: Hershey, PA : IGI Global Scientific Publishing, [2025] | Includes bibliographical references and index. | Summary: "This book aims to explore the synergy between AI and LA in the context of distance learning. It will provide a comprehensive overview of the key concepts, technologies, and methodologies involved"-- Provided by publisher.
Identifiers: LCCN 2024054520 (print) | LCCN 2024054521 (ebook) | ISBN 9798369371954 (hardcover) | ISBN 9798369371961 (paperback) | ISBN 9798369371978 (ebook)
Subjects: LCSH: Distance education. | Artificial intelligence. | Learning.
Classification: LCC LC5803.L43 A53 2025 (print) | LCC LC5803.L43 (ebook) | DDC 371.35--dc23/eng/20250211
LC record available at https://lccn.loc.gov/2024054520
LC ebook record available at https://lccn.loc.gov/2024054521
British Cataloguing in Publication Data
A Cataloguing in Publication record for this book is available from the British Library.

Table of Contents

Detailed Table of Contents

The integration of artificial intelligence (AI) into distance learning presents significant challenges and opportunities. While AI can enhance personalized learning, improve engagement, and streamline administrative processes, it also poses obstacles such as data privacy concerns, lack of infrastructure, and resistance to change among educators. This chapter explores these dynamics by examining current literature and case studies on AI applications in distance education. By identifying best practices and potential pitfalls, this study aims to provide a framework for institutions looking to harness AI's transformative potential while addressing ethical, technical, and pedagogical challenges in online learning environments.

E-learning assessments play a crucial role in evaluating the progress and understanding of students in online education. Properly crafted evaluations aid in quantifying learning objectives, pinpointing opportunities for enhancement, and guaranteeing that learners are gaining the essential abilities and comprehension. The study's ensembled machine learning model offers a useful prediction model for a supportive learning environment. Minmax normalization is a common technique used prior to model fitting to normalize the pre-processed data. For the variables or input data to contribute equally to the model fitting, they must be regulated since they are restrained at different scales. The evaluation plan's recommended prediction model for end user satisfaction. There are 150 male and 150 female participants in the 300-person ensembled classifier. comprising professors, Ph.D. research scholars, UG and PG students, and other students.

This chapter examines the satisfaction levels of distance education students in accounting programs regarding the quality of their educational experience. As online learning becomes increasingly prevalent, understanding the factors that influence student satisfaction is crucial for educational institutions striving to enhance their offerings. Through a mixed-methods approach, including quantitative surveys and qualitative interviews, this research identifies key elements impacting satisfaction, such as course content, instructional quality, technological support, and community interaction. Findings reveal that while students value the flexibility of distance education, challenges related to engagement and support persist. The chapter emphasizes the importance of continuous improvement in curriculum design, faculty training, and student services to foster a more satisfying learning environment. By addressing these factors, institutions can enhance student outcomes and retention in distance accounting programs.

The integration of artificial intelligence (AI) technologies into education has emerged as a promising avenue to revolutionize the learning experience. With the use of AI tools and methodologies, teachers can tailor educational pathways to suit their students' individual needs, respond to differences in teaching style and provide prompt feedback so that they are more engaged and comprehended. Various applications of artificial intelligence in the field of education such as intelligent tutoring systems, adaptive learning platforms, and natural language processing tools are examined to highlight their effectiveness for dealing with educational challenges and supporting student success. This chapter looks at the potential of artificial intelligence for improving education practices, with a focus on increasing learning processes and optimising student results. It highlights the importance of responsible use of AI to reduce biases and ensure equal opportunities for all in order to address concerns about ethics and possible problems related to integration of AI into education.

This chapter dives into the extraordinary capability of artificial intelligence driven customized learning in upgrading understudy commitment and results, especially inside the setting of distance training. The chapter begins by outlining the significance of personalized learning in fostering individualized educational experiences and addressing the diverse requirements of students. It investigates key parts and advantages of customized getting the hang of, outlining how simulated intelligence innovations, for example, AI, versatile calculations, and regular language handling customize and upgrade the educational experience. The section likewise features different computer-based intelligence driven apparatuses, including versatile learning stages and smart coaching frameworks, that altogether add to understudy inspiration and interest. It also looks at how AI can simplify grading and assessment, provide real-time feedback, and overcome obstacles when implementing AI in education.

This chapter delves into how AI and learning analytics are reshaping distance learning by enabling a more personalized, adaptive, and data-informed educational experience. AI-driven tools allow educators to analyze student behavior, engagement, and performance, facilitating timely support and targeted interventions that enhance learning outcomes. Learning analytics helps predict challenges, enabling proactive measures that keep students on track, while also providing insights into diverse learning needs. Through AI, online education becomes more interactive and efficient, as automation handles routine tasks and customizes content to suit individual progress and preferences. This approach not only improves the efficacy of distance learning but also drives a shift in traditional educational methods toward a more inclusive and responsive framework. As educational institutions adopt these technologies, understanding their capabilities and limitations becomes essential for effectively advancing digital learning and supporting diverse learner success.

access and fair learning outcomes. The future of distance learning lies in responsible integration of AI and LA, creating immersive and inclusive educational experiences.

Preface

INTRODUCTION

In today's rapidly evolving educational landscape, the integration of Artificial Intelligence (AI) and learning analytics into distance learning represents not merely a technological upgrade but a paradigm shift. As institutions worldwide grapple with the challenges and opportunities presented by digital transformation, this book—AI and Learning Analytics in Distance Learning—emerges as a timely and essential resource. It compiles a series of peer-reviewed articles that explore innovative strategies, cutting-edge research, and practical implementations at the intersection of AI, learning analytics, and distance education.

Over the past decade, the realm of distance learning has grown from a marginal educational alternative into a mainstream platform that redefines how we access, consume, and engage with knowledge. The convergence of AI and learning analytics with distance learning not only enhances the quality and personalization of education but also addresses critical questions about accessibility, engagement, and quality assurance in a globalized learning environment. This volume seeks to capture the essence of these transformative processes, offering readers a comprehensive insight into current trends, methodologies, and forward-thinking applications that are reshaping the future of education.

At its core, this book examines the dynamic interplay between AI, learning analytics, and distance learning. AI encompasses a broad array of technologies—from machine learning algorithms to natural language processing and intelligent tutoring systems—that are being deployed to enrich educational experiences. Learning analytics, on the other hand, involves the collection, analysis, and application of data derived from learners' interactions with digital platforms. When combined, these disciplines provide the analytical backbone and adaptive intelligence necessary to create learning environments that are both personalized and scalable.

The articles presented in this volume cover a spectrum of topics: from high-level theoretical discussions to practical case studies. They address essential questions such as how AI can be leveraged to overcome traditional educational challenges, how learning analytics can drive continuous improvement, and how these technologies can be integrated to offer innovative, data-informed approaches to teaching and learning. By bringing together diverse perspectives and methodologies, the book underscores the importance of an interdisciplinary approach to harnessing technology in education.

In the current era, digital transformation is reshaping every facet of society, and education is no exception. The shift toward online platforms, accelerated by global events and technological advancements, has propelled distance learning to the forefront of modern pedagogy. As educators and administrators seek to ensure that learning remains engaging, effective, and accessible, AI and learning analytics have become indispensable tools. They offer the potential to not only tailor educational content to individual needs but also to identify and address gaps in learning in real time.

This subject matter resonates across various domains—from higher education and K–12 systems to corporate training and lifelong learning initiatives. The ubiquity of digital devices, widespread internet access, and the increasing sophistication of data collection techniques have created an unprecedented opportunity to rethink traditional educational paradigms. In this context, the strategies, research findings, and innovative practices explored in this volume are not isolated academic exercises; they are part of a broader movement that is fundamentally transforming how education is delivered and experienced across the globe.

This book is intended for a diverse audience that spans multiple sectors of the education ecosystem. Educators, academic administrators, and policymakers will find practical insights into how AI and learning analytics can be integrated into curriculum design, instructional delivery, and institutional strategy. Researchers and scholars in the fields of educational technology, data science, and instructional design will appreciate the rigorous methodologies and evidence-based discussions that underpin the contributions in this volume. Additionally, technology developers and practitioners involved in creating e-learning solutions will discover innovative approaches that can inform the design and implementation of next-generation educational tools.

By addressing both the theoretical foundations and the pragmatic applications of these technologies, the book serves as a bridge between research and practice. Whether you are involved in strategic decision-making at an institutional level, engaged in scholarly research, or directly implementing digital learning solutions in your classroom or organization, the insights contained within these pages are designed to inspire, inform, and challenge conventional approaches to education.

BOOK ORGANIZATION

The opening chapter lays the groundwork for the entire volume. It features a singular, yet comprehensive article—"Challenges and Opportunities of Implementing AI in Distance Learning"—that provides a critical overview of the field. This article addresses the multifaceted challenges that institutions face when integrating AI into existing distance learning frameworks, from infrastructural limitations and pedagogical shifts to ethical and privacy concerns. Simultaneously, it highlights the myriad opportunities that AI presents, such as enhanced personalization, improved student outcomes, and the potential to democratize education. By establishing a robust contextual framework, this chapter primes readers for a deeper exploration of subsequent topics, emphasizing both the transformative promise and the inherent complexities of adopting AI in educational settings.

After, the book delves into the practical dimensions of integrating advanced technologies into distance learning environments. It features two pivotal articles:

"Ensembled Machine Learning Approach to Check User Satisfaction Towards Assessment Evaluation in E-Learning"

This article introduces an innovative methodological framework that utilizes ensemble machine learning techniques to assess and improve user satisfaction. By employing a multi-model approach, the research demonstrates how nuanced data analysis can yield actionable insights into user experience, thereby informing the design and delivery of more effective assessment strategies. The findings offer significant implications for educators seeking to enhance the reliability and validity of online evaluations.

"Distance Education Students' Satisfaction with Education Quality in Accounting Programs"

Complementing the technical focus of the first article, this study provides an empirical analysis of student satisfaction within the context of accounting programs offered through distance education. By exploring the variables that influence perceptions of educational quality, the article contributes to a deeper understanding of how institutional practices and digital platform design can impact learner outcomes. Together, these articles offer a balanced perspective on the strategic and operational aspects of implementing AI and learning analytics in distance education.

Recognizing that one of the most compelling promises of AI in education is its capacity for personalization, Chapter 3 is dedicated to exploring strategies for enhancing student engagement through tailored learning experiences. This chapter is comprised of four articles, each contributing a unique perspective to the discourse on personalization:

"Personalized Learning and Student Engagement: Leveraging AI for Enhanced Learning Experiences in Distance Education"

This article examines how AI can be harnessed to design learning environments that adapt to the individual needs of students. By analyzing case studies and deploying theoretical models, the authors illustrate how adaptive algorithms can transform generic course content into personalized learning journeys that boost both engagement and achievement.

"Creating Engaging and Personalized Learning Experiences in Distance Education: AI and Learning Analytics"

Building on the previous discussion, this article highlights the symbiotic relationship between AI and learning analytics. It discusses how real-time data can inform the customization of content and instructional strategies, thereby creating an immersive learning environment that is both dynamic and responsive to student feedback.

"Personalised Learning Experiences in Distance Learning"

This contribution delves into the operational aspects of personalization, discussing practical methodologies and technological frameworks that can be implemented to achieve individualized learning outcomes. It provides educators with a roadmap for integrating personalization into their teaching practices, emphasizing both the benefits and the challenges of this approach.

"AI-Driven Personalized Learning-Enhancing Student Engagement and Outcomes"

Rounding out the chapter, this article presents empirical evidence on the impact of AI-driven personalization on student engagement and academic performance. Through rigorous analysis, it demonstrates how targeted interventions and customized learning pathways can lead to measurable improvements in learner satisfaction and success.

Collectively, these articles underscore the transformative potential of personalized learning in distance education. They provide a comprehensive exploration of how AI-driven approaches can be implemented to create more engaging, effective, and learner-centered educational experiences.

The final part of the book shifts focus to the critical role of data in informing educational practices and driving continuous improvement. With an emphasis on evidence-based decision-making, this chapter includes three articles that explore the processes of data collection, analysis, and application in the context of learning analytics:

"Leveraging AI and Learning Analytics for Enhanced Distance Learning: Transformation in Education"

This article lays the foundation for understanding how AI and learning analytics serve as catalysts for educational transformation. It explores the overarching trends and technological advancements that are redefining the digital learning landscape, emphasizing the strategic importance of data-driven innovation in shaping future educational practices.

"Integrating AI and Learning Analytics in Distance Learning: Strategies for Educators and Institutions"

Focusing on the practical integration of technology, this contribution provides a detailed roadmap for educators and administrators. It outlines actionable strategies for embedding AI and learning analytics into existing educational frameworks, highlighting the operational, technical, and pedagogical considerations that must be addressed to ensure a seamless transition.

"From Data to Action: How AI and Learning Analytics are Shaping the Future of Distance Education"

Concluding the chapter, this article bridges the gap between theoretical data analysis and practical application. It discusses how insights derived from data can be translated into concrete actions that enhance the quality and effectiveness of distance education. The article serves as a call to action for institutions to embrace data-informed practices as a means to drive continuous improvement and innovation.

CONCLUSION: IMPACT AND CONTRIBUTIONS TO THE FIELD

The confluence of AI, learning analytics, and distance learning represents one of the most significant shifts in the educational landscape in recent years. This book not only documents the state-of-the-art in these domains but also provides a comprehensive roadmap for educators, researchers, and policymakers aiming to navigate the complexities of digital transformation. Each chapter contributes a vital piece to the puzzle—ranging from theoretical frameworks and empirical analyses to practical strategies and future directions.

By synthesizing diverse perspectives and methodologies, AI and Learning Analytics in Distance Learning serves as a catalyst for both reflection and action. It challenges traditional paradigms, encourages innovative thinking, and provides evidence-based strategies that can be implemented across a variety of educational contexts. The insights offered within these pages have far-reaching implications, fostering a deeper understanding of how AI and learning analytics can be leveraged to enhance educational quality, improve learner engagement, and promote equitable access to knowledge.

For educators and administrators, the practical strategies outlined in this volume offer tangible guidance on how to design and implement technology-driven initiatives that cater to the evolving needs of diverse learner populations. For researchers, the rigorous methodologies and data-driven analyses presented here open new avenues for exploration, paving the way for further innovations and breakthroughs in the field. And for policymakers and technology developers, the insights provided serve as a reminder of the profound impact that well-integrated technological solutions can have on the future of education.

In a world where education is increasingly mediated by digital technologies, the challenges are as significant as the opportunities. This book makes a substantial contribution by addressing both the promise and the pitfalls of integrating AI and learning analytics into distance learning. It stands as a testament to the potential of these technologies to transform educational practices, ensuring that learning remains accessible, engaging, and effective in an era defined by rapid technological change.

As you embark on this journey through the diverse and dynamic chapters of this volume, I invite you to reflect on the implications of these advances for your own practice, research, and vision of the future of education. May the insights contained herein inspire you to not only adopt new technologies but also to reimagine what is possible in the pursuit of knowledge and lifelong learning.

In closing, it is our sincere hope that this volume will serve as both a resource and an inspiration—a bridge between theoretical inquiry and practical application that ultimately enriches the field of distance education. By engaging with the challenges and opportunities presented by AI and learning analytics, we are not merely adapting to change; we are actively shaping the future of education for generations to come.

Henrique S. Mamede
Universidade Aberta, Portugal

Arnaldo Santos
Universidade Aberta, Portugal

Chapter 1
Challenges and Opportunities of Implementing AI in Distance Learning

Anthony Savio Herminio da Piedade Fernandes
Trading Equations, India

ABSTRACT

The integration of artificial intelligence (AI) into distance learning presents significant challenges and opportunities. While AI can enhance personalized learning, improve engagement, and streamline administrative processes, it also poses obstacles such as data privacy concerns, lack of infrastructure, and resistance to change among educators. This chapter explores these dynamics by examining current literature and case studies on AI applications in distance education. By identifying best practices and potential pitfalls, this study aims to provide a framework for institutions looking to harness AI's transformative potential while addressing ethical, technical, and pedagogical challenges in online learning environments.

LITERATURE REVIEW

Introduction

The rapid advancement of technology has revolutionized various sectors, with education being no exception. The integration of Artificial Intelligence (AI) in distance learning offers promising opportunities, yet it also presents substantial challenges.

DOI: 10.4018/979-8-3693-7195-4.ch001

This literature review examines the existing body of research on the challenges and opportunities associated with implementing AI in distance learning environments.

Opportunities of AI in Distance Learning

1. Personalized Learning: Personalized learning is one of the most significant opportunities presented by AI in distance learning. By analyzing learners' behavior and preferences, AI systems can tailor educational content to meet individual needs (Chen et al., 2020). Studies have shown that personalized learning pathways can enhance student engagement and academic performance (Kumar et al., 2021).
2. Enhanced Engagement: AI can increase student engagement through intelligent tutoring systems and chatbots that provide real-time assistance and feedback (Gonzalez et al., 2021). These technologies can facilitate interactive learning experiences, making distance education more appealing to students.
3. Administrative Efficiency: AI can streamline administrative processes, reducing the burden on educators and allowing them to focus more on teaching (Zawacki-Richter et al., 2019). Automated grading systems and enrollment management tools can enhance institutional efficiency, leading to better resource allocation.
4. Data-Driven Insights: The integration of AI in distance learning provides valuable data analytics that can inform instructional design and curriculum development (Almulla et al., 2022). Institutions can leverage these insights to enhance teaching strategies and improve learning outcomes.

Challenges of AI in Distance Learning

1. Data Privacy Concerns: The use of AI in distance learning raises significant data privacy issues. The collection and analysis of students' personal data may lead to potential breaches of privacy (Williamson & Piattoeva, 2021). Institutions must ensure compliance with data protection regulations while fostering trust among students.
2. Infrastructure Limitations: Implementing AI technologies requires robust digital infrastructure, which may not be available in all educational settings (Pappano, 2020). Limited access to high-speed internet and modern devices can hinder the effective integration of AI in distance learning.
3. Resistance to Change: Educators and institutions may resist adopting AI technologies due to fear of job displacement or a lack of familiarity with the technology (Brynjolfsson & McAfee, 2014). Overcoming this resistance necessitates comprehensive training and professional development initiatives.

4. Ethical Considerations: The use of AI in education raises ethical concerns regarding bias and equity (O'Neil, 2016). AI systems can perpetuate existing biases if not carefully designed and monitored, potentially leading to unequal learning opportunities for marginalized groups.

Conclusion

The integration of AI in distance learning presents a complex landscape of challenges and opportunities. While AI has the potential to enhance personalized learning, improve engagement, and increase administrative efficiency, it also poses significant challenges related to data privacy, infrastructure limitations, resistance to change, and ethical considerations. Future research should focus on developing best practices for implementing AI in distance learning, addressing the identified challenges, and exploring innovative solutions to harness the full potential of AI in education.

RESEARCH METHODOLOGY

The research methodology for this chapter will primarily involve a systematic literature review of secondary data sources. This will include:

1. Data Sources: The study will utilize peer-reviewed journal articles, conference papers, government reports, and credible online databases such as Google Scholar, JSTOR, and ERIC.
2. Data Selection: The selection criteria will include studies published within the last ten years focusing on AI applications in distance learning, emphasizing empirical research, case studies, and theoretical frameworks.
3. Data Analysis: The analysis will involve thematic coding to identify recurring themes and trends regarding the challenges and opportunities of AI in distance learning. This qualitative analysis will allow for a comprehensive understanding of the subject matter.
4. Synthesis: The findings from the literature will be synthesized to create a cohesive narrative that addresses the research questions, highlighting key challenges and opportunities.

1. INTRODUCTION

1.1 Background of AI in Education

Artificial Intelligence (AI) has significantly reshaped many industries, and education is no exception. In the context of education, AI refers to technologies that simulate human intelligence, performing tasks such as problem-solving, learning, and adapting over time. While AI has already transformed various sectors, its potential in distance learning is particularly notable. Distance learning, which allows students to learn from remote locations, has historically relied on technology to bridge the gap between educators and students. AI's ability to provide personalized learning experiences, automate administrative tasks, and offer data-driven insights makes it a valuable asset in this domain.

Distance learning has evolved significantly since its inception. Early distance education models involved correspondence courses that relied on postal services. With advancements in technology, particularly the internet, distance education transitioned into online learning platforms, virtual classrooms, and interactive educational tools. AI further enhances this transformation by offering intelligent systems that can personalize content, predict student performance, and facilitate more dynamic interactions between teachers and students.

1.2 Rationale for the Study

With the growing demand for flexible, accessible education, especially after the COVID-19 pandemic, distance learning has become more prominent than ever before. AI offers opportunities to address many of the challenges in traditional distance learning, such as lack of engagement, difficulty in personalizing instruction, and limitations in scalability. As more educational institutions adopt AI technologies, understanding the opportunities and challenges of implementing AI in distance learning becomes increasingly essential. This study seeks to fill this knowledge gap by exploring the dual facets of AI's impact on distance learning—its potential to enhance education and the hurdles that must be overcome to implement it effectively.

The successful integration of AI into distance learning offers an opportunity to significantly improve learning outcomes, access to education, and overall student satisfaction. However, challenges such as ethical concerns, privacy issues, and the need for appropriate infrastructure cannot be overlooked. Thus, a balanced exploration of both challenges and opportunities is necessary to develop strategies that maximize the benefits while mitigating the risks of AI in distance learning.

1.3 Objectives of the Chapter

The objectives of this chapter are as follows:

1. To explore how AI can enhance personalized learning experiences, increase engagement, and improve administrative processes in distance learning.
2. To analyze the barriers to effective AI integration, including data privacy concerns, infrastructure limitations, resistance to change among educators, and ethical considerations.
3. To offer practical recommendations for educational institutions seeking to implement AI in distance learning, addressing both challenges and opportunities.
4. To add to the existing body of knowledge regarding AI in education by providing a comprehensive analysis of its implications in distance learning.

1.4 Structure of the Chapter

The chapter will be organized into several key sections:

- Chapter 2 will provide an overview of distance learning, tracing its historical development, key characteristics, and current trends.
- Chapter 3 will delve into the opportunities that AI brings to distance learning, highlighting real-world applications and case studies.
- Chapter 4 will focus on the challenges of implementing AI, discussing critical issues such as data privacy, ethical concerns, and resistance from educators.
- Chapter 5 will analyze case studies of AI integration in distance learning, examining both successes and failures to identify best practices.
- Chapter 6 will present practical strategies for effectively implementing AI in distance learning, including training, ethical guidelines, and evaluation methods.
- Chapter 7 will offer conclusions and insights into the future of AI in distance education, along with policy recommendations.

This introduction sets the foundation for the rest of the chapter, outlining the importance of the topic and what the reader can expect in the subsequent sections. The balance between challenges and opportunities is emphasized, as well as the need for practical, data-driven recommendations for educators and policymakers.

2. OVERVIEW OF DISTANCE LEARNING

2.1 Definition and Characteristics of Distance Learning

Distance learning refers to an educational system where students and teachers are physically separated, relying on technology to facilitate interaction and instruction. This mode of learning typically allows students to engage in education from remote locations without needing to attend a physical classroom. Over the years, the defining characteristics of distance learning have evolved, and modern iterations incorporate various digital tools to make learning more flexible, accessible, and efficient.

Key characteristics of distance learning include:

a) Flexibility: Learners can access content at their convenience, making it easier for those balancing education with work or family responsibilities.
b) Accessibility: Distance learning breaks down geographical barriers, allowing learners from different regions to access the same educational materials.
c) Scalability: Institutions can scale their courses to accommodate larger numbers of students than in traditional classroom settings.
d) Self-Paced Learning: Many distance learning programs allow students to learn at their own pace, fostering a personalized learning experience.
e) Learner Autonomy: Since the physical presence of teachers is absent, students must take more responsibility for their learning, developing independent study skills.

Distance learning can take several forms, including synchronous (real-time interaction between teachers and students, such as live video classes) and asynchronous (students access pre-recorded lectures or course materials at their own convenience) methods. Many distance learning programs today use a hybrid model that combines both approaches, leveraging the benefits of real-time engagement and the flexibility of self-paced learning.

2.2 Historical Context

The concept of distance learning is not new. It can be traced back to the 19th century when correspondence courses were introduced to provide education to individuals in remote areas. These early programs relied on postal services to deliver educational materials and assignments to students, who would then return completed work to their instructors.

The late 20th century saw significant advances in distance learning due to the proliferation of television, radio, and early computer systems. Open universities, such as the UK's Open University (established in 1969), pioneered the use of broadcast media to reach learners across the nation. As personal computers became more widespread in the 1980s and 1990s, educational software and CD-ROMs became common tools for distance education, enhancing the interactive element of learning.

With the advent of the internet in the 1990s, distance learning entered a new phase. Online learning platforms allowed students to access content and interact with instructors and peers from anywhere in the world. This marked the beginning of e-learning as we know it today. The rise of massive open online courses (MOOCs) in the 2010s further democratized education by offering free or low-cost courses to learners globally.

2.3 Current Trends in Distance Learning

In recent years, distance learning has evolved rapidly, driven by technological advances and changing societal needs. The COVID-19 pandemic accelerated the shift toward online learning, forcing educational institutions across the globe to adopt remote teaching methods on an unprecedented scale. This sudden transition highlighted both the potential and challenges of distance learning, leading to innovations in educational technology (EdTech).

Some key trends in distance learning today include:

a) Learning Management Systems (LMS): Platforms like Moodle, Blackboard, and Google Classroom have become essential tools for managing courses, tracking student progress, and facilitating communication between students and teachers. LMS platforms enable educators to organize content, assignments, quizzes, and discussions in a streamlined, user-friendly manner.
b) Video Conferencing Tools: Applications such as Zoom, Microsoft Teams, and Google Meet have become integral to synchronous distance learning, allowing students and teachers to interact in real-time through virtual classrooms. These platforms offer features like breakout rooms, polls, and chat functions to enhance engagement.
c) Mobile Learning: With the increasing use of smartphones and tablets, many students now access educational content on mobile devices. Mobile-friendly courses and apps, such as Coursera and Duolingo, cater to this growing demand by providing learners with on-the-go access to materials.

d) Gamification: Educational platforms are incorporating gamification strategies, using game-like elements such as points, badges, and leaderboards to motivate learners and improve engagement. This has been particularly effective in fields such as language learning and STEM education.
e) Microlearning: Short, focused learning modules, or microlearning, have gained popularity, particularly for professional development and corporate training. These bite-sized lessons are designed to fit into the busy schedules of learners and often focus on specific skills or knowledge areas.
f) AI-Powered Learning: AI is increasingly being used to deliver personalized learning experiences by analyzing student performance and adjusting content accordingly. Adaptive learning platforms can modify course difficulty based on individual learner needs, offering tailored recommendations to enhance the learning experience.
g) Interactive Multimedia Content: Modern distance learning often involves interactive content, such as simulations, virtual labs, and augmented reality (AR). These tools provide students with practical, hands-on learning experiences that can mimic real-world scenarios.

2.4 The Role of AI in Distance Learning

AI plays a transformative role in modern distance learning by enabling personalized, efficient, and scalable education solutions. Some specific roles of AI include:

a) Personalized Learning: AI algorithms analyze data on student performance, learning preferences, and behavior to customize learning experiences. For instance, AI can recommend specific content to help a student struggling with a particular concept or adjust the pace of learning to match their needs. This level of personalization is difficult to achieve in traditional classrooms but is a natural fit for distance learning environments.
b) Virtual Teaching Assistants: AI-powered virtual assistants, such as chatbots, can handle routine tasks like answering frequently asked questions, grading assignments, or providing guidance on course materials. These assistants free up teachers' time, allowing them to focus on more complex tasks that require human intervention.
c) Predictive Analytics: AI can use historical data to predict student success and identify learners at risk of falling behind. By analyzing patterns of engagement, test scores, and other metrics, AI-driven analytics can offer timely interventions to improve student outcomes.

d) Content Creation: AI is also being used to generate content, such as practice tests, quizzes, or even written responses, helping to ease the workload on educators and offering students additional resources to reinforce their learning.

2.5 The Importance of AI in the Future of Distance Learning

As distance learning continues to grow, AI will likely play an even more prominent role in shaping educational practices. The integration of AI into distance education offers significant opportunities for improving student engagement, creating personalized learning experiences, and enhancing the overall efficiency of educational systems.

However, the successful implementation of AI in distance learning also requires addressing challenges such as ensuring equitable access to technology, safeguarding data privacy, and training educators to effectively use AI tools. Institutions must strike a balance between leveraging AI's potential and maintaining the human elements that are crucial to a meaningful educational experience.

The history of distance learning demonstrates a continuous evolution driven by technological advancements. As AI technologies become more integrated into educational systems, they offer the potential to revolutionize distance learning by making education more accessible, personalized, and efficient. However, understanding the unique characteristics, trends, and challenges associated with distance learning is essential to leveraging AI's full potential. This foundational understanding sets the stage for exploring the opportunities and challenges of AI in the subsequent chapters.

3. OPPORTUNITIES OF AI IN DISTANCE LEARNING

3.1 Introduction to AI Opportunities in Distance Learning

Artificial Intelligence (AI) has emerged as a powerful tool to transform various sectors, including education. In the context of distance learning, AI presents unique opportunities that have the potential to revolutionize teaching, learning, and educational management. By leveraging AI technologies, institutions can overcome traditional barriers of distance learning, such as limited interactivity, one-size-fits-all instruction, and lack of real-time feedback. The opportunities offered by AI in distance education are vast and multifaceted, encompassing areas such as personalized learning, enhanced engagement, administrative efficiency, and improved learning outcomes.

This chapter will explore the key opportunities of AI in distance learning and discuss how institutions, educators, and students can benefit from integrating AI technologies. These opportunities can address specific challenges in distance learning, providing innovative solutions that can make remote education more dynamic, efficient, and equitable.

3.2 Personalized Learning and Adaptive Instruction

One of the most significant opportunities AI brings to distance learning is the ability to deliver personalized learning experiences. Traditional classroom settings often rely on a one-size-fits-all approach, which may not be effective for all learners. Students have different learning preferences, paces, and prior knowledge, which makes it difficult to cater to individual needs in large classes. However, AI algorithms can analyze student data, such as performance metrics, engagement levels, and learning behaviors, to tailor educational content and delivery to each student's unique needs.

3.2.1 Tailored Content Delivery

AI can automatically adjust the learning materials presented to students based on their performance and preferences. For example, if a student is struggling with a particular topic, AI can recommend additional resources, such as tutorials, videos, or practice exercises, to reinforce their understanding. On the other hand, if a student demonstrates proficiency in a subject, AI can introduce more challenging material to keep them engaged and motivated. This level of customization helps ensure that each student progresses at an optimal pace and receives the support they need.

Adaptive learning platforms, such as DreamBox, Smart Sparrow, and Knewton, are examples of AI-powered tools that use data-driven insights to adapt instruction in real-time. These platforms continuously assess student performance and adjust the difficulty, content, and delivery method accordingly. This personalization is particularly beneficial in distance learning environments, where students often work independently and may not have immediate access to instructor support.

3.2.2 Intelligent Tutoring Systems

AI-powered intelligent tutoring systems (ITS) simulate one-on-one tutoring by providing students with personalized guidance and feedback. These systems can interact with students, ask questions, provide hints, and explain concepts based on their responses. ITS can identify knowledge gaps and misconceptions, offering targeted interventions to help students improve. By mimicking the role of a human tutor, AI systems can provide individualized attention to learners, even in large-scale distance learning programs.

One notable example of ITS is Carnegie Learning's Cognitive Tutor, which uses AI to deliver personalized math instruction. The system analyzes student responses and adapts the instruction to address areas of difficulty, providing hints and feedback to guide learners through problem-solving processes. The use of ITS in distance learning helps to replicate the benefits of personalized tutoring, even when students are learning remotely.

3.2.3 AI-Driven Assessment and Feedback

Another critical aspect of personalized learning is providing timely and relevant feedback. In traditional distance learning, feedback is often delayed, which can hinder student progress. AI-powered assessment tools can automatically evaluate student work, such as quizzes, essays, and assignments, and provide immediate feedback. These tools use natural language processing (NLP) to analyze written responses and offer constructive suggestions for improvement.

By delivering real-time feedback, AI helps students understand their mistakes, reflect on their learning, and make necessary adjustments before moving on to new material. This continuous feedback loop is essential for improving learning outcomes in distance education, where students may not have regular face-to-face interactions with instructors.

3.3 Enhancing Engagement and Motivation

Student engagement is a critical factor in the success of distance learning. Without the physical presence of instructors and peers, distance learners may struggle to stay motivated and engaged in their coursework. AI technologies offer innovative solutions to enhance engagement and create more interactive and immersive learning experiences.

3.3.1 Gamification and Interactive Learning

AI-powered platforms can incorporate gamification techniques to make learning more engaging and enjoyable. Gamification involves integrating game-like elements, such as points, badges, leaderboards, and rewards, into the learning process. These elements tap into students' intrinsic motivation by introducing competition, challenges, and a sense of achievement.

For example, Duolingo, a popular language-learning platform, uses AI-driven gamification strategies to keep learners motivated. The app offers daily challenges, unlockable achievements, and personalized learning paths, all while adapting content based on individual performance. This approach makes learning more dynamic and encourages students to stay engaged with the material.

Gamified learning environments can also include simulations and role-playing scenarios, where students apply their knowledge in real-world contexts. AI can create adaptive simulations that change based on student actions, providing instant feedback and new challenges. These interactive experiences help students develop critical thinking skills and retain information more effectively.

3.3.2 Virtual Reality (VR) and Augmented Reality (AR)

AI, when combined with VR and AR technologies, can create immersive learning environments that simulate real-world experiences. VR and AR allow students to explore virtual worlds, interact with digital objects, and engage in hands-on learning activities, even in a remote setting. For instance, medical students can practice surgeries in a virtual operating room, or engineering students can build and test virtual models of structures.

AI enhances these experiences by adjusting the difficulty of simulations based on student progress, providing personalized feedback, and offering guidance in real-time. By making learning more interactive and engaging, VR and AR can increase motivation and deepen understanding, especially in subjects that require practical application.

3.3.3 AI-Driven Chatbots for Real-Time Support

AI-powered chatbots are another tool that can enhance engagement in distance learning. These chatbots serve as virtual assistants, answering student questions, providing reminders, and offering support throughout the learning process. Chatbots are available 24/7, allowing students to receive help whenever they need it, even outside of traditional class hours.

For example, Georgia State University implemented an AI chatbot called "Pounce" to assist students with administrative tasks, such as registration, financial aid, and enrollment. The chatbot was highly effective in increasing student engagement and reducing dropout rates by providing timely information and addressing student concerns. In an educational context, AI chatbots can answer questions about course content, clarify concepts, and guide students through assignments, creating a more interactive and supportive learning experience.

3.4 Improving Accessibility and Inclusivity

One of the core advantages of distance learning is its ability to provide education to students regardless of their location or circumstances. However, ensuring that distance learning is accessible to all students, including those with disabilities, can be challenging. AI has the potential to make distance education more inclusive by offering tools that accommodate diverse learning needs and disabilities.

3.4.1 Assistive Technologies for Students with Disabilities

AI-powered assistive technologies can significantly enhance accessibility for students with disabilities. For instance, students with visual impairments can benefit from AI-driven screen readers that convert text into speech, while students with hearing impairments can use real-time transcription tools to follow along with lectures. AI can also offer speech-to-text services for students with physical disabilities, enabling them to participate in online discussions and complete assignments without typing.

Microsoft's AI-powered accessibility tools, such as Seeing AI and Immersive Reader, are examples of how technology can create more inclusive learning environments. These tools provide personalized assistance to students with diverse needs, making it easier for them to engage with course materials and participate in learning activities.

3.4.2 Adaptive Learning for Diverse Learning Styles

AI's ability to analyze and adapt to individual learning preferences also promotes inclusivity by catering to diverse learning styles. Some students may learn best through visual aids, while others may prefer auditory or kinesthetic approaches. AI-powered platforms can offer multiple modes of content delivery, allowing students to choose the format that suits their learning preferences.

For example, AI can present the same information in different formats, such as videos, podcasts, infographics, or interactive quizzes, to accommodate various learning styles. This flexibility ensures that all students, regardless of their preferred learning methods, can access and engage with the content effectively.

3.5 Administrative Efficiency and Scalability

In addition to enhancing the learning experience, AI offers significant opportunities for improving the administrative efficiency of distance education programs. By automating routine tasks, AI frees up time for educators and administrators to focus on higher-order responsibilities, such as curriculum design, student support, and strategic planning.

3.5.1 Automated Grading and Assessment

One of the most time-consuming tasks for educators is grading assignments and assessments. AI can automate grading for objective assessments, such as multiple-choice quizzes, and even analyze more complex tasks like essays and research papers using NLP algorithms. Automated grading systems not only save time but also provide students with immediate feedback, allowing them to track their progress and make improvements more quickly.

Platforms like Gradescope use AI to grade assignments, provide detailed feedback, and identify patterns in student responses. This automation improves scalability, enabling institutions to handle larger class sizes without compromising the quality of instruction or feedback.

3.5.2 Data-Driven Decision Making

AI can also assist administrators in making data-driven decisions to improve the overall efficiency and effectiveness of distance learning programs. By analyzing student performance data, engagement metrics, and other relevant information, AI can provide insights into areas where students are struggling or excelling. These insights can inform curriculum adjustments, instructional strategies, and resource allocation, ensuring that the educational program meets the needs of all students.

AI-powered analytics platforms, such as Brightspace and Canvas, offer dashboards that provide real-time insights into student engagement, learning outcomes, and course completion rates. These tools help administrators make informed decisions about program improvements, faculty support, and student interventions, contributing to the overall success of distance learning initiatives.

3.6 Conclusion

AI presents a range of opportunities that can transform distance learning by making it more personalized, engaging, accessible, and efficient. From adaptive learning systems and intelligent tutoring to AI-driven chatbots and assistive technologies,

AI has the potential to enhance the learning experience for students, regardless of their location or circumstances. Additionally, AI's ability to automate administrative tasks and provide data-driven insights helps institutions scale their programs while maintaining high-quality instruction and support.

By embracing AI, educators and institutions can overcome some of the traditional challenges of distance learning and create more dynamic, inclusive, and effective educational environments. As AI technology continues to evolve, its potential to improve distance education will only grow, offering new ways to engage learners, support diverse needs, and ensure successful learning outcomes.

4. CHALLENGES OF IMPLEMENTING AI IN DISTANCE LEARNING

Artificial intelligence (AI) holds tremendous potential to transform distance learning, but its implementation comes with a range of significant challenges. These challenges span technical, ethical, institutional, and pedagogical dimensions, impacting how effectively AI can be integrated into educational systems. In this chapter, we will explore these challenges in detail, shedding light on the complexities involved in adopting AI in distance learning. Understanding these hurdles is crucial for educators, administrators, and policymakers as they navigate the evolving landscape of AI-powered education.

4.1 Technological Infrastructure and Access

4.1.1 Digital Divide and Inequitable Access to Technology

One of the most fundamental challenges of implementing AI in distance learning is the issue of technological infrastructure and access. The effectiveness of AI-driven tools in education relies heavily on the availability of reliable internet connections, high-quality devices, and sufficient computational resources. However, there is a significant digital divide between students in urban areas with access to high-speed internet and cutting-edge devices, and students in rural or low-income areas who may lack such resources.

The disparity in access to technology exacerbates educational inequality. While AI has the potential to make learning more personalized and accessible, students without adequate technology are left behind. The requirement for high-speed internet and devices capable of running AI-driven platforms creates a barrier to entry, limiting the reach and effectiveness of AI in distance learning. Institutions must grapple with this digital divide to ensure that the benefits of AI are equitably distributed.

4.1.2 Insufficient Technological Infrastructure in Educational Institutions

Beyond individual access, educational institutions themselves may lack the necessary infrastructure to implement AI effectively. Deploying AI-driven learning systems requires significant investments in hardware, software, and cloud-based infrastructure. Many institutions, particularly in developing countries or underfunded areas, may not have the financial resources or technical expertise to adopt and maintain these systems.

Inadequate infrastructure can result in poor performance of AI tools, leading to frustration for both educators and students. Issues such as slow processing speeds, system crashes, and compatibility problems can disrupt the learning experience, making it difficult to rely on AI technologies consistently. Therefore, improving technological infrastructure is a critical challenge that institutions must address to realize the full potential of AI in distance education.

4.2 Data Privacy and Security Concerns

4.2.1 Handling of Sensitive Student Data

The implementation of AI in distance learning often requires the collection and analysis of large amounts of student data. AI systems use this data to personalize learning experiences, track student progress, and predict outcomes. However, the collection of such sensitive information raises significant concerns regarding data privacy and security.

Students' personal information, including learning habits, performance metrics, and even behavioral patterns, can be vulnerable to breaches or misuse if not properly protected. Educators and institutions must ensure that AI systems comply with data protection regulations, such as the General Data Protection Regulation (GDPR) in Europe or the Family Educational Rights and Privacy Act (FERPA) in the United States. Failure to safeguard student data could result in serious ethical and legal consequences, as well as a loss of trust in AI-driven educational tools.

4.2.2 Cybersecurity Risks

AI systems, like any other digital technology, are vulnerable to cybersecurity threats. Distance learning platforms are often targets for cyberattacks, including data breaches, hacking, and ransomware attacks. The implementation of AI further complicates cybersecurity by introducing additional layers of complexity in data storage, processing, and access.

Cybersecurity risks are particularly concerning in AI-powered learning environments because of the sensitive nature of the data being handled. For instance, AI-driven proctoring tools used in online exams collect video, audio, and biometric data, which could be exploited by malicious actors if not adequately secured. Educational institutions must invest in robust cybersecurity measures to protect AI systems from potential threats, which may be costly and resource-intensive.

4.3 Bias and Fairness in AI Algorithms

4.3.1 Bias in Data Sets and AI Algorithms

AI algorithms are only as good as the data they are trained on. One of the major challenges in using AI for distance learning is the risk of bias in AI algorithms, which can lead to unfair or discriminatory outcomes. AI systems often rely on historical data to make predictions or tailor learning experiences, but if this data contains biases—such as racial, gender, or socioeconomic biases—the AI system can perpetuate or even amplify these inequities.

For example, if an AI system is trained on data that reflects historical academic performance trends favoring certain groups, it may unfairly disadvantage students from underrepresented or marginalized communities. AI systems could also misinterpret the learning behaviors of non-native speakers or students with disabilities, leading to inaccurate assessments of their abilities. Addressing bias in AI algorithms requires careful curation of data sets and ongoing monitoring to ensure that AI-driven tools provide equitable learning experiences for all students.

4.3.2 Lack of Transparency and Explainability in AI Decision-Making

Another challenge related to bias is the lack of transparency in AI decision-making processes. AI systems, particularly those using machine learning or deep learning techniques, can be "black boxes," meaning that their decision-making processes are opaque even to the developers who created them. This lack of explainability raises concerns about how AI tools make judgments about student learning and performance.

In an educational context, transparency is crucial. Students and educators need to understand how AI systems arrive at certain conclusions—whether it's determining a student's grade, identifying a learning gap, or recommending specific interventions. Without this transparency, it becomes difficult to identify and correct instances of bias or errors in the system. There is a growing demand for AI models that provide clear, explainable outputs to ensure fairness and accountability in educational settings.

4.4 Pedagogical and Ethical Concerns

4.4.1 Teacher-Student Relationship and Reduced Human Interaction

One of the core pedagogical concerns of implementing AI in distance learning is the potential reduction of human interaction between teachers and students. While AI can automate many aspects of teaching, such as grading, feedback, and content delivery, the absence of human interaction can detract from the overall learning experience. In traditional education, the teacher-student relationship is vital for fostering engagement, providing emotional support, and motivating students. AI cannot replicate the empathetic and intuitive aspects of human teaching.

Distance learning already poses challenges in terms of student isolation, and the use of AI may exacerbate this issue. AI systems, while efficient, cannot fully replace the nuances of face-to-face communication, such as reading body language, detecting emotional cues, or offering personalized encouragement. This raises important questions about the balance between AI-driven automation and the need for meaningful human interaction in education.

4.4.2 Ethical Implications of AI in Learning Assessment

AI is increasingly used to assess student learning, from grading essays to monitoring behavior during exams. However, the ethical implications of using AI for assessment are a growing concern. AI systems that assess student performance may lack the contextual understanding necessary to evaluate complex or creative work. For instance, AI may struggle to accurately grade essays that involve subjective interpretations or cultural nuances, leading to potentially unfair evaluations.

Furthermore, the use of AI for remote proctoring during exams has raised ethical concerns regarding student privacy and autonomy. AI-powered proctoring systems use webcams, microphones, and other monitoring tools to detect cheating behaviors, but these systems are not infallible. False positives, where AI misidentifies normal student behaviors as cheating, can lead to undue stress and unfair penalties for students. Additionally, the continuous surveillance inherent in AI proctoring tools raises concerns about the invasion of privacy, particularly when used in students' homes.

4.5 Cost and Resource Constraints

4.5.1 High Costs of AI Implementation

Implementing AI in distance learning requires substantial financial investment. The costs associated with developing, deploying, and maintaining AI-powered systems can be prohibitive for many educational institutions. AI technologies often require specialized hardware, cloud-based services, and ongoing technical support, all of which add to the operational costs.

For smaller institutions or those in developing countries, these costs can be a significant barrier to adoption. Even when institutions have access to AI technologies, the need for regular updates, training for staff, and system maintenance can strain budgets. The high upfront and ongoing costs make it difficult for many institutions to fully integrate AI into their distance learning programs.

4.5.2 Lack of AI Expertise Among Educators

Another resource-related challenge is the lack of AI expertise among educators. Many teachers and administrators may not have the technical skills or knowledge to effectively use AI tools in their classrooms. This gap in expertise can lead to underutilization or improper implementation of AI technologies, limiting their potential impact on learning outcomes.

To address this challenge, institutions must invest in professional development and training programs to equip educators with the necessary skills to leverage AI tools effectively. However, providing such training requires time, resources, and institutional support, which may not always be available.

4.6 Legal and Regulatory Challenges

4.6.1 Navigating Legal Frameworks for AI in Education

As AI technologies become more prevalent in distance learning, legal and regulatory challenges are emerging. Many countries have yet to establish comprehensive legal frameworks governing the use of AI in education. This regulatory uncertainty creates challenges for institutions seeking to implement AI responsibly.

For example, the use of AI in learning assessment and student monitoring may raise legal questions related to academic integrity, privacy rights, and intellectual property. Institutions must navigate these legal complexities while ensuring compliance with existing educational regulations. The lack of clear legal guidelines can hinder the widespread adoption of AI in distance learning, as institutions may be reluctant to implement technologies that could expose them to legal risks.

4.6.2 Intellectual Property Concerns

The use of AI in content creation and assessment raises important questions about intellectual property (IP). AI tools that generate educational content, such as personalized study materials or automatically graded assignments, may create ambiguity around who owns the rights to these materials. In some cases, the AI developer, the educational institution, or the student may all have a stake in the IP generated by AI systems.

Institutions must develop clear policies to address intellectual property issues related to AI in education. These policies should define ownership rights, usage permissions, and compensation for content created or assessed by AI tools. Without clear guidelines, disputes over intellectual property could arise, complicating the implementation of AI in distance learning.

4.7 Conclusion

While AI offers exciting opportunities to enhance distance learning, its implementation is fraught with challenges that must be carefully addressed. From the digital divide and technological infrastructure gaps to concerns over data privacy, bias, and ethical implications, these hurdles highlight the complexities of adopting AI in education. Institutions must be proactive in addressing these challenges by investing in infrastructure, developing policies for fairness and transparency, and providing training for educators.

By navigating these challenges, educational institutions can harness the transformative potential of AI while ensuring that the benefits are accessible, equitable, and ethically sound. As AI continues to evolve, addressing these barriers will be essential for creating a future of distance learning that is inclusive, effective, and secure.

5. CASE STUDIES OF AI IMPLEMENTATION IN DISTANCE LEARNING

Examining real-world applications of AI in distance learning provides valuable insights into both the challenges and opportunities that come with its implementation. This chapter presents in-depth case studies from different educational institutions and countries that have integrated AI into their distance learning programs. These examples highlight successful strategies, innovative practices, and the barriers encountered along the way. Through these case studies, readers will gain a clearer understanding of the practical aspects of AI in education and the lessons learned from various implementations.

5.1 Case Study 1: AI in Adaptive Learning Systems - Arizona State University

5.1.1 Overview of Implementation

Arizona State University (ASU) is a pioneer in using AI to enhance distance learning, particularly through its adaptive learning platform, "Smart Sparrow." Smart Sparrow uses AI algorithms to deliver personalized content and adjust to students' learning needs in real time. The platform's AI-driven approach allows for a tailored learning experience where students receive customized feedback, individualized resources, and adaptive problem sets based on their performance.

5.1.2 Impact on Student Learning

Smart Sparrow significantly improved student outcomes, particularly in STEM courses. In one notable example, the platform was used for an introductory biology course. The AI-driven adaptive system helped students of varying ability levels, offering more challenging content to advanced learners while providing additional support for those struggling. As a result, ASU saw a significant reduction in dropout rates and an increase in student retention and pass rates.

5.1.3 Challenges and Lessons Learned

Despite its success, the implementation of Smart Sparrow at ASU faced several challenges. One major hurdle was the need for instructors to spend considerable time developing content that could be effectively integrated with the AI platform. Faculty had to undergo extensive training to use the platform to its full potential, and technical support was critical in the early stages. Additionally, ensuring equity in access was a challenge, as not all students had the same level of access to devices or internet connectivity. This case illustrates the importance of investing in training and support for educators and ensuring that all students have access to the necessary technology.

5.2 Case Study 2: AI-Powered Tutoring System - Carnegie Learning

5.2.1 Overview of Implementation

Carnegie Learning, an AI-driven tutoring system, is widely recognized for its use in distance learning environments. The system uses AI to provide students with step-by-step guidance and hints as they work through mathematical problems. The AI analyzes student responses in real-time, adjusting the difficulty of questions based on their progress and identifying areas where students need additional practice. This AI-driven approach mimics the one-on-one support typically provided by a tutor.

5.2.2 Improvement in Learning Outcomes

The AI-powered tutoring system significantly enhanced student achievement, particularly for students who required extra support in mathematics. Carnegie Learning was used in both blended and fully online environments, allowing students to learn at their own pace. Research showed that students who used the AI-powered tutoring system outperformed their peers on standardized math tests, particularly those in underserved communities, where access to quality math instruction was limited.

5.2.3 Challenges and Ethical Considerations

One of the challenges encountered with Carnegie Learning was ensuring that the AI system provided accurate and unbiased feedback to students. There were concerns about how the system could potentially reinforce learning biases if it misinterpreted student data. For example, students from different cultural or socioeconomic backgrounds may approach problem-solving differently, and the AI system had to be trained to account for such diversity.

To address these concerns, Carnegie Learning incorporated a feedback loop that allowed human instructors to review AI-generated reports and provide additional support when necessary. This case underscores the importance of continuous monitoring and human oversight to ensure AI systems provide fair and accurate assessments.

5.3 Case Study 3: AI and Automated Assessment Tools - University of New South Wales

5.3.1 Overview of Implementation

The University of New South Wales (UNSW) implemented AI-driven automated assessment tools in their distance learning programs, particularly in large-scale courses. The university adopted a system called "Gradescope," which uses AI to grade assignments and exams. The AI system could process both multiple-choice questions and more complex assignments like essays and programming tasks.

5.3.2 Efficiency Gains and Impact on Faculty Workload

Gradescope allowed UNSW to handle large volumes of student submissions efficiently, significantly reducing the time required for grading. The system's ability to grade consistently and accurately made it particularly valuable in courses with hundreds or thousands of students. Faculty members appreciated the reduction in administrative workload, which allowed them to focus more on course development and student engagement.

In terms of student outcomes, automated grading provided quicker feedback, allowing students to understand their mistakes and improve in real-time. The ability to receive immediate feedback positively influenced student learning outcomes, particularly in technical courses like engineering and computer science.

5.3.3 Challenges with AI Assessment

Despite the advantages, the implementation of automated assessment tools raised concerns about fairness and transparency. One major issue was the AI's difficulty in grading assignments that required subjective judgment, such as creative writing or open-ended responses. There were also instances where the AI made errors in grading, prompting students and faculty to question the system's reliability.

UNSW addressed these issues by introducing a system where human instructors reviewed the AI-generated grades, especially for more complex assignments. Additionally, the university emphasized the importance of transparency, ensuring that students understood how the AI grading system worked and had the opportunity to contest any unfair evaluations.

5.4 Case Study 4: AI-Enhanced Learning Analytics - Open University UK

5.4.1 Overview of Implementation

The Open University in the UK, one of the largest providers of distance learning, adopted AI-enhanced learning analytics to improve student support and retention. The university's "OU Analyse" platform uses AI to predict student performance and identify those at risk of dropping out. By analyzing data from student activities, such as log-ins, assignment submissions, and engagement with course materials, the AI system identifies patterns that indicate whether a student is struggling.

5.4.2 Impact on Student Retention

OU Analyse has had a significant impact on student retention rates at the Open University. The AI system sends alerts to both students and academic advisors when it identifies at-risk students, prompting timely interventions. These interventions include personalized support, additional tutoring, and changes in study plans to help students stay on track.

The AI system's predictive capabilities allowed the university to allocate resources more efficiently, focusing support on students who needed it most. As a result, the Open University saw an increase in student retention, particularly in courses with traditionally high dropout rates.

5.4.3 Challenges of Data Privacy and Ethics

One of the primary challenges in implementing AI-driven learning analytics was ensuring that the system complied with data privacy regulations. Collecting and analyzing large amounts of student data raised ethical concerns, particularly regarding how data was used and who had access to it. Students expressed concerns about being constantly monitored and how their data might be used for purposes beyond their education.

The Open University addressed these concerns by being transparent about the data collection process and offering students the ability to opt out of certain analytics features. They also ensured that all data was anonymized and used solely for educational purposes. This case study highlights the importance of addressing ethical considerations when implementing AI systems that rely heavily on student data.

5.5 Case Study 5: AI for Language Learning - Duolingo

5.5.1 Overview of Implementation

Duolingo, a leading language-learning platform, has successfully integrated AI into its distance learning program to provide personalized learning experiences for its millions of users. Duolingo's AI-driven algorithms adapt lessons based on each learner's progress, helping to identify strengths and weaknesses. The platform uses machine learning to analyze user behavior and tailor lessons to suit individual learning styles.

5.5.2 Personalization and Engagement

The AI-driven personalization on Duolingo has significantly increased learner engagement and completion rates. Users are more likely to continue learning when lessons are tailored to their pace and preferences. Duolingo's AI system also employs gamification strategies, such as rewards and levels, to keep users motivated. The platform's ability to dynamically adjust difficulty levels based on real-time performance has been a key factor in its success.

5.5.3 Challenges and Limitations

One limitation of Duolingo's AI system is its reliance on short, multiple-choice questions for language assessment, which may not fully capture the complexities of language learning, such as conversation skills or cultural context. Additionally, the platform's AI system is limited in its ability to provide personalized feedback on spoken language or writing tasks, which are crucial components of language acquisition.

To address these limitations, Duolingo has introduced more advanced AI features, such as speech recognition for pronunciation practice and the ability to analyze written responses. However, fully replicating the nuances of human language instruction remains a challenge for AI-driven systems.

5.6 Conclusion: Lessons Learned from Case Studies

The case studies presented in this chapter highlight both the successes and challenges of implementing AI in distance learning. While AI has the potential to enhance personalization, efficiency, and engagement in education, its implementation requires careful consideration of issues such as data privacy, bias, and the need for human oversight.

These examples demonstrate that AI works best when it complements, rather than replaces, traditional educational methods. Institutions that have successfully integrated AI into their distance learning programs have done so by providing ongoing support for educators, addressing ethical concerns, and ensuring equitable access to technology. As AI continues to evolve, these case studies provide valuable insights into how it can be effectively implemented to improve the distance learning experience for students around the world.

6. BEST PRACTICES FOR IMPLEMENTING AI IN DISTANCE LEARNING

In this chapter, we explore best practices for implementing artificial intelligence (AI) in distance learning environments. The insights provided here are based on real-world case studies, theoretical frameworks, and evolving trends in AI-driven education. Institutions and educators looking to incorporate AI into their teaching methods can leverage these practices to maximize the potential of AI while mitigating challenges such as bias, data privacy concerns, and technical infrastructure limitations.

6.1 Understanding the Role of AI in Distance Learning

AI is transforming distance learning by offering personalized learning paths, automating administrative tasks, and facilitating data-driven decision-making. However, the successful integration of AI requires a clear understanding of its capabilities and limitations. Educators and institutions need to recognize AI as a tool that enhances, rather than replaces, traditional pedagogical approaches. AI systems can support the learning process by adapting to individual student needs, but human oversight remains essential to ensure accuracy, fairness, and inclusivity.

Key considerations:

a) AI as a support tool: AI should assist educators in their tasks, not replace them. Automation in grading, feedback, or content delivery helps reduce workload but must be monitored for accuracy.
b) Customizing AI tools: Institutions must tailor AI tools to meet the specific needs of their students and courses. Off-the-shelf solutions may not fit every learning environment.
c) Addressing AI's limitations: Acknowledging AI's inability to interpret context, emotion, or complex, open-ended responses is crucial to setting realistic expectations.

6.2 Building a Strong Technological Infrastructure

A robust technological foundation is essential for implementing AI in distance learning. This includes ensuring high-speed internet access, reliable servers, and seamless integration between AI platforms and existing Learning Management Systems (LMS). Without the right infrastructure, AI tools may underperform, leading to frustration for both students and educators.

Key components:

a) Scalable cloud-based systems: AI tools require processing large datasets in real-time, necessitating scalable cloud-based systems that can handle these demands.
b) User-friendly interfaces: Students and educators need intuitive interfaces to interact with AI-powered systems. A complex or unintuitive system can hinder adoption and reduce engagement.
c) Regular maintenance and updates: Continuous technological support is essential for resolving bugs, maintaining system security, and ensuring the AI system evolves with changing educational needs.

Recommendations:

a) Institutions should perform regular audits of their technological infrastructure and update systems as needed to ensure they remain compatible with AI tools.
b) Collaborate with AI vendors to customize solutions and maintain seamless integration with current learning platforms.
c) Provide students and educators with clear training materials and technical support.

6.3 Training Educators to Use AI Tools Effectively

One of the most significant barriers to implementing AI in distance learning is the lack of training for educators. Many instructors may feel uncomfortable using AI technologies, particularly if they are unfamiliar with their functionality. Institutions need to prioritize comprehensive training to ensure educators understand how to use AI tools effectively, interpret the data provided by these systems, and integrate AI into their pedagogical practices.

Best Practices for Training:

a) Professional development programs: Institutions should create mandatory training sessions to help educators become proficient in using AI tools and understanding AI-driven analytics.
b) Ongoing support: Even after the initial training, educators should have access to continuous professional development and technical support.
c) Incorporating AI literacy into faculty development: Training programs should emphasize AI literacy, helping educators understand AI's underlying algorithms, potential biases, and data processing methods to empower informed decision-making.

Benefits:

a) Reduced faculty workload: Educators who are well-trained in AI can offload time-consuming tasks such as grading or content recommendations, allowing them to focus on personalized student interactions.
b) Enhanced teaching strategies: AI can provide educators with detailed data about student engagement and performance, enabling more tailored instructional approaches.

6.4 Fostering Student Familiarity and Engagement with AI

Students also need to understand how to effectively interact with AI-driven learning platforms. While younger students may have more familiarity with technology, not all learners are proficient with AI systems, especially older or non-traditional students. As such, institutions should focus on fostering student engagement by offering training, resources, and support on how to leverage AI tools in their studies.

Strategies to Enhance Student Engagement:

a) Clear onboarding process: Create tutorials and guides for students to help them navigate AI-driven platforms.
b) Accessible user interfaces: Prioritize user-friendly designs that do not require extensive technical knowledge.
c) Encouraging active learning: AI systems should be used to promote active learning, where students can engage in personalized learning experiences and receive tailored feedback in real-time.

Overcoming Barriers:

a) Digital literacy training: Students who are less familiar with AI technologies should be provided with digital literacy courses, ensuring they can maximize the benefits of AI-driven platforms.
b) Student feedback loops: Establish a feedback mechanism where students can report difficulties or concerns with AI systems, allowing for iterative improvements based on user experience.

6.5 Ensuring Data Privacy and Security

Data privacy is one of the most critical issues when implementing AI in distance learning. AI-driven systems rely heavily on data, often including sensitive student information such as personal details, performance analytics, and engagement patterns. Institutions must ensure that robust data privacy protocols are in place to protect this information and comply with relevant regulations such as the General Data Protection Regulation (GDPR) or the Family Educational Rights and Privacy Act (FERPA).

Best Practices for Data Privacy:

a) Adherence to legal frameworks: Institutions must follow global and local data privacy regulations, ensuring compliance and protection for student data.
b) Encryption and anonymization: Personal data should be encrypted, and where possible, anonymized to prevent misuse or unauthorized access.
c) Transparency in data usage: Institutions must clearly communicate to students and educators how their data is being collected, stored, and used by AI systems.

Establishing Trust:

a) User consent: Obtain explicit consent from students regarding the use of their data for AI analytics and feedback.
b) Data minimization: Collect only the data necessary for AI functionality and educational improvement to minimize risks associated with data breaches.

6.6 Mitigating Bias and Ensuring Fairness

One of the most significant challenges with AI in education is the potential for algorithmic bias, which can exacerbate inequalities rather than resolve them. For instance, if AI systems are trained on datasets that reflect biases (such as gender, racial, or socioeconomic biases), they may perpetuate these issues in their recommendations or evaluations. Educational institutions need to prioritize fairness and inclusivity when implementing AI.

Best Practices to Mitigate Bias:

a) Diverse data sets: AI systems should be trained on diverse datasets that represent a broad range of student experiences, demographics, and learning styles to reduce bias.
b) Human oversight: AI-driven assessments and feedback should always include a human review component to catch any instances of bias or errors in the system.
c) Regular audits: Institutions should conduct regular audits of AI systems to check for bias and adjust the algorithms if necessary.

Promoting Fairness:

a) Inclusive design principles: Ensure that the design of AI systems accounts for the diverse needs of all learners, including those with disabilities or from marginalized communities.
b) Bias awareness training: Educators and developers must be trained to recognize potential biases in AI systems and actively work to mitigate their impact on student outcomes.

6.7 Creating Policies for AI in Education

For AI to be successfully implemented in distance learning, institutions need to develop clear policies regarding the use of AI tools, data privacy, intellectual property, and ethical considerations. Policies should outline the rights and responsibilities of both students and educators when interacting with AI systems.

Policy Areas to Consider:

a) Data ownership: Define who owns the data generated by AI systems—whether it's the student, institution, or the AI service provider.
b) Usage of AI-generated content: Clarify intellectual property rights over content created or graded by AI tools.
c) Ethical guidelines: Institutions should create ethical frameworks to ensure AI is used responsibly, particularly in high-stakes situations like grading or admissions.

Implementation:

a) Institution-wide adoption: Ensure that AI policies are implemented across the entire institution, with clear guidelines provided to all stakeholders.
b) Stakeholder involvement: Involve educators, students, IT professionals, and legal experts in the policy-making process to ensure a holistic approach.

6.8 Promoting Collaboration Between Educators and AI Developers

Successful AI implementation in distance learning requires ongoing collaboration between educators and the developers who create AI tools. Developers often lack a deep understanding of the unique needs of distance education, while educators may not be familiar with the technical intricacies of AI. By fostering partnerships between these groups, institutions can create AI tools that are better suited to the educational context.

Best Practices for Collaboration:

a) Co-design AI systems: Engage educators in the design and development process to ensure that AI systems align with pedagogical needs and challenges.
b) Feedback loops: Developers should continuously gather feedback from educators and students to improve AI tools over time.
c) Cross-disciplinary teams: Institutions should create cross-functional teams that include educators, AI developers, and data privacy experts to oversee the implementation and monitoring of AI systems.

6.9 Conclusion: Navigating the Future of AI in Distance Learning

Implementing AI in distance learning offers significant opportunities for personalized education, efficiency, and scalability. However, the success of AI integration depends on thoughtful planning, robust infrastructure, educator training, and ethical considerations. By adhering to these best practices, educational institutions can maximize the benefits of AI while ensuring that its use remains fair, inclusive, and beneficial to all learners.

As AI continues to evolve, institutions must stay adaptable and responsive to new challenges, such as emerging technologies, changing student expectations, and ongoing developments in AI ethics. By fostering a culture of continuous learning and collaboration, educational institutions can navigate the complexities of AI and ensure its long-term success in distance learning environments.

7. FUTURE DIRECTIONS AND CONCLUSION

As the landscape of education evolves, the integration of artificial intelligence (AI) in distance learning presents both significant opportunities and formidable challenges. This chapter explores future directions for AI in distance learning and provides a comprehensive conclusion, emphasizing the implications of AI adoption, the need for continued research, and the importance of ethical considerations in shaping a sustainable educational environment.

7.1 Emerging Trends in AI and Distance Learning

The intersection of AI and distance learning is continually advancing, driven by technological innovations and shifting educational paradigms. Several key trends are emerging that will shape the future of AI in education.

a) Increased Personalization: AI's ability to analyze vast amounts of data will enable even more personalized learning experiences. Advanced algorithms will adapt educational content to match individual learning styles, preferences, and progress rates. As AI systems learn from student interactions, they will provide real-time feedback and adjust instructional materials accordingly, fostering deeper engagement and improved outcomes.
b) Enhanced Collaboration: AI tools will facilitate collaboration among students and educators across geographical boundaries. Virtual classrooms powered by AI will enable seamless communication, group projects, and peer-to-peer

learning opportunities, creating a global learning community that transcends traditional educational constraints.

c) Intelligent Tutoring Systems: The development of intelligent tutoring systems (ITS) will provide students with personalized support outside of the traditional classroom. These AI-driven platforms will offer targeted assistance, answering questions, providing explanations, and guiding learners through complex concepts in real time.
d) Integration of Virtual and Augmented Reality: Combining AI with virtual and augmented reality technologies will create immersive learning experiences. Students will be able to explore virtual environments that enhance their understanding of complex subjects, from historical events to scientific concepts. These technologies can help bridge the gap between theoretical knowledge and practical application.
e) Predictive Analytics for Student Success: AI will play a crucial role in predicting student performance and identifying at-risk learners. By analyzing patterns in data, institutions can intervene early with tailored support, helping to ensure that students remain engaged and on track to achieve their academic goals.

7.2 Ethical Considerations for AI in Education

As the integration of AI in distance learning accelerates, it is essential to address the ethical implications of its use. Ethical considerations must guide the development and implementation of AI systems to ensure that they promote equity, accessibility, and student well-being.

a) Equity and Access: While AI has the potential to enhance educational experiences, it also risks exacerbating existing inequalities. Institutions must strive to ensure that all students have access to AI tools and that these systems are designed to meet the diverse needs of learners from various backgrounds.
b) Data Privacy and Security: The reliance on data-driven approaches raises significant concerns regarding data privacy and security. Institutions must implement robust data protection policies that safeguard student information and comply with relevant regulations. Transparency in data usage is essential to build trust among students and educators.
c) Algorithmic Bias: AI systems can inadvertently perpetuate biases present in training data. To mitigate this risk, developers must prioritize fairness and inclusivity when designing algorithms. Regular audits and updates to AI systems are necessary to identify and rectify potential biases, ensuring equitable treatment of all learners.

d) Human Oversight: While AI can enhance educational processes, it should not replace human judgment. Educators must remain involved in decision-making processes related to assessment and support, ensuring that AI tools complement their expertise and insights.

7.3 Recommendations for Future Research

To fully harness the potential of AI in distance learning, further research is needed to explore various dimensions of its implementation and impact. Key areas for future research include:

a) Longitudinal Studies: Conducting longitudinal studies will provide insights into the long-term effects of AI integration in distance learning. Understanding how AI influences student performance, retention rates, and overall educational experiences over time will inform best practices.
b) Impact Assessment: Research should focus on assessing the impact of AI tools on various student demographics. By examining how different groups respond to AI-driven interventions, researchers can identify best practices that promote inclusivity and equity.
c) Technological Advancements: As AI technology continues to evolve, researchers must investigate emerging tools and platforms that can enhance distance learning. Exploring innovative applications of AI, such as natural language processing and machine learning, will contribute to the development of more effective educational solutions.
d) Faculty Development: Future research should evaluate the effectiveness of faculty development programs aimed at enhancing educators' understanding and use of AI tools. Investigating how training impacts teaching practices and student outcomes will help institutions design more effective professional development initiatives.

7.4 Conclusion: Navigating the Future of AI in Distance Learning

The integration of AI in distance learning presents a unique opportunity to transform education, making it more personalized, accessible, and effective. By leveraging the power of AI, educational institutions can enhance student engagement, improve learning outcomes, and streamline administrative processes.

However, realizing the full potential of AI requires a commitment to ethical considerations, equitable access, and ongoing research. Institutions must prioritize transparency, data privacy, and the mitigation of algorithmic bias to build trust and ensure that AI serves the best interests of all learners.

As the field of AI in education continues to evolve, stakeholders—including educators, policymakers, researchers, and technologists—must collaborate to navigate the challenges and seize the opportunities that lie ahead. By working together, we can create an educational landscape where AI serves as a valuable partner in fostering learning, growth, and success for all students.

The future of AI in distance learning is bright, filled with potential for innovation and improvement. By embracing best practices, prioritizing ethical considerations, and engaging in continuous research, educational institutions can ensure that AI enhances rather than disrupts the learning experience, paving the way for a more equitable and effective education system.

REFERENCES

Allen, I. E., & Seaman, J. (2017). *Digital learning compass: Distance education enrollment report 2017*. Babson Survey Research Group. https://www.onlinelearningsurvey.com/reports/digtiallearningcompass.pdf

Almarashdeh, I., & Alzahrani, A. (2021). The impact of artificial intelligence on higher education: A review of the literature. *Journal of Education and Learning*, *10*(4), 61–73. DOI: 10.5539/jel.v10n4p61

Almulla, M., Alanazi, H., & Alshammari, S. (2022). The impact of artificial intelligence on education: A systematic review. *Educational Technology Research and Development*, *70*(4), 757–778. DOI: 10.1007/s11423-022-10140-1

Brynjolfsson, E., & McAfee, A. (2014). *The second machine age: Work, progress, and prosperity in a time of brilliant technologies*. W. W. Norton & Company.

Chen, L., Xie, H., & Zhu, X. (2020). Personalized learning in higher education: An artificial intelligence perspective. *International Journal of Educational Technology in Higher Education*, *17*(1), 1–19. DOI: 10.1186/s41239-020-00217-5

Czerkawski, B. C., & Lyman, E. W. (2016). Beyond the "one size fits all": Differentiating instruction using artificial intelligence in online learning environments. *International Journal of Educational Technology in Higher Education*, *13*(1), 1–10. DOI: 10.1186/s41239-016-0004-5

Gonzalez, A. I., Caballero, R., & Nunez, A. (2021). AI and student engagement: A case study in higher education. *Journal of Computer Assisted Learning*, *37*(1), 23–32. DOI: 10.1111/jcal.12475

Huang, R. H., & Liaw, S. S. (2021). Artificial intelligence in education: A review. *Journal of Educational Technology & Society*, *24*(1), 10–22. https://www.jstor.org/stable/26996858

Kim, K. J., & Park, J. H. (2021). The role of artificial intelligence in promoting student engagement in online learning environments. *Computers & Education*, *162*, 104059. DOI: 10.1016/j.compedu.2020.104059

Kumar, V., Das, S., & Choudhary, A. (2021). The role of AI in enhancing student engagement in online learning environments. *Journal of Educational Computing Research*, *59*(1), 45–60. DOI: 10.1177/0735633120944516

Luckin, R., Holmes, W., Griffiths, M., & Forcier, L. B. (2016). Intelligence unleashed: An argument for AI in education. *Pearson.* https://www.pearson.com/content/dam/one-dot-com/one-dot-com/pedagogical-services/Intelligence-Unleashed-Paper.pdf

McFarlane, A., & Sakai, K. (2018). The challenges of artificial intelligence in education: A critical perspective. *AI & Society*, *33*(4), 503–515. DOI: 10.1007/s00146-018-0852-4

O'Neil, C. (2016). *Weapons of math destruction: How big data increases inequality and threatens democracy*. Crown Publishing Group.

Pappano, L. (2020). The learning future: 5 ways AI can help students. *The New York Times*. Retrieved from https://www.nytimes.com/2020/03/05/education/learning-future-ai.html

Shadiev, R., & Liu, M. (2020). The role of artificial intelligence in distance education: A review. *Computers & Education*, *150*, 103835. DOI: 10.1016/j.compedu.2020.103835

Siemens, G. (2014). Learning analytics: The emerging role of artificial intelligence in education. *Educational Technology Magazine*, 54(6), 24-28. https://www.learntechlib.org/p/147905/

Williamson, B., & Piattoeva, N. (2021). Education governance and datafication: The challenges of data privacy. *International Journal of Education Policy and Leadership*, *16*(1), 1–15. DOI: 10.22230/ijepl.2021v16n1a404

Zawacki-Richter, O., Marín, V. I., Bond, M., & Gouverneur, A. (2019). Systematic review of research on artificial intelligence applications in higher education – Where are we now and where are we going? *International Journal of Educational Technology in Higher Education*, *16*(1), 1–20. DOI: 10.1186/s41239-019-0171-0

Zhao, Y., & Watter, M. (2020). Artificial intelligence in education: Trends and challenges. *International Journal of Artificial Intelligence in Education*, *30*(3), 366–387. DOI: 10.1007/s40593-020-00210-3

Chapter 2
Ensembled ML Approach to Check User Satisfaction Towards Assessment Evaluation in E-Learning

G. Revathy
https://orcid.org/0000-0002-0691-1687
Sastra University, India

A. Sairam
Saveetha University, India

C. Nithiya
Aadhi Engineering College, India

P. G. Palanimani
https://orcid.org/0000-0003-4886-103X
Erode Sengunthar Engineering College, India

ABSTRACT

E-learning assessments play a crucial role in evaluating the progress and understanding of students in online education. Properly crafted evaluations aid in quantifying learning objectives, pinpointing opportunities for enhancement, and guaranteeing that learners are gaining the essential abilities and comprehension. The study's ensembled machine learning model offers a useful prediction model for a supportive learning environment. Minmax normalization is a common technique

DOI: 10.4018/979-8-3693-7195-4.ch002

used prior to model fitting to normalize the pre-processed data. For the variables or input data to contribute equally to the model fitting, they must be regulated since they are restrained at different scales. The evaluation plan's recommended prediction model for end user satisfaction. There are 150 male and 150 female participants in the 300-person ensembled classifier. comprising professors, Ph.D. research scholars, UG and PG students, and other students.

1. INTRODUCTION

E-learning holds significant importance in the modern educational landscape and professional development. E-learning assessments are a crucial component of online education that help measure the progress, comprehension, and achievement of learners. The types of assessments used in e-learning can vary, ranging from traditional quizzes to more interactive and innovative methods. One of the biggest innovations in the IS sector in recent years is electronic learning, or e-learning by Kumar et. al (2024). Schools and businesses face a distinct difficulty as a consequence of the proliferation of asynchronous e-learning platforms. A crucial topic in both practice and research is how to evaluate the efficacy of e-learning systems by Aljawarneh, N. M. (2024). Unfortunately, a single-item measure like global satisfaction cannot be cast-off to evaluate the usefulness of e-learning systems. For the valuation of e-learning systems to be a treasured diagnostic tool, it necessity gross into version numerous facets of electronic learner (e-learner) satisfaction.

2. TYPES OF E-LEARNING ASSESSMENTS

1. Quizzes and Exams:
   - Objective: Measure knowledge and understanding of specific topics.
   - Best Practices: Include a mix of question types (multiple-choice, true/false, etc.), set time limits, and provide instant feedback.
2. Assignments and Projects:
   - Objective: Evaluate application of knowledge and critical thinking skills.
   - Best Practices: Clearly define expectations, use rubrics for grading consistency, and encourage creativity.
3. Discussions and Forums:
   - Objective: Assess participation, collaboration, and critical thinking.
   - Best Practices: Establish clear discussion guidelines, set participation expectations, and provide constructive feedback.

4. Peer Reviews:
   - Objective: Foster collaborative learning and provide feedback from peers.
   - Best Practices: Clearly outline evaluation criteria, ensure anonymity, and guide students on providing constructive feedback.
5. Interactive Simulations and Labs:
   - Objective: Evaluate hands-on skills and practical application.
   - Best Practices: Provide clear instructions, ensure accessibility, and offer support for technical issues.
6. Reflections and Journals:
   - Objective: Encourage self-reflection and metacognition.
   - Best Practices: Set reflective prompts, emphasize the connection to real-world experiences, and offer feedback on reflections.
7. Online Assessments with Adaptive Learning:
   - Objective: Personalize assessments based on individual learning needs.
   - Best Practices: Use adaptive learning platforms, monitor student progress, and adjust difficulty levels dynamically.

3. BEST PRACTICES FOR E-LEARNING ASSESSMENTS

1. Clear Learning Objectives:
   - Clearly define learning objectives and align assessments with those objectives.
2. Diverse Assessment Formats:
   - Use a variety of assessment types to cater to different learning styles and objectives.
3. Transparent Assessment Criteria:
   - Clearly communicate assessment criteria and expectations to students.
4. Timely and Constructive Feedback:
   - Provide prompt and constructive feedback to aid learning and improvement.
5. Technology Accessibility:
   - Ensure that assessments are accessible to all students, considering different devices and assistive technologies.
6. Security Measures:
   - Implement measures to prevent cheating and maintain the integrity of assessments.
7. Engaging Content:

- Design assessments with engaging content, visuals, and interactive elements.

8. Flexible Timing:
    - Provide flexibility in assessment timing to accommodate diverse student schedules.
9. Regular Updates:
    - Regularly update assessments based on feedback and changes in course content.
10. Training for Instructors:
    - Provide instructors with training on effective online assessment practices.
11. Data Privacy:
    - Ensure the privacy and security of student data in accordance with regulations.
12. Encourage Collaboration:
    - Foster collaboration through group projects, discussions, and peer reviews.
13. Continuous Improvement:
    - Gather feedback from students and instructors to continually enhance assessment strategies.

Effective e-learning assessments contribute to a meaningful and engaging learning experience, ensuring that students achieve the desired learning outcomes.

4. E-LEARNING NEED

Liu et.al(2024) justifies that E-learning, or electronic learning, has become increasingly important in today's educational landscape and professional development. Several factors contribute to the growing need for e-learning

1. Accessibility:
    - E-learning enables learners to access instructional information anytime, anywhere, breaking down geographical barriers and enabling flexibility for various schedules.
2. Global Reach:
    - Wider Audience: E-learning enables educational institutions and businesses to reach a worldwide spectators, contravention outmoded limitations associated with physical classrooms or training centers.
3. Cost-Effectiveness:

- Reduced Expenses: E-learning often decreases expenses related with outmoded education, such as travel, accommodation, and printed materials. It canister be a more cost-effective solution for both learners and educational institutions.

4. Flexibility:
    - E-learning allows learners to learn at their own pace and style. This adaptability is especially advantageous for those with varying learning styles.
5. Personalization:
    - Adaptive Learning: E-learning systems may use technology to provide individualized learning experiences by modifying information depending on individual progress, strengths, and shortcomings.
6. Up-to-Date Content:
    - Real-Time Updates: E-learning content can be rationalized additional rapidly than outdated textbooks, safeguarding that beginners have admittance to the latest information and resources.
7. Interactive Learning:
    - Engagement: E-learning often incorporates interactive elements, multimedia, and simulations, enhancing engagement and providing a more dynamic learning experience.
8. Career Advancement:
    - Professional Development: E-learning allows professionals to acquire new skills and knowledge, facilitating career advancement and staying competitive in rapidly evolving industries.
9. Lifelong Learning:
    - Continuous Education: E-learning supports the concept of lifelong learning by offering opportunities for individuals to continually update their knowledge and skills throughout their lives.
10. Scalability:
    - Scalable Solutions: E-learning platforms can easily scale to accommodate a growing number of learners without significant infrastructure challenges, making it suitable for both small and large-scale education initiatives.
11. Assessment and Analytics:
    - Data-Driven Insights: E-learning platforms often provide tools for tracking learner progress and performance, allowing educators and organizations to make data-driven decisions to improve teaching strategies and content delivery.
12. Environmental Impact:

- Reduced Environmental Footprint: E-learning reduces the need for printed materials and minimizes the environmental impact associated with commuting to physical locations, contributing to sustainability efforts.

13. Inclusivity:
    - Accommodating Diverse Learners: E-learning can be designed to accommodate various learning styles, preferences, and abilities, making education more inclusive.
14. Collaboration:
    - Virtual Collaboration: E-learning platforms often incorporate collaborative tools, fostering interaction and teamwork among learners, even if they are geographically dispersed.

The increasing need for flexible, accessible, and efficient education and training options has made e-learning a vital component of contemporary learning ecosystems. It addresses the demands of a rapidly changing world and provides opportunities for individuals to acquire knowledge and skills throughout their lives given by Khasawneh et.al(2024).

5. CONSIDERATIONS FOR EFFECTIVE E-LEARNING ASSESSMENTS

- Clear Instructions: Provide clear and concise instructions for each assessment.
- Fair Evaluation: Ensure assessments are fair, free from bias, and aligned with learning objectives.
- Timely Feedback: Provide prompt and constructive feedback to aid learning and improvement.
- Technology Compatibility: Ensure that the assessment platform is compatible with various devices and browsers.
- Data Security: Implement measures to protect the privacy and security of student data.
- Accessibility: Design assessments to be accessible to learners with diverse needs and abilities.

6. CREATING AN ENSEMBLED LEARNING

Creating an ensemble machine learning approach to assess user satisfaction towards assessment evaluation in e-learning cannister be a multi-step process. Ensembling involves uniting the forecasts of multiple machine learning replicas to progress overall performance and robustness. Here's a general guide on how you might approach this:

1. Data Collection and Preprocessing:

Collect relevant data on user satisfaction in e-learning, including features related to assessment evaluation. Features might include the type of assessment, time spent, user demographics, etc. Clean and preprocess the data to handle missing values, outliers, and format issues.

2. Feature Engineering:

Create meaningful features from the raw data that can enhance the performance of your models. For instance, you strength excerpt features related to the difficulty level of assessments, user engagement, or historical performance.

3. Model Selection:

Choose a diversity of machine learning replicas that are appropriate for your problem. Common models for user satisfaction prediction include:

- Logistic Regression
- Decision Trees
- Random Forests
- Support Vector Machine
- Neural Networks

4. Model Training:

Train each selected model on your preprocessed dataset using a portion of your data for training and another portion for validation. Adjust hyperparameters for each model to optimize performance.

The architecture diagram for the proposed ensembled model is given below in Figure 1.

Figure 1. Architecture diagram

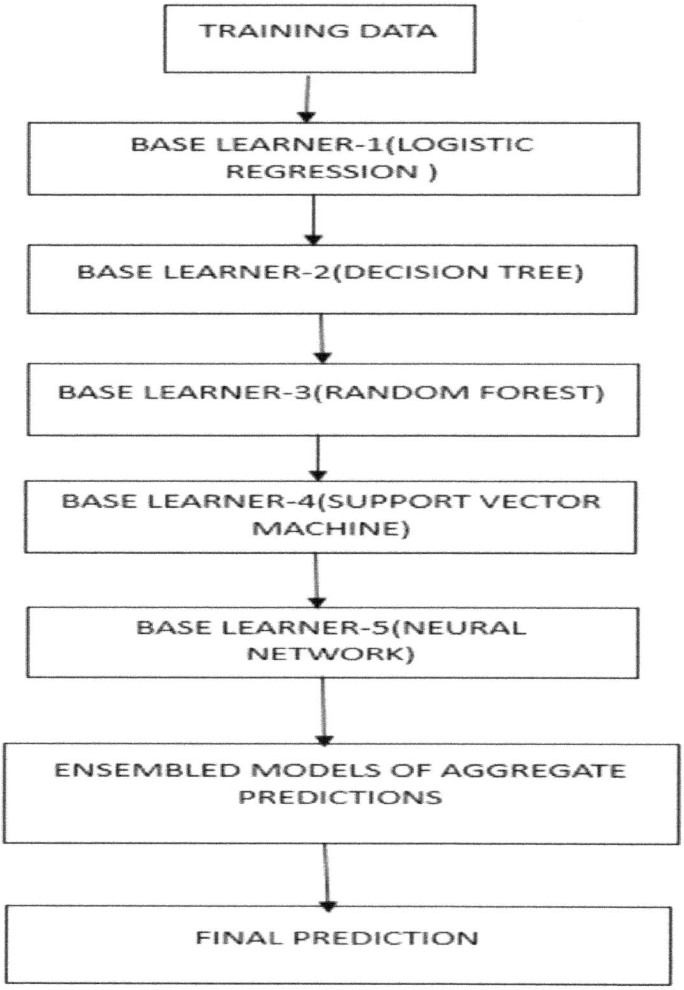

In the figure 1 Architecture diagram Base Learner 1 uses logistic regression, Base Learners 2, 3,4 and 5 use different algorithms Decision tree, random forest, support vector machine and Neural Network respectively. The ensemble model aggregates the forecasts from all sordid learners to make the final prediction. Including logistic regression as a base learner in an ensemble model allows for diversity in the types of models contributing to the ensemble, potentially leading to improved performance and robustness.

5.MinMax Normalization:

MinMax normalization is a data preprocessing technique used to scale numeric features in a dataset to a specific range, typically between 0 and 1. It is a simple and generally castoff technique for normalizing numerical variables, making them comparable and preventing the dominance of large-scale features over smaller-scale ones. The formula for MinMax normalization is:

$$X_{Norm} = \frac{X - X_{min}}{X_{max} - X_{min}} \quad \text{Eq.1}$$

Where X original value of feature

X_{min} is the minimum value of feature in dataset

X_{max} is the maximum value of feature in dataset

X_{Norm} is the normalized value of feature

The resulting values after MinMax normalization will fall within the range [0, 1]. This normalization method preserves the circulation of the innovative data and is useful when the spreading of the features is unknown or non-Gaussian.

MinMax normalization is particularly advantageous for machine learning algorithms that rely on distance calculations or gradient-based optimization, such as k-nearest neighbors (KNN), support vector machines (SVM), and neural networks. By scaling the features to a common range, MinMax normalization can improve the convergence of these algorithms and prevent numerical instabilities.

6. Ensemble Techniques:

Combine the predictions of individual models using various ensemble methods. Common ensemble methods include:

- **Voting Classifier:** Combine predictions through majority voting.
- **Bagging (Bootstrap Aggregating):** Train multiple models on dissimilar subsections of the data and average their predictions.
- **Boosting:** Combine weak learners into a strong learner sequentially.

Voting Classifier

The Voting Classifier is a machine learning collaborative technique that syndicates the predictions of multiple individual classifiers to kind a final prediction. It aggregates the predictions of apiece improper classifier and outputs the class with the most votes (mode) or computes the average probability across all classifiers. This approach often leads to improved predictive performance compared to any single classifier in the ensemble. The Voting Classifier can include various types of base classifiers, including decision trees, support vector machines (SVM), logistic regression, k-nearest neighbors (KNN), etc. It can combine classifiers with different algorithms or hyperparameters to exploit their diverse strengths and improve overall performance.

The Voting Classifier is a authoritative procedure for ensemble learning, especially when individual classifiers have different biases or perform well on diverse subsections of the data. It can lead to more robust and accurate predictions, particularly in situations where no single classifier consistently outperforms others.

Bagging (Bootstrap Aggregating)

Bagging, brief for Bootstrap Aggregating, is a machine learning ensemble practice that aims to improve the steadiness and accurateness of models by combining the predictions of multiple base learners proficient on dissimilar subsections of the training data. It reduces the modification of the model and helps prevent overfitting.

Key features and benefits of bagging include:

- **Reduction of Variance:** Bagging reduces the alteration of the model by combining multiple models skilled on diverse subsections of data. This leads to more stable and reliable predictions.
- **Prevention of Overfitting:** By training base learners on diverse subsets of data, bagging helps prevent overfitting, especially in models with high variance or complex decision boundaries.
- **Robustness to Noise:** Bagging can improve the robustness of the classical to noisy data or outliers by reducing the inspiration of individual instances on the final prediction.
- **Parallelization:** Because sordid learners are trained independently, bagging can be parallelized efficiently, making it suitable for distributed computing environments.

Common algorithms that utilize bagging include Random Forest for decision trees, Bagged Decision Trees, Bagged SVM, and Bagged Neural Networks.

Overall, bagging is a influential procedure for edifice robust and accurate predictive models, predominantly when collective with weak learners or when dealing with high-dimensional or noisy datasets.

Boosting Top of Form

Boosting is a machine learning ensemble method that combines multiple weak learners sequentially to create a strong learner. Unlike bagging, which trains base learners independently, boosting focuses on training base learners consecutively, with each succeeding model correcting the errors of its predecessors. Boosting aims to reduce bias and variance simultaneously, leading to improved predictive performance.

Key features and assistances of boosting include:

- **Improved Predictive Performance:** Boosting often leads to higher predictive accuracy compared to individual base learners, especially when using weak learners.
- **Reduction of Bias and Variance:** Boosting aims to reduce both bias and variance by sequentially correcting errors made by previous base learners, leading to improved generalization performance.
- **Adaptation to Complex Data:** Boosting can handle complex datasets and capture intricate relations between topographies and the board adjustable by iteratively focusing on hard-to-predict instances.

Common algorithms that utilize boosting include AdaBoost (Adaptive Boosting), Gradient Boosting Machines (GBM), XGBoost, and LightGBM.

Overall, boosting is a authoritative practice for building precise and vigorous predictive models, predominantly when production with structured data or classification and regression tasks.

6. Cross-Validation:

Cross-validation is a resampling technique used in machine learning to assess the performance and generalization ability of a predictive model. It is particularly useful when the available dataset is limited, and splitting it into separate training and testing sets might lead to unreliable estimates of model performance.

The basic idea behind cross-validation is to partition the dataset into multiple subsets, or "folds," where each fold serves as both a training set and a testing set at diverse phases of the evaluation process. This permits for a more comprehensive valuation of the model's performance by averaging the results obtained from multiple evaluations. Perform cross-validation to assess the generalization performance of your ensemble model. This involves excruciating your data into multiple folds, training on subsets, and validating on the remaining data.

Here's how cross-validation typically works:

1. **Data Partitioning:**
   - The dataset is divided into k approximately equal-sized folds, where k is usually chosen based on the extent of the dataset and computational resources. Common choices include 5-fold and 10-fold cross-validation.
2. **Model Training and Evaluation:**
   - For each iteration (or fold) of the cross-validation process, one fold is held out as the testing set, while the residual folds are used for exercise the model.
   - The model is qualified on the training set and appraised on the testing set to obtain a performance metric, such as accuracy, precision, recall, or F1-score.
3. **Performance Aggregation:**
   - The performance metric obtained from each iteration is averaged to obtain an overall estimate of the model's performance.
   - Additionally, the variability of the performance metric across folds can be calculated to assess the stability of the model's performance.
4. **Cross-Validation Variants:**
   - Several variants of cross-validation exist, including:
   - **Stratified Cross-Validation:** Guarantees that apiece fold contains a representative distribution of the target variable classes.
   - **Repeated Cross-Validation:** Repeats the cross-validation procedure manifold times with dissimilar random splits of the data to obtain more reliable estimates of model performance.
   - **Leave-One-Out Cross-Validation (LOOCV):** A special case of k-fold cross-validation where k equals the quantity of occurrences in the dataset. In each iteration, one instance is left out as the testing set.

Cross-validation helps address issues such as overfitting and data leakage by providing a more accurate estimate of a model's performance on unseen data. It is frequently cast-off for model selection (e.g., hyperparameter tuning) and comparing the performance of different algorithms on a given dataset.

7. Evaluation Metrics:

When evaluating ensemble models, it is critical to utilize relevant measures that represent the ensemble's overall performance, including its capacity to produce correct predictions and deal with uncertainty. Here are some commonly used assessment measures for ensemble models:

1. **Accuracy:**

- Accuracy procedures the quantity of appropriately classified occurrences out of the total number of instances.
- While accuracy is a straightforward metric, it may not be suitable for imbalanced datasets, where the class distribution is skewed.

2. **Precision:**
   - Precision refers to the fraction of genuine positive predictions provided by the model. It is especially beneficial when the cost of false positives is significant, such as in medical diagnostics and fraud detection.
3. **Recall (Sensitivity):**
   - Recall assesses the fraction of genuine positive predictions in a dataset.
   - It is crucial in situations where missing positive occurrences (false negatives) might be expensive or have serious repercussions.
4. **F1-Score:**
   - The F1-score represents the harmonic average of accuracy and recall. It strikes a balance between accuracy and recall.
   - The F1-score is beneficial for unequal class distributions or when false positives and false negatives are equally relevant.
5. **ROC Curve and AUC:**
   - The Receiver Operating Characteristic (ROC) curve compares the true positive rate (TPR) and false positive rate (FPR) at different thresholds.
   - Area Under the ROC Curve (AUC) measures the classifier's overall performance across all potential threshold settings.
   - The ROC curve and AUC are effective for testing binary classification models, particularly when class distributions are skewed.
6. **Confusion Matrix:**
   - A confusion matrix provides a detailed breakdown of the model's predictions across different classes.
   - It includes metrics such as true positives, true negatives, false positives, and false negatives, which canister be cast-off to compute various evaluation metrics.
7. **Log Loss:**
   - Log Loss (or cross-entropy loss) measures the accuracy of the probabilities predicted by the model. It penalizes incorrect predictions founded on the confidence of the prediction.
   - It is commonly used for evaluating probabilistic classifiers, such as those producing class probabilities (e.g., logistic regression, neural networks).
8. **Mean Squared Error (MSE) or Mean Absolute Error (MAE):**
   - For regression tasks, MSE or MAE container be used to appraise the correctness of the predicted continuous values.

- MSE procedures the typical formed alteration between the forecast and definite values, while MAE procedures the regular absolute difference.

When evaluating ensemble models, it's crucial to consider the specific characteristics of the dataset and the problem domain to indicate the most appropriate evaluation metrics. Additionally, it's often beneficial to use multiple metrics to gain a comprehensive understanding of the model's performance from different perspectives.

Indicate suitable appraisal metrics for your problem. For user satisfaction, you might consider metrics like accuracy, precision, recall, F1 score, or area under the ROC curve (AUC-ROC).

8. Hyperparameter Tuning:

Fine-tune the hyperparameters of your ensemble model for optimal performance. This step might involve grid search, random search, or more advanced techniques like Bayesian optimization.

Here's a general overview of the hyperparameter tuning process:

1. **Define Hyperparameters:**
   - Identify the hyperparameters that need to be tuned for the specific machine learning algorithm. Common examples include learning rate, number of trees in a random forest, regularization strength, kernel type in support vector machines, and depth of a decision tree.
2. **Choose a Search Space:**
   - Define the range of values or distribution from which to sample hyperparameters during the tuning process. This search space can be specified manually or using automated procedures like grid search, random search, or Bayesian optimization.
3. **Select a Validation Strategy:**
   - Decide on a validation strategy to appraise the routine of different hyperparameter configurations. Common validation techniques include k-fold cross-validation, holdout validation, and nested cross-validation.
4. **Perform Hyperparameter Search:**
   - Use the chosen search strategy to discover the hyperparameter space and appraise the presentation of different configurations. This involves training the model with each set of hyperparameters and appraising its presentation on the validation data.
5. **Evaluate Performance:**
   - Measure the recital of each model configuration using appropriate evaluation metrics. This can comprise metrics such as accuracy, precision,

recall, F1-score, ROC AUC, or others liable on the specific problem domain.

6. **Select Best Hyperparameters:**
   - Choose the hyperparameters that result in the best performance on the validation data. This could be based on the performance of the model on a single validation set or the average performance across multiple folds in cross-validation.
7. **Final Model Evaluation:**
   - Evaluate the performance of the final model with the selected hyperparameters on an independent test set to assess its generalization ability. This provides an estimate of how well the model will perform on unseen data.
8. **Iterate if Necessary:**
   - If the performance of the model is not satisfactory, refine the hyperparameter search space or validation strategy and repeat the process until a satisfactory model is obtained.

Hyperparameter tuning is an essential step in the machine learning pipeline and can significantly impact the performance of a model. By systematically exploring the hyperparameter space and selecting the best configurations, practitioners can build models that achieve better generalization and improve predictive accuracy.

9. Interpretability:

Consider the interpretability of your ensemble model. Some ensemble methods, like decision trees, offer interpretability. This is important for understanding the factors contributing to user satisfaction.

10. Deployment and Monitoring:

Once satisfied with the model's performance, deploy it to your e-learning platform. Continuously monitor the model's performance and update it as needed.

Remember, the effectiveness of your ensemble model depends on the quality of your data, the diversity of your base models, and the proper tuning of hyperparameters

7. RESULTS AND DISCUSSION

There are totally 300 people in different E-Learning platform and different modes of assessment. There are certain questions that are asked to the people in terms of need of e learning, benefits of e-leanring, various modes of e-learning and based on the queries the results are recorded. Based on the queries a dataset is created and is been trained with Ensembled models of machine learning. The testing set composed of streamlit GUI which ask the unknown user about 5 to 8 Questions and predicts the results in more accurate mode.

The various GUI testing results are recorded for state of art models such as RF, NB and SVM and our proposed Ensembled model. The ensembled models shows better results than the state of art models.

The various questions are posted to the users regarding content clarity, overall satisfaction, content question justifications, user interface experience, assessment format and structure, flexibility and suggestions for improvement.

These questionnaires cover various aspects of the e-learning experience, including content clarity, user interface, feedback, engagement, and suggestions for improvement. You can modify these questions based on your specific requirements and context:

Overall Satisfaction:

- How satisfied are you with the e-learning assessment experience?
- Did the assessment questions clearly align with the learning objectives?
- Were the assessment questions relevant to the course content?
- How easy was it to navigate through the assessment interface?
- Did you encounter any technical issues while taking the assessment? (Please specify)

Assessment Format and Structure:

- Did the format of the assessment suit your learning style?
- Were the instructions for the assessment clear and easy to understand?

Feedback and Guidance:

- Did you receive timely and constructive feedback on your assessment performance?
- Were additional resources or guidance provided to help you prepare for the assessment?

Engagement and Interactivity:

- Did the assessment questions engage your interest and promote critical thinking?
- Were there interactive elements (e.g., multimedia, simulations) that enhanced your learning experience?

Flexibility and Accessibility:

- Did the assessment allow for flexibility in terms of timing and completion?
- Were accommodations made for learners with diverse needs or accessibility requirements?
- Do you feel that the assessment accurately assessed your understanding of the course material?
- Did the assessment contribute to your overall learning and knowledge retention?

Suggestions for Improvement:

- What aspects of the e-learning assessment could be improved to enhance user satisfaction?

Open-ended response

- Do you have any suggestions for future assessments or enhancements to the e-learning platform?

These sample questionnaires can be distributed to learners after completing e-learning assessments to gather feedback and insights for improving the assessment experience. Adjust the wording and format as needed to suit your specific requirements and preferences.

The users results of the proposed models are more accurate when compared with state of models such as Random forest, SVM, Neural network and KNN.

Figure 2. Assessment comparison

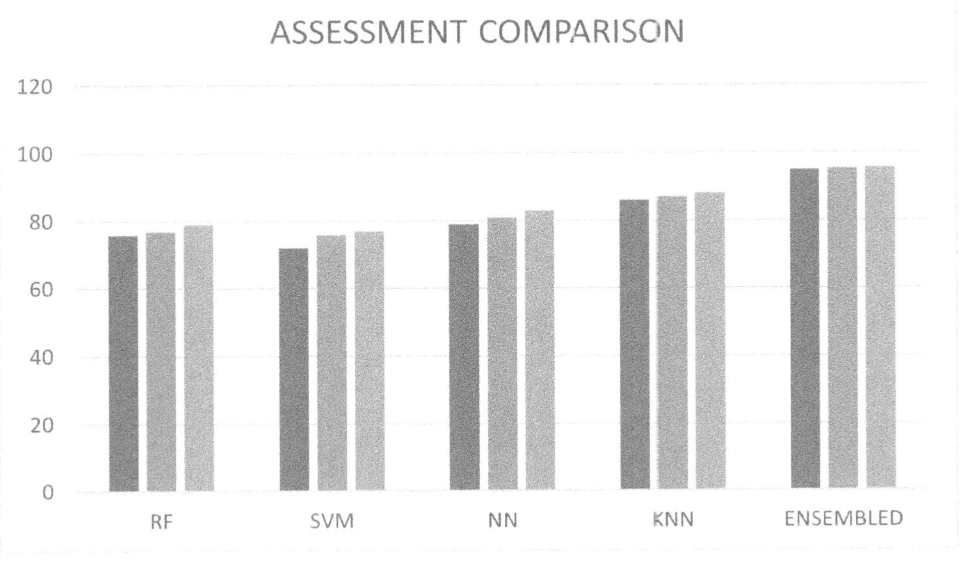

Figure 2 explains the ensembled model comparison of assessment user satisfaction with various state of art models. The ensembled models gets the accurate results from the users and the average of 96%.

8. CONCLUSION

E-Learning plays an important role in most of the people in the current world scenario. But various people at various crisis are satisfied with various mode of assessments. Hence the Prediction model will help us to utilize the need of e-learning and the satisfied assessment points on each user view. The predicted model provides accurate results when compared with state of art models.

REFERENCES

Aljawarneh, Nader Mohammad. "Effect of User Satisfaction between Cloud Learning Applications & University Education Agility." (2024).

Khasawneh, N. A. S., Khasawneh, A. J., Khasawneh, D. M. A. S., & Khasawneh, D. Y. (2024). Improving Arabic Content Delivery on Cloud Computing Platforms for Jordanian E-learning Environments. *Migration Letters : An International Journal of Migration Studies*, *21*(S1), 575–585. DOI: 10.59670/ml.v21iS1.6181

Kumar, A., Bala, P. K., Chakraborty, S., & Behera, R. K. (2024). Exploring antecedents impacting user satisfaction with voice assistant app: A text mining-based analysis on Alexa services. *Journal of Retailing and Consumer Services*, *76*, 103586. DOI: 10.1016/j.jretconser.2023.103586

Liu, H., Zhao, J., Zhou, L., Yang, J., & Liang, K. (2024). Intelligent performance evaluation of e-commerce express services using machine learning: A case study with quantitative analysis. *Expert Systems with Applications*, *240*, 122511. DOI: 10.1016/j.eswa.2023.122511

Chapter 3
Distance Education Students' Satisfaction With Education Quality in Accounting Programs

Priyanka Vemburaj
https://orcid.org/0000-0002-6581-7543
Rathinam College of Arts and Science, India

T. M. Hemalatha
https://orcid.org/0000-0002-3360-8501
Rathinam College of Arts and Science, India

ABSTRACT

This chapter examines the satisfaction levels of distance education students in accounting programs regarding the quality of their educational experience. As online learning becomes increasingly prevalent, understanding the factors that influence student satisfaction is crucial for educational institutions striving to enhance their offerings. Through a mixed-methods approach, including quantitative surveys and qualitative interviews, this research identifies key elements impacting satisfaction, such as course content, instructional quality, technological support, and community interaction. Findings reveal that while students value the flexibility of distance education, challenges related to engagement and support persist. The chapter emphasizes the importance of continuous improvement in curriculum design, faculty training, and student services to foster a more satisfying learning environment. By addressing these factors, institutions can enhance student outcomes and retention in distance accounting programs.

DOI: 10.4018/979-8-3693-7195-4.ch003

INTRODUCTION

The rapid evolution of technology has transformed the landscape of higher education, making distance education a prominent choice for students worldwide. This chapter explores the satisfaction levels of distance education students in accounting programs concerning the quality of education they receive. Understanding these factors is crucial for educational institutions aiming to improve their offerings and retain students.

Objectives of this study:

- Evaluate the overall satisfaction levels of distance education students enrolled in accounting programs, focusing on their perceptions of educational quality.
- Identify and analyze the key factors that contribute to student satisfaction, including course content, instructional quality, technological support, and opportunities for interaction.
- Compare the experiences and satisfaction levels of distance education students with those in traditional face-to-face accounting programs.

REVIEW OF LITERATURE

The shift toward distance education has been propelled by technological advancements and a growing demand for flexible learning options. Allen and Seaman (2017) report a significant increase in enrollment in online courses, highlighting the necessity for institutions to adapt to this new landscape. The report emphasizes that quality education delivered remotely can meet students' needs while providing access to a broader audience.

Research indicates that student satisfaction is influenced by several interconnected factors. Kahu (2013) discusses the concept of student engagement, positing that a student's sense of belonging and connection to their learning environment directly impacts their overall satisfaction and academic success. Engaged students tend to perform better academically, further reinforcing the need for institutions to focus on engagement strategies in their distance education programs.

While technology enables distance education, it can also pose challenges. Muilenburg and Berge (2005) identify common barriers students face, such as access to reliable internet and familiarity with learning management systems. Addressing these barriers is essential for enhancing student satisfaction and ensuring a smooth learning experience.

Building a sense of community is crucial in distance education. Rovai (2002) argues that online learners often feel isolated, which can negatively affect their satisfaction and retention. Establishing opportunities for interaction—through discussion forums, group projects, and networking events—can mitigate feelings of isolation and foster a supportive learning environment.

Background of Distance Education in Accounting

Overview of Distance Education

Distance education has evolved significantly over the past few decades, driven by advancements in technology and changing student demographics. This mode of learning enables students to pursue their education from remote locations, often at their own pace, through online platforms, video lectures, and interactive digital resources. The flexibility offered by distance education appeals to a diverse range of learners, including working professionals, parents, and international students.

Evolution of Accounting Education

Historically, accounting education has been delivered through traditional face-to-face classroom settings, emphasizing rigorous curricula and direct faculty-student interactions. However, as the demand for flexible learning options grew, many institutions began to adapt their programs for online delivery. This transition has enabled institutions to reach a broader audience and accommodate the diverse needs of students.

The Role of Technology in Accounting Education

Technology plays a crucial role in distance education, especially in accounting programs where practical applications of theoretical knowledge are essential. Learning management systems (LMS), online simulations, and accounting software allow students to engage with course material dynamically and interactively. These tools not only facilitate learning but also prepare students for the technological demands of the accounting profession.

Challenges in Distance Accounting Education

Despite its advantages, distance education in accounting faces several challenges. These include ensuring the quality and rigor of the curriculum, maintaining student engagement, providing adequate support services, and addressing technological barriers. Additionally, students may experience feelings of isolation due to the lack of in-person interactions, which can impact their overall satisfaction with the program.

The Importance of Accreditation and Quality Assurance

Accreditation is a critical factor in maintaining the quality of accounting programs, whether delivered in-person or online. Accredited programs are often viewed as more credible by employers and can enhance students' job prospects. As distance education grows, ensuring that online accounting programs meet the same rigorous standards as traditional programs is essential for maintaining educational quality and student satisfaction.

Importance of Student Satisfaction

Definition of Student Satisfaction

Student satisfaction refers to the degree to which students' expectations and experiences align with their perceptions of the educational process. This encompasses various aspects, including course content, teaching quality, support services, and the overall learning environment. High levels of satisfaction indicate that students feel their needs are met and their educational experiences are valuable.

Impact on Retention and Success

Student satisfaction is closely linked to retention rates in educational programs. Satisfied students are more likely to continue their studies, complete their degrees, and achieve their academic goals. Conversely, dissatisfaction can lead to higher dropout rates, negatively impacting both students and institutions. Understanding the factors that contribute to satisfaction can help institutions implement strategies that enhance student retention.

Influence on Academic Performance

Research suggests a positive correlation between student satisfaction and academic performance. When students feel supported and engaged, they are more likely to perform better academically. Satisfaction fosters a sense of belonging and motivation, encouraging students to invest time and effort into their studies. This is particularly important in fields like accounting, where the curriculum can be demanding and requires consistent engagement.

Role in Institutional Reputation

The reputation of an educational institution is significantly influenced by student satisfaction. Positive experiences lead to favorable word-of-mouth recommendations and higher enrollment rates. Institutions that prioritize student satisfaction are often viewed as more attractive to prospective students, enhancing their competitive edge in the market.

Feedback for Continuous Improvement

Student satisfaction surveys provide valuable feedback that institutions can use to improve their programs and services. By actively seeking student input, institutions can identify areas of strength and opportunities for enhancement. This iterative process not only boosts satisfaction but also ensures that the educational offerings remain relevant and effective.

Contribution to Professional Outcomes

Satisfied students are more likely to become engaged alumni who contribute positively to their fields. In accounting, for example, graduates who feel well-prepared and satisfied with their education are more likely to excel in their careers, which reflects positively on their alma mater. Strong professional outcomes for graduates enhance the institution's reputation and can lead to increased recruitment of future students.

Factors Influencing Satisfaction in Distance Education

Course Content and Curriculum

The relevance and rigor of the course content are critical to student satisfaction in distance education programs. A well-structured curriculum that aligns with industry standards and incorporates practical applications enhances the learning experience. Students value courses that not only cover theoretical concepts but also prepare them for real-world scenarios, especially in a field like accounting where practical skills are paramount.

Instructional Quality

The quality of instruction plays a significant role in shaping student satisfaction. Factors such as the clarity of teaching, the engagement of instructors, and their responsiveness to student queries are essential. In distance education, where face-to-face interaction is limited, instructors must leverage various online teaching strategies to maintain student engagement and foster a supportive learning environment. Effective communication and timely feedback are crucial components of high-quality instruction.

Technological Support and Resources

Access to reliable technology and adequate support services is vital for distance education students. Students need to be equipped with the necessary tools and resources to engage with course materials effectively. Technical issues can lead to frustration and decreased satisfaction. Institutions should provide robust technical support, online libraries, and resources that facilitate learning, ensuring that students can navigate their courses with confidence.

Interaction and Community

Opportunities for interaction, both with peers and instructors, significantly influence student satisfaction. Distance education can sometimes lead to feelings of isolation, making it essential for institutions to create a sense of community. This can be achieved through online discussion forums, group projects, and virtual networking events. Engaging students in collaborative activities helps build relationships and enhances the overall learning experience.

Feedback Mechanisms

Regular feedback on assignments, assessments, and overall performance is crucial for student development and satisfaction. Constructive feedback allows students to understand their strengths and areas for improvement, fostering a sense of progress and achievement. Institutions that implement effective feedback mechanisms, including formative assessments and timely responses, can enhance student satisfaction and promote a culture of continuous learning.

Flexibility and Personalization

The flexibility of distance education is one of its key advantages, allowing students to learn at their own pace and balance their studies with personal and professional commitments. However, the degree of flexibility offered can vary among programs. Institutions that provide options for personalized learning paths, scheduling, and course selection tend to enhance student satisfaction, as this empowers students to tailor their education to their individual needs.

Institutional Support Services

Comprehensive support services, including academic advising, counseling, and career services, are critical for distance education students. Access to these resources can significantly impact student satisfaction by helping them navigate academic challenges and plan for their futures. Institutions that prioritize holistic support for their students demonstrate a commitment to their success, fostering a more positive educational experience.

METHODOLOGY

- **Research Design:** This chapter employs a mixed-methods approach, combining quantitative surveys and qualitative interviews to gather comprehensive data on student satisfaction.
- **Respondents:** The study includes current students enrolled in distance education accounting programs across various institutions. Demographic factors such as age, prior education, and work experience will be considered.
- **Data Collection:** Data will be collected through online surveys assessing various dimensions of satisfaction and semi-structured interviews to gain deeper insights into student experiences.

FINDINGS AND DISCUSSION

Survey Results

The quantitative data collected through student satisfaction surveys reveal a nuanced picture of the distance education experience in accounting programs. Key findings indicate that:

- **Overall Satisfaction Levels**: A significant percentage of students (approximately 75%) reported being satisfied or very satisfied with their distance education experience. However, around 25% expressed dissatisfaction, highlighting areas for improvement.
- **Course Content**: The majority of respondents (82%) rated the relevance and applicability of the course content highly, noting that the curriculum effectively prepares them for the accounting profession.
- **Instructional Quality**: While many students praised the instructors' expertise, only 60% felt that the online teaching methods were engaging. This suggests a need for improved pedagogical strategies in distance learning environments.
- **Technological Support**: Approximately 70% of students reported satisfaction with technological resources and support services, but 30% encountered issues with access and usability, indicating room for enhancement in this area.
- **Interaction and Community**: Students expressed mixed feelings about interaction opportunities; while 65% appreciated the availability of online discussion forums, many felt that the sense of community was lacking, leading to feelings of isolation.

Thematic Analysis of Interviews

Qualitative interviews provided deeper insights into student experiences and satisfaction levels. Several recurring themes emerged:

- **Value of Engagement**: Students highlighted the importance of engaging teaching methods. Many emphasized that interactive elements, such as live Q&A sessions and group discussions, significantly enhanced their learning experience.
- **Need for Personalized Support**: Participants expressed a desire for more personalized academic support and mentorship. Students indicated that one-on-one interactions with instructors could provide clearer guidance and foster a stronger connection.
- **Technological Frustrations**: While most students appreciated the online learning environment, several reported frustrations with technological glitches and the learning management system's usability. These challenges sometimes hindered their ability to engage fully with course materials.
- **Community Building Efforts**: Many students suggested that initiatives aimed at building a sense of community—such as virtual networking events,

peer study groups, and social activities—would greatly enhance their overall experience.

Comparison with Traditional Education

When comparing the experiences of distance education students with those in traditional classroom settings, several distinctions emerged:

- **Engagement Levels**: Students in traditional programs often reported higher levels of engagement due to face-to-face interactions with peers and instructors. This suggests that distance education may benefit from implementing more interactive and synchronous learning opportunities.
- **Support Services**: Traditional students generally felt they had more immediate access to support services, such as advising and tutoring. Distance education programs must enhance their support structures to provide comparable resources.
- **Networking Opportunities**: The networking opportunities available in traditional settings, such as in-person events and informal interactions, are often perceived as lacking in online programs. Creating virtual networking opportunities could help bridge this gap.

Implications for Improvement

The findings of this study highlight several key areas for improvement in distance education accounting programs:

- **Enhancing Instructional Quality**: Training faculty in effective online teaching strategies and integrating more interactive elements can improve engagement and satisfaction levels.
- **Strengthening Technological Support**: Investing in user-friendly technologies and robust support services can alleviate technical frustrations and enhance the learning experience.
- **Fostering Community**: Developing initiatives to promote interaction and community-building among students can combat feelings of isolation and increase satisfaction.
- **Personalized Academic Support**: Implementing more personalized support mechanisms, such as mentorship programs and one-on-one advising, can help students feel more connected and supported in their educational journey.

Implications for Educational Institutions

The findings from this study reveal several critical implications for educational institutions offering distance education in accounting programs. By addressing the factors influencing student satisfaction, institutions can enhance the quality of their programs and improve student retention and success. The following strategies are recommended:

Enhancing Course Design

- **Curriculum Relevance**: Institutions should ensure that course content is continuously updated to reflect current industry practices and standards. This includes integrating real-world case studies and practical applications that resonate with students' future careers in accounting.
- **Engagement Strategies**: Incorporating diverse teaching methods, such as interactive modules, multimedia resources, and gamification, can make learning more engaging and effective.

Investing in Instructional Quality

- **Faculty Training**: Providing professional development opportunities for instructors in online teaching strategies is essential. Training should focus on fostering engagement, utilizing technology effectively, and delivering constructive feedback.
- **Peer Collaboration**: Encouraging faculty collaboration can lead to the sharing of best practices and innovative teaching methods, enhancing the overall instructional quality.

Strengthening Technological Support

- **User-Friendly Platforms**: Institutions should invest in intuitive learning management systems (LMS) that are easy for students to navigate. Regular updates and maintenance can help prevent technical issues that hinder learning.
- **Comprehensive Technical Support**: Establishing robust technical support services, including live chat options and tutorial resources, can assist students in overcoming technological barriers and enhance their learning experience.

Fostering Community and Interaction

- **Virtual Networking Opportunities**: Creating structured opportunities for student interaction—such as online study groups, discussion forums, and networking events—can help build a sense of community and reduce feelings of isolation.
- **Mentorship Programs**: Implementing mentorship initiatives that connect students with faculty or industry professionals can provide valuable guidance and foster stronger relationships within the learning environment.

Implementing Effective Feedback Mechanisms

- **Regular Surveys and Assessments**: Conducting periodic surveys to gauge student satisfaction and gather feedback on specific aspects of the program can inform continuous improvement efforts.
- **Actionable Feedback**: Providing students with clear, constructive feedback on their performance fosters a culture of learning and helps them identify areas for growth.

Holistic Support Services

- **Academic and Career Advising**: Institutions should ensure that comprehensive academic advising and career services are readily available to distance education students, offering guidance tailored to their individual needs.
- **Mental Health and Well-Being Support**: Recognizing the importance of mental health, institutions should provide access to counseling services and resources to support students' well-being throughout their educational journey.

CONCLUSION

This study highlights the critical importance of student satisfaction in distance education accounting programs, revealing both the strengths and challenges of this learning modality. While many students appreciate the flexibility and relevance of the curriculum, several areas require attention to enhance their educational experience. Key findings demonstrate that course content, instructional quality, technological support, community engagement, and personalized services significantly influence student satisfaction. To foster a more effective distance education environment, educational institutions must prioritize continuous improvement in these areas.

By enhancing course design and instructional practices, investing in user-friendly technology, and promoting community-building initiatives, institutions can create a more engaging and supportive learning atmosphere. Additionally, implementing robust support services and feedback mechanisms will ensure that students feel valued and connected throughout their educational journey.

REFERENCES

Allen, I. E., & Seaman, J. (2013). *Changing Course: Ten Years of Tracking Online Education in the United States*. Babson Survey Research Group. Retrieved from https://www.babson.edu

Allen, I. E., & Seaman, J. (2017). *Digital Learning Compass: Distance Education Enrollment Report 2017*. Babson Survey Research Group. Retrieved from https://www.babson.edu

Muilenburg, L. Y., & Berge, Z. L. (2005). Student Barriers to Online Learning: A Factor Analytic Study. *The Distance Education Report*, *9*(4), 7–8.

Rovai, A. P. (2002). Building Sense of Community at a Distance. *International Review of Research in Open and Distance Learning*, *3*(1). https://www.irrodl.org/index.php/irrodl/article/view/79

Chapter 4
Personalized Learning and Student Engagement:
Leveraging AI for Enhanced Learning Experiences in Distance Education

C. V. Suresh Babu
https://orcid.org/0000-0002-8474-2882
Hindustan Institute of Technology and Science, India

M. Yuvansankar
Hindustan Institute of Technology and Science, India

K. Tharuneshwaran
Hindustan Institute of Technology and Science, India

ABSTRACT

The integration of artificial intelligence (AI) technologies into education has emerged as a promising avenue to revolutionize the learning experience. With the use of AI tools and methodologies, teachers can tailor educational pathways to suit their students' individual needs, respond to differences in teaching style and provide prompt feedback so that they are more engaged and comprehended. Various applications of artificial intelligence in the field of education such as intelligent tutoring systems, adaptive learning platforms, and natural language processing tools are examined to highlight their effectiveness for dealing with educational challenges and supporting student success. This chapter looks at the potential of artificial intelligence for improving education practices, with a focus on increasing learning processes and optimising student results. It highlights the importance of responsible use of AI to reduce biases and ensure equal opportunities for all in order to address concerns

DOI: 10.4018/979-8-3693-7195-4.ch004

about ethics and possible problems related to integration of AI into education.

1. INTRODUCTION

1.1 Background of Personalized Learning in Distance Education

With the deepening of distance education research, distance education researchers increasingly realize that comprehensive and systematic learning support services are the core elements to maintain the success of distance education. Compared with full-time distance education students, distance learners are confronted with the following three difficulties in learning under the premise of taking into account both work and life: (1) Interaction difficulties. One of the characteristics of distance education is that teachers, distance education students and teaching institutions are separated geographically, and the process of teaching and learning depends on various media and media to complete, so there is a lack of timely and effective communication and exchange between teachers and distance education students, and between distance education students and distance education students. (2) Lack of learning skills. The success of distance education requires not only the development and provision of well-designed and diverse learning resources by educational institutions, but also the learners' high autonomous learning ability and time management ability. Secondly, distance education is mainly based on online autonomous learning, so it requires learners to have certain computer skills and information technology foundation. (3) Lack of time. Distance learners need to balance work, study and life, and can only study in leisure time and holidays, so they need higher learning efficiency. Kaur, S., Budhraja, K., Pahuja, A., Nayyar, V., & Saluja, S. (2024). Leveraging Artificial Intelligence in Education: Enhancing Learning Experience. In *Ethical AI and Data Management Strategies in Marketing* (pp. 125-140). IGI Global. DOI: 10.4018/979-8-3693-6660-8. Once the distance education students encounter difficulties, they will have corresponding needs. If the needs are not met, these difficulties will lead to the loss of interest in the course, the gradual loss of learning passion, the disordered learning arrangement and plan, and finally the failure.

An important way to solve these difficulties is to develop and provide perfect and systematic personalized learning path service for distance education students. As a bridge to maintain distance education institutions and learners, personalized learning path construction refers to the development of various services to meet the needs of distance education students, help distance education students solve learning difficulties, provide them with learning navigation, information consultation, resource search, facilities and technology, learning evaluation and other services to help them overcome various difficulties in pre-school, school and post-school. Therefore, this study uses Internet technology to enable education and artificial intelligence methods such as data mining and machine learning to conduct personalized learning research, so as to provide distance education students with personalized learning path navigation that ADAPTS to their knowledge background, learning preference, cognitive ability and learning goals, so as to effectively motivate and maintain the learning motivation of distance education students. The purpose of improving student's academic performance and promoting their development.

1.2 Role of AI in Enhancing Learning Experiences

The integration of Artificial Intelligence (AI) in education has a profound impact on learning experiences by transforming traditional classrooms into dynamic and personalized learning environments. AI technologies offer individualized support, real-time feedback, and adaptive learning pathways, leading to enhanced student engagement, motivation, and academic achievements. Firstly, it has a positive impact on the personalization of learning and enhancement of engagement. AI-powered personalized learning experiences cater to students' unique learning needs, styles, and paces. By analyzing individual performance data and learning preferences, AI algorithms recommend learning materials and activities that align with each student's strengths and weaknesses (Binns, R. 2018; Bobadilla, J., et. al. 2013; Kapp, K. M., 2012). Consequently, students are more engaged in their studies as they find relevance and value in the educational content. It also helps to improve decision-making, especially considering that data analytics can be incorporated. Educational data analytics powered by AI offer educators comprehensive insights into student learning patterns, strengths, and areas for improvement (Xu, Z., 2024). These data-driven insights enable evidence-based decision-making, empowering educators to implement targeted instructional strategies and interventions. As a result, students receive tailored support and resources that align with their individual needs, promoting academic success and fostering a sense of belonging and support within the educational community (Nissenbaum, H.,2010). Finally, it also has the ability to lead to experiential learning through immersive technologies like VR and AR. Students can explore virtual worlds, conduct experiments, and interact with simulated environments, enhancing their understanding of complex concepts (Holmes et al. 2019). In fact, AR simulations exhibited deeper critical thinking skills and improved problem-solving abilities, underlining the impact of experiential learning through immersive technologies (Holmes et al. 2019).

1.3 Importance of Student Engagement

The importance of student engagement becomes clearer if we consider the relationship of teacher to student in contrast to professional client relationships in other professions such as law, engineering, finance, management, and, in some cases, medicine. In other professions the client often recognizes a problem and voluntarily seeks the help of a professional. The professional is trusted to have important knowledge that will have clear benefits for the client, usually within a reasonably short period of time. The teaching of children, however, is more coercive. Children are told by society that they have a problem (ignorance) that must be solved regardless of whether they feel a need for education. They are subjected to a program of labor that the teacher prescribes. (Lamborn, S.,et. al. 1992). The significance and sources of student engagement.. The benefits of this labor are rarely self-evident to the student, partly because they are projected far into the future. These circumstances seem to diminish student trust in the professional, which is necessary if the student is to invest the considerable effort required for learning. Client effort is also required in other professions, especially, for example, mental health fields, but teaching stands out as the profession whose success depends on exceptionally long-term committed participation of its clients.

2. UNDERSTANDING PERSONALIZED LEARNING

2.1 Definition and Key Concepts

Personalized learning is an educational approach that tailors the learning experience to meet the unique needs, strengths, and interests of each student. Key concepts include learner agency, where students take an active role in their education; differentiated instruction, which adapts teaching methods to diverse learning styles; and data-driven decision-making, which uses insights from assessments to inform instructional strategies. (Topping, K. J., Ehly, S. W., 1998). In the context of leveraging AI for enhanced learning experiences in distance education, these principles become particularly powerful. AI can analyze vast amounts of data to identify individual learning patterns, providing personalized content and support that enhances engagement and retention. By integrating AI into distance education, educators can create customized learning pathways that foster a more effective and responsive educational environment, ultimately leading to improved student outcomes.

2.2 Historical Context and Evolution

The evolution of personalized learning has been shaped by significant shifts in educational philosophy and technological advancements. Early education systems predominantly relied on traditional, one-size-fits-all approaches, emphasizing standardized curricula and assessments. However, as educational theories progressed throughout the 20th century, the importance of catering to individual learning styles began to gain traction, influenced by theorists like John Dewey and Lev Vygotsky, who advocated for experiential and social learning. (Woolf, B. P. 2010). The rise of computer-assisted instruction in the late 20th century marked a pivotal moment, introducing more adaptive learning technologies that allowed for personalized experiences.

With the advent of the internet and online learning platforms in the 21st century, the concept of personalized learning gained further momentum, allowing for flexible learning environments and access to diverse resources. (Suresh Babu, C. V. & Rohan, B. 2023). Today, the integration of artificial intelligence has revolutionized this landscape, enabling real-time data analysis and personalized feedback in distance education. AI tools can assess student performance and adapt content accordingly, creating tailored learning experiences that were previously unimaginable. This evolution underscores the transformative potential of personalized learning in enhancing educational outcomes, particularly in distance education contexts where traditional face-to-face interactions are limited.

2.3 Relevance in Distance Learning Environments

In today's increasingly digital educational landscape, the relevance of personalized learning in distance learning environments cannot be overstated. As traditional classrooms evolve into online platforms, the challenge of meeting diverse student needs becomes more pronounced. Personalized learning offers a solution by allowing educators to tailor the educational experience to individual learners, enhancing engagement and effectiveness. (Chen, C. M., & Hwang, G. J., 2018). Leveraging AI in this context amplifies these benefits; AI systems can analyze student interactions, performance data, and preferences to create customized learning pathways that adapt in real time. This means that students can work at their own pace, accessing resources that align with their learning styles and interests, which is particularly crucial in remote settings where students may feel isolated or disconnected.

Furthermore, AI-driven analytics enable educators to identify at-risk students early on, facilitating timely interventions that can significantly improve retention and success rates. (Luckin, R., 2017). The ability to provide immediate feedback and adjust instructional strategies based on individual progress empowers both students and teachers, fostering a more interactive and responsive learning environment. Ultimately, the integration of personalized learning through AI not only enhances the distance education experience but also prepares students for lifelong learning in an ever-changing world.

3. ARTIFICIAL INTELLIGENCE TECHNIQUES FOR PERSONALIZED LEARNING

3.1 Overview of AI Technologies for Personalized Learning

Artificial intelligence encompasses a range of technologies that can significantly enhance personalized learning in distance education. (Suresh Babu, C. V. & Rohan, B. 2023). This capability allows educational platforms to adapt content dynamically, providing tailored resources and activities that align with each learner's unique needs. Natural language processing (NLP) is another vital AI technology that enables more interactive and engaging learning experiences. Through chatbots and virtual assistants, NLP facilitates real-time communication, offering instant feedback and support to students as they navigate their coursework. (Suresh Babu, C. V. & Rohan, B. 2023).

Additionally, adaptive learning systems leverage AI to customize the pace and difficulty of learning materials based on individual progress. These systems monitor student interactions and outcomes, adjusting the learning pathway to ensure optimal challenge without causing frustration.

Furthermore, AI-powered analytics tools provide educators with insights into student engagement and achievement, helping them make informed decisions about instructional strategies and interventions.

Overall, the integration of these AI technologies not only enhances the personalization of learning experiences but also creates a more responsive and supportive educational environment, ultimately leading to improved student outcomes in distance learning settings.

3.1.1 Machine Learning

Machine learning, a subset of artificial intelligence, plays a pivotal role in enhancing personalized learning experiences in distance education. By leveraging algorithms that can learn from and make predictions based on data, machine learning systems can analyze student interactions and performance in real time. This capability allows educational platforms to adaptively tailor content to meet individual learner needs, ensuring that students receive the right level of challenge and support. For instance, machine learning can identify patterns in a student's engagement and mastery of concepts, automatically adjusting the difficulty of assignments or recommending supplementary resources that target specific knowledge gaps. Additionally, these systems can predict potential struggles, enabling educators to intervene proactively and provide timely assistance. As a result, machine learning not only personalizes the learning journey for each student but also enhances overall engagement and retention in distance education environments, creating a more effective and responsive learning experience.

3.1.2 Natural Language Processing

Natural language processing (NLP) is a powerful AI technology that significantly enhances learning experiences in distance education by facilitating better communication and interaction between students and educational platforms (Suresh Babu, C. V., Anniyappa, C. S, et. al . 2024).

Through NLP, educational tools can understand and process human language, enabling features such as chatbots and virtual assistants that provide instant support and feedback (Suresh Babu, C. V., Anniyappa, C. S, et. al . 2024). For instance, students can ask questions in natural language and receive immediate, contextually relevant answers, fostering a more interactive learning environment. Additionally, NLP can analyze student-written responses to gauge understanding, offering personalized feedback and resources to help improve writing skills or conceptual comprehension. Furthermore, sentiment analysis can help educators monitor student emotions and engagement levels, allowing for timely interventions when students may be struggling or disengaged. By integrating NLP into distance education, institutions can create a more engaging, responsive, and supportive learning atmosphere, ultimately enhancing student satisfaction and success.

3.1.3 Computer Vision

Computer vision, another vital AI technology, has the potential to transform distance education by enabling more interactive and immersive learning experiences. This technology allows computers to interpret and process visual information from the world, facilitating applications such as automated grading of visual assignments, real-time feedback on presentations, and even monitoring student engagement during virtual classes. (Suresh Babu, C. V., Anniyappa, C. S, et. al . 2024). For instance, computer vision can analyze students' facial expressions and body language during video lectures to gauge their level of engagement, allowing educators to adapt their teaching methods accordingly.

Additionally, computer vision can enhance learning through augmented reality (AR) and virtual reality (VR) experiences, providing students with immersive environments where they can explore complex concepts in a hands-on manner. (Kour, A., et. al. 2019).. For example, students in science or engineering fields can visualize intricate models or simulations that enhance their understanding of challenging material. By leveraging computer vision in distance education, institutions can create more dynamic and engaging learning experiences, ultimately promoting deeper understanding and retention of knowledge.

3.2 Applications of AI in Distance Education

3.2.1 Intelligent Tutoring Systems

Intelligent Tutoring Systems (ITS) are sophisticated AI-driven platforms designed to provide personalized instruction to learners, mimicking the benefits of one-on-one tutoring in a distance education setting. By employing advanced algorithms, ITS can assess a student's knowledge level, learning style, and progress in real time. (VanLehn, K., 2011).

This allows the system to adaptively present tailored content, exercises, and feedback that specifically address each learner's unique needs (Suresh Babu, C. V. and A. Auroshaa, 2024). For example, if a student struggles with a particular concept, the ITS can offer additional explanations, practice problems, and hints to reinforce understanding, while also guiding them through progressively challenging materials as they gain mastery.

Moreover, ITS can track and analyse a student's interactions over time, providing educators with valuable insights into individual performance and learning patterns. This data enables instructors to identify areas where students may need further support and to intervene when necessary, thereby enhancing the overall learning experience. By integrating ITS into distance education, institutions can create a more engaging and effective learning environment, ultimately leading to improved student outcomes and greater satisfaction.

3.2.2 Adaptive Learning Platforms

Adaptive learning platforms represent a transformative application of AI in distance education, designed to create personalized learning experiences that cater to the diverse needs of students. These platforms utilize sophisticated algorithms to continuously assess individual learner data, including performance metrics, engagement levels, and learning preferences (Suresh Babu, C. V. & Rohan, B. 2023). As students interact with the content, the system dynamically adjusts the learning pathway, presenting tailored resources, exercises, and assessments that align with each learner's unique strengths and weaknesses.

For instance, if a student excels in certain subjects but struggles in others, the adaptive learning platform can provide advanced materials in their areas of strength while offering additional practice and support in more challenging topics. This personalized approach not only enhances mastery of concepts but also keeps students engaged by ensuring that they are neither bored with overly simplistic content nor overwhelmed by excessive difficulty. Furthermore, adaptive learning platforms can offer real-time feedback, allowing learners to track their progress and make informed decisions about their study habits.By leveraging adaptive learning technologies, distance education can foster a more inclusive and effective learning environment, accommodating various learning styles and paces. This ultimately leads to improved educational outcomes, as students are empowered to take charge of their own learning journeys, supported by systems that understand and respond to their individual needs.

3.2.3 Recommendation Engines

Recommendation engines are a powerful AI application that significantly enhances the learning experience in distance education by providing personalized content suggestions tailored to individual students. These systems analyze a learner's past interactions, preferences, and performance data to curate resources such as courses, videos, articles, and exercises that align with their interests and learning goals. (Pazzani, M. J., & Billsus, D. 2007). By utilizing collaborative filtering and content-based filtering techniques, recommendation engines can identify patterns in user behavior and recommend materials that similar learners have found beneficial.

The impact of recommendation engines extends beyond merely suggesting resources; they actively encourage students to explore new topics and deepen their understanding of subjects. For instance, if a student shows a strong interest in a particular field, the engine can recommend advanced courses or complementary materials, fostering a sense of agency and promoting lifelong learning. Additionally, these engines can help identify gaps in knowledge by suggesting foundational resources when a learner struggles with advanced topics.

In a distance education context, where students may feel isolated or disengaged, recommendation engines play a crucial role in maintaining motivation and enhancing engagement. (Bobadilla, J., et. al. 2013). By providing a personalized learning pathway that resonates with each student, these systems not only improve educational outcomes but also create a more dynamic and supportive online learning environment. Ultimately, recommendation engines empower learners to take control of their educational journey, ensuring that they receive the right content at the right time.

4. ENHANCING STUDENT ENGAGEMENT THROUGH AI AND LEARNING ANALYTICS

4.1 Importance of Student Engagement in Learning

Student engagement is a critical component of effective learning, particularly in distance education, where the absence of face-to-face interactions can lead to feelings of isolation and disconnection. Engaged students are more likely to be motivated, participate actively in their learning, and retain information, all of which contribute to improved academic outcomes. Engagement fosters a sense of belonging and investment in the educational process, encouraging learners to take ownership of their studies and explore topics more deeply. In distance learning environments, where traditional motivators may be less accessible, enhancing engagement becomes even more vital.

AI and learning analytics play a significant role in boosting student engagement by providing personalized experiences that resonate with individual learners. Through real-time data analysis, educators can gain insights into student behavior, identifying when learners are struggling or disengaged. (Fredricks, J. A., et. al.). This allows for timely interventions and tailored support that can rekindle interest and motivation. Additionally, AI-driven tools can create interactive and adaptive learning experiences, ensuring that content is relevant and challenging, thus capturing students' attention and encouraging active participation. By leveraging these technologies, educators can foster a more engaging learning environment, ultimately leading to better retention, satisfaction, and success in distance education.

4.2Techniques for Increasing Engagement

4.2.1 Gamification and AI

Gamification, the integration of game design elements into non-gaming contex Construction and Innovative Exploration of Personalized Learning Systems in the (Context of Educational Data Mining). Its, is a powerful technique for increasing student engagement in distance education, especially when combined with AI. By incorporating elements such as points, badges, leaderboards, and challenges, gamification transforms traditional learning experiences into more interactive and enjoyable activities. (Suresh Babu, C. V. & Adhithya, S., 2023). This approach taps into students' intrinsic motivations, encouraging them to participate actively and persist through challenges.

AI enhances gamification by personalizing the experience for each learner. For instance, AI algorithms can analyze individual performance data to adjust the difficulty of challenges, ensuring that tasks are neither too easy nor overly difficult. (Kapp, K. M., 2012). This adaptability keeps students in a state of flow, where they feel challenged yet capable, which is crucial for maintaining motivation. Additionally, AI can provide instant feedback on performance, allowing students to see their progress in real time and motivating them to improve.

Moreover, gamified learning environments foster social interaction and collaboration through team-based challenges and competitions. AI can facilitate these interactions by pairing students with similar interests or complementary skills, creating opportunities for peer learning and support. Overall, the combination of gamification and AI not only makes learning more engaging and enjoyable but also promotes a sense of community and collaboration among distance learners, leading to enhanced educational outcomes.

4.2.2 Interactive Learning Environments

Interactive learning environments are essential in distance education, as they actively engage students and facilitate meaningful learning experiences despite physical separation. (Baker, R. S., 2016). These environments leverage various technologies and pedagogical strategies to create dynamic, immersive educational experiences that promote collaboration, critical thinking, and active participation.

1. **Collaborative Tools**: Platforms such as discussion forums, virtual classrooms, and group projects enable students to collaborate in real time. These tools foster communication and teamwork, allowing learners to share ideas, ask questions, and work together on assignments, which helps build a sense of community.
2. **Multimedia Content**: Incorporating videos, interactive simulations, and gamified elements can make learning more engaging and accessible. Multimedia resources cater to different learning styles and help clarify complex concepts, enhancing student understanding and retention.
3. **Adaptive Learning Technologies**: These technologies personalize the learning experience by adjusting content based on individual performance and preferences. By continuously analyzing student interactions, adaptive learning platforms ensure that each learner receives the right level of challenge and support.

4. **Feedback Mechanisms**: Immediate feedback is crucial for maintaining engagement. Interactive environments often include quizzes and assessments that provide real-time insights into student performance, enabling learners to identify strengths and areas for improvement quickly.
5. **Hands-On Activities**: Virtual labs, simulations, and project-based learning opportunities allow students to apply their knowledge in practical contexts. These hands-on experiences deepen understanding and make learning more relevant and engaging.
6. **Gamification**: Introducing game-like elements such as points, badges, and leaderboards can motivate students to participate actively. Gamification encourages healthy competition and makes the learning process more enjoyable.
7. **Flexible Learning Pathways**: Providing students with choices in their learning pathways fosters autonomy and encourages exploration of topics that interest them. This flexibility enhances motivation and investment in the learning process.

4.3 Data-Driven Insights from Learning Analytics

4.3.1 Collecting and Analyzing Learning Data

Collecting and analyzing learning data is fundamental to leveraging learning analytics in distance education. This process involves gathering various types of data from student interactions with online platforms, including participation rates, assignment submissions, quiz scores, and time spent on different activities. By employing tools such as learning management systems (LMS), educators can track not only academic performance but also engagement levels and learning behaviors.

Once the data is collected, advanced analytics techniques, including machine learning and statistical analysis, can be applied to identify patterns and trends. (Baker, R. S., 2016). For instance, educators can analyze which resources or activities lead to higher engagement and success rates, as well as pinpoint students who may be at risk of falling behind. This data-driven approach enables instructors to make informed decisions about curriculum design and instructional strategies, ensuring that the learning experience is tailored to meet the needs of all students.

Furthermore, visualizing learning data through dashboards can provide immediate insights for both educators and students. Instructors can quickly assess class performance and adapt their teaching accordingly, while students can track their own progress and set goals for improvement. Overall, the effective collection and analysis of learning data empower educators to create more personalized and responsive learning environments, ultimately enhancing student engagement and success in distance education.

4.3.2 Personalization of Content and Feedback

Personalization of content and feedback is a critical component of effective learning analytics in distance education. By utilizing data collected from student interactions, educators can tailor educational materials and feedback to meet the specific needs and preferences of individual learners. (Wang, F., & Wang, Q., 2019). This personalized approach not only enhances student engagement but also fosters a deeper understanding of the subject matter.

Learning analytics enables the identification of students' strengths and weaknesses through detailed performance tracking. For example, if a student struggles with a particular concept, the system can automatically suggest targeted resources—such as supplementary readings, instructional videos, or practice exercises—that address those gaps. (Baker, R. S. J. D., 2014). This adaptive content delivery ensures that learners receive the right support at the right time, facilitating mastery of challenging topics.

Additionally, personalized feedback is crucial in helping students understand their progress and areas for improvement. Rather than receiving generic comments, learners can benefit from specific, actionable insights based on their performance data. This feedback loop encourages self-reflection and empowers students to take ownership of their learning journey.

By leveraging learning analytics for content personalization and feedback, distance education can become more responsive and effective, ultimately leading to improved educational outcomes and a more satisfying learning experience for students.

5. CASE STUDIES OF PERSONALIZED LEARNING IN ACTION

5.1 Overview of Selected Case Studies

Personalized learning has been successfully implemented in various educational settings, demonstrating its effectiveness in enhancing student engagement and achievement. This section provides an overview of selected case studies that highlight innovative approaches to personalized learning in action.

1. Khan Academy: This widely recognized platform uses adaptive learning technologies to tailor educational experiences for students. Through personalized dashboards, learners can progress at their own pace, receiving recommendations for exercises based on their mastery of topics. (Kizilcec, R. F., & Schneider, E. F. 2015).

Case studies from schools utilizing Khan Academy have shown significant improvements in student performance, particularly in math, as students can focus on areas where they need more practice.

2. Summit Learning: This program emphasizes personalized learning through a combination of project-based learning and technology. In schools implementing Summit Learning, students set individual goals, engage in self-directed projects, and receive real-time feedback from teachers and peers. Case studies indicate that this approach fosters a strong sense of ownership over learning, leading to increased motivation and academic success.
3. DreamBox Learning: This adaptive math program is designed for K-8 students and utilizes real-time data to adjust lessons based on individual performance. The platform personalizes instruction by analyzing student interactions and providing tailored feedback and challenges. Schools using DreamBox report increased student engagement and improved math scores, particularly among struggling learners. (Dream Box Learning. (2021).

These case studies illustrate the diverse applications of personalized learning across various contexts and highlight the positive impact on student engagement, mastery, and overall educational outcomes. By leveraging technology and data-driven insights, these programs demonstrate how personalized learning can create more responsive and effective educational environments.

5.2.1 Case Study 1: AI Implementation in K-12 Education

In a K-12 education setting, a school district implemented an AI-powered personalized learning platform aimed at enhancing student engagement and improving academic outcomes. The initiative began with an extensive needs assessment, identifying the varying levels of proficiency among students in subjects such as math and reading. European Commission. (2018). The AI system utilized adaptive learning algorithms that adjusted the curriculum in real time based on individual student performance.

Upon implementation, the platform provided students with diagnostic assessments to gauge their initial skills. As students interacted with the content, the AI continuously analyzed their responses, offering tailored exercises and resources that targeted specific areas where they struggled. For instance, if a student struggled with fractions, the system would provide additional practice problems and instructional videos focused on that concept.

Teachers received access to detailed analytics that highlighted student progress and areas needing attention. This enabled them to intervene promptly, offering additional support to students who required it. The platform also facilitated communication between teachers, students, and parents, creating a collaborative environment for monitoring progress.

The results were compelling: the school district reported an average improvement of 20% in standardized test scores among students using the AI platform compared to those in traditional classrooms. Teachers noted increased engagement levels, with students taking greater ownership of their learning journeys. The combination of real-time feedback, personalized content, and targeted interventions proved effective in addressing the diverse needs of learners.

Overall, this case study illustrates how AI implementation in K-12 education can create a more responsive and engaging learning environment, ultimately leading to enhanced student performance and satisfaction.

5.2.2 Case Study 2: AI in Higher Education

In a higher education context, a university adopted an AI-based learning analytics system to enhance student success in large lecture courses. The system collected data on student interactions with course materials, attendance, and performance on assessments. Using this data, the AI provided personalized feedback and resources tailored to each student's learning behaviors and progress.

The results were promising: the university observed a notable increase in course completion rates, especially among first-year students who often struggle in large classes. Faculty could identify at-risk students early and provide targeted support, such as tutoring sessions or supplementary resources. This case demonstrates how AI can be leveraged in higher education to create a supportive learning environment that promotes student retention and success.

5.2.3 Case Study 3: AI in Adult Learning Programs

In adult learning programs, an organization implemented an AI-driven platform to facilitate personalized learning for working professionals pursuing skill development. The system assessed individual learning goals, career aspirations, and prior knowledge to recommend tailored courses and learning pathways.

Feedback from participants indicated increased satisfaction and engagement, as the platform provided relevant, real-time feedback and allowed learners to progress at their own pace. Additionally, completion rates for courses rose significantly, with many participants reporting that the personalized approach helped them apply what they learned directly to their jobs. This case underscores the effectiveness of AI in adult education, highlighting its ability to meet the diverse needs of adult learners and support their professional development.

These success stories illustrate the transformative impact of AI in various educational contexts, showcasing its potential to enhance personalized learning experiences, increase engagement, and improve outcomes across K-12, higher education, and adult learning programs.

5.3 Lessons Learned from Case Studies

The analysis of various case studies on the implementation of personalized learning through AI in K-12, higher education, and adult learning programs offers valuable insights into best practices and potential challenges. Here are some key lessons learned:

1. Emphasize Data-Driven Decision Making: Successful implementations rely heavily on the effective collection and analysis of learning data. Educational institutions must prioritize establishing robust data systems that can provide real-time insights into student performance and engagement. This data is crucial for tailoring instructional approaches and identifying at-risk students early.
2. Focus on Personalized Learning Paths: One of the most significant advantages of AI is its ability to personalize learning experiences. Educators should leverage AI tools to create individualized learning paths that address each student's strengths, weaknesses, and interests. This tailored approach not only improves engagement but also fosters a sense of ownership in learners.
3. Ensure Teacher Training and Support: For AI and personalized learning initiatives to succeed, teachers must be adequately trained to utilize these technologies effectively. Ongoing professional development and support are essential for educators to integrate AI tools into their teaching practices and to interpret data insights meaningfully.
4. Foster Collaboration and Communication: Effective communication among students, teachers, and parents is vital for the success of personalized learning initiatives. Platforms that facilitate collaboration and feedback create a supportive learning community, enhancing student motivation and accountability.
5. Adaptability and Flexibility are Key: AI-driven systems should be flexible enough to adapt to changing educational needs and student dynamics. Institutions should regularly assess and update their technologies and approaches to ensure they remain relevant and effective in meeting diverse learner needs.
6. Monitor and Evaluate Outcomes Continuously: Continuous monitoring and evaluation of the impact of personalized learning initiatives are essential. Institutions should establish metrics for success and regularly assess both academic outcomes and student satisfaction to identify areas for improvement.

7. Cultivate a Culture of Innovation: Successful case studies often involve a culture that embraces innovation and experimentation. Educational institutions should encourage educators to explore new teaching methodologies and technologies, fostering an environment where creative solutions to learning challenges can thrive.

By incorporating these lessons learned from case studies, educational institutions can enhance their approaches to personalized learning through AI, ultimately leading to improved engagement, satisfaction, and academic success for students across various educational settings.

6. ETHICAL CONSIDERATIONS AND CHALLENGES

6.1 Data Privacy and Security Concerns

The integration of AI in distance education introduces critical ethical challenges, particularly regarding data privacy and security. As educational institutions collect vast amounts of student data—including personal identifiers, academic performance, and engagement metrics—ensuring informed consent becomes paramount. Nissenbaum, H. (2010). Binns, R. (2018). Students must understand what data is collected, how it will be used, and the implications of sharing it. Compliance with legal frameworks like FERPA and GDPR is essential to safeguard sensitive information and protect students' rights.

Moreover, robust cybersecurity measures are necessary to prevent data breaches, which could expose personal information and undermine trust in educational institutions. This includes implementing encryption, secure access controls, and regular security audits. The potential for algorithmic bias in AI systems also poses risks; biased algorithms can lead to unequal educational experiences for different student demographics. To mitigate this, transparency in AI design and ongoing evaluation for fairness are crucial.

Additionally, clear policies around data ownership and the rights of students to access, correct, or delete their information are vital in promoting a culture of accountability. While AI can enhance learning through personalized experiences, excessive surveillance may infringe on privacy, creating a need for balance between monitoring for academic support and respecting individual autonomy. Addressing these data privacy and security concerns is essential for fostering an ethical and supportive learning environment in distance education.

6.2 Bias and Fairness in AI Algorithms

The use of AI in distance education raises significant concerns about bias and fairness in algorithms, which can adversely affect student learning outcomes. AI systems, often trained on historical data, may inadvertently reflect and perpetuate existing biases present in that data, leading to unequal treatment of different student demographics based on race, gender, socioeconomic status, or learning abilities. This can manifest in various ways, such as biased recommendations for resources or differential access to support services, ultimately disadvantaging certain groups. To address these challenges, it is essential for educational institutions to prioritize transparency in AI algorithms, ensuring that stakeholders understand how decisions are made. Implementing diverse training datasets and conducting regular audits for bias can help mitigate these risks. Additionally, involving a diverse range of voices in the development and evaluation of AI tools can promote fairness and inclusivity. By actively addressing bias in AI systems, institutions can create more equitable learning environments that support all students in achieving their full potential.

6.3 Recommendations for Ethical AI Practices

To foster ethical AI practices in distance education, institutions should implement several key strategies. First, establishing clear guidelines for data privacy and consent is essential, ensuring that students are fully informed about data collection, usage, and their rights. Regular audits of AI algorithms for bias should be conducted to identify and mitigate unfair practices, promoting transparency and accountability in decision-making processes. (Jobin, A., Ienca, M., & Andorno, R., 2019). Engaging diverse stakeholders—students, educators, and technologists—in the development and evaluation of AI tools can help create more inclusive systems. (Dignum, V., 2019).

Additionally, providing training for educators on the ethical use of AI will empower them to integrate these technologies responsibly while being mindful of potential biases and privacy concerns. Finally, creating mechanisms for student feedback and oversight can help institutions remain responsive to the ethical implications of their AI applications, fostering a culture of continuous improvement and ethical accountability in leveraging AI for enhanced learning experiences.

7. IMPLEMENTATION STRATEGIES FOR EDUCATORS

7.1 Practical Steps for Integrating AI into Distance Learning

To effectively integrate AI into distance learning, educators can follow a structured approach that starts with assessing their technological readiness and identifying areas where AI can add value, such as by personalizing learning or automating tasks like grading. Selecting tools aligned with the school's goals and budget is essential at this stage, as noted by Holmes et al. (2019), who discuss the importance of targeted AI implementation in educational settings. Beginning with small pilot programs allows educators to test AI applications in controlled environments, gather feedback, and make data-informed adjustments to enhance tool efficacy (Zawacki-Richter et al., 2019). Training educators is critical for effective AI integration; providing ongoing professional development ensures they can confidently use AI tools and interpret the data these tools provide (Luckin et al., 2016). An ethical, inclusive approach to AI is also necessary to address concerns around privacy and bias, as highlighted by UNESCO (2021), which emphasizes transparency and equitable digital literacy in AI-enabled education. Finally, educators should establish key performance indicators to track the impact of AI on student engagement and academic progress, refining strategies as needed and gradually expanding successful tools across more classrooms. This methodical approach not only enhances the learning experience but also ensures AI integration is adaptive and aligned with the diverse needs of students.

7.2 Technical and Administrative Considerations

Integrating AI into distance learning requires addressing both technical and administrative aspects to ensure a smooth and secure implementation. Robust technical infrastructure, including reliable internet, adequate devices, and secure data storage, is essential to support AI tools effectively (UNESCO, 2021). Administrators must also prioritize data privacy by establishing strict protocols for data management and security, safeguarding students' personal information, and ensuring compliance with ethical standards, including bias detection and transparency in AI-driven processes (Holmes et al., 2019). Moreover, dedicated IT support is crucial to promptly resolve technical issues, thereby minimizing disruptions and fostering a reliable learning environment.

7.3 Professional Development and Training for Educators

Professional development and training are equally vital, as educators need to be equipped with the skills to operate and maximize AI's potential in teaching. Luckin et al. (2016) underscore the importance of comprehensive training programs that familiarize educators with AI functionalities while enhancing their ability to interpret AI-generated data insights. This training should be ongoing, with support networks like peer collaborations or online communities that enable educators to share experiences and best practices (Zawacki-Richter et al., 2019). Such resources build teachers' confidence in using AI tools, ultimately supporting a learning environment where AI enhances educational outcomes and adapts to student needs effectively.

8. FUTURE TRENDS AND RESEARCH DIRECTIONS

8.1 Emerging Technologies in AI and Learning Analytics

The integration of AI in distance education is reshaping the learning landscape with advancements in emerging technologies and learning analytics, paving the way for highly personalized educational experiences. Emerging technologies such as natural language processing (NLP), machine learning (ML), and predictive analytics are rapidly transforming distance learning by enabling more responsive, data-driven, and individualized approaches to education. NLP, for instance, facilitates real-time interaction between students and AI-driven platforms, offering immediate feedback and guidance, thereby enhancing engagement and making remote learning more interactive (Holmes et al., 2019). Furthermore, ML algorithms analyze patterns in student engagement and performance, providing insights into learning behaviors and enabling predictive modeling to identify students at risk of falling behind. This early intervention allows teachers to provide timely support, effectively bridging gaps in learning before they widen (Zawacki-Richter et al., 2019).

8.2 Predictions for Personalized Learning in Distance Education

Personalized learning in distance education is another key trend, with AI poised to enable tailored educational paths for individual students. AI-driven adaptive learning systems are capable of customizing both content and assessments to meet the unique needs of each learner, facilitating a student-centered approach that allows learners to progress at their own pace. For example, an AI-powered platform could adjust the complexity of assignments based on a student's mastery of the material, ensuring they are neither overwhelmed nor unchallenged. This customization supports competency-based learning, where students move forward based on skill proficiency rather than the time spent on tasks, creating a more efficient and engaging educational experience (UNESCO, 2021). Additionally, personalized learning tools in AI can track students' preferences, learning styles, and areas of interest, using this information to curate content that is not only relevant but also motivating. The ability of AI to process and analyze vast amounts of data allows for a nuanced understanding of each student's strengths and areas for growth, which can result in a highly flexible and adaptive educational journey (Luckin et al., 2016).

8.3 Areas for Further Research and Exploration

However, the advancement of AI in education also introduces a variety of complex challenges, pointing to critical areas for further research. One pressing issue is the ethical dimension of AI, particularly concerning privacy, equity, and algorithmic bias. Since AI systems rely heavily on student data to provide personalized experiences, ensuring data security and transparency in data use is paramount. AI-driven systems need to be designed with fairness in mind to avoid biases that could unfairly disadvantage certain student groups. Further research is needed to develop frameworks that address these ethical considerations, ensuring that AI is deployed in ways that are both safe and equitable for all students (UNESCO, 2021). Moreover, studies on the long-term outcomes of AI-powered personalized learning are essential to assess its actual impact on student success and retention. These studies can provide valuable insights into whether AI-driven education genuinely supports learning objectives and enhances student outcomes over time.

Another key area for exploration is professional development for educators. As AI tools become more complex and integral to the educational process, educators must be adequately trained to leverage these tools effectively. Research is needed to identify best practices for AI training programs that not only build teachers' technical skills but also enhance their ability to interpret data insights and integrate AI-driven resources into their pedagogy effectively (Luckin et al., 2016). Training programs should also address the ethical considerations surrounding AI in education, equipping educators to make informed decisions about data use and student privacy.

9. CONCLUSION

9.1 Summary of Key Findings

The integration of AI in distance education has illuminated transformative ways to make education more accessible, responsive, and adaptive to individual learning needs. Key findings from the research indicate that AI technologies, including natural language processing (NLP), machine learning (ML), and predictive analytics, are invaluable in tailoring educational content, monitoring student progress, and providing real-time support (Holmes et al., 2019). AI-driven adaptive learning systems enable personalized learning pathways, which allow students to advance at their own pace based on competency rather than time, thereby supporting a shift toward a mastery-focused education model (UNESCO, 2021). Furthermore, the capabilities of AI to analyze large volumes of data in real time allow educators to make data-informed decisions that can close learning gaps, identify struggling students, and customize intervention strategies. However, ethical challenges associated with data privacy, security, and algorithmic bias persist, requiring careful oversight and responsible deployment (Luckin et al., 2016). These challenges underscore the need for structured training for educators, as well as for ongoing research and development to ensure that AI use remains safe, ethical, and inclusive.

9.2 Final Thoughts on the Future of AI in Distance Education

AI's role in shaping the future of distance education is promising, with the potential to foster inclusivity and engagement, and to support personalized learning on a broader scale. By automating repetitive tasks, AI frees up educators to focus more on interactive and supportive roles, enhancing the quality of education students receive (Zawacki-Richter et al., 2019). Additionally, as AI technologies advance, they can bridge significant educational gaps by providing accessible learning opportunities to underserved or remote communities. However, realizing this future requires a commitment to responsible AI practices that address ethical considerations, such as data security and the reduction of algorithmic bias. The benefits AI promises can only be fully realized if these technologies are deployed thoughtfully, with an emphasis on accessibility and equity, ensuring they do not exacerbate existing disparities. Continuous collaboration between educators, policymakers, and AI developers is essential to create standards that guide ethical AI use in education, ensuring a supportive environment where technology complements rather than disrupts learning.

9.3 Call to Action for Educators and Policymakers

To harness AI's full potential in distance learning, both educators and policymakers must play active, collaborative roles. For educators, this means engaging in ongoing professional development to stay updated on AI advancements and their potential applications in teaching. Teachers should strive to build digital literacy within the classroom, helping students understand AI's role in their education and its ethical implications. This proactive approach can cultivate an adaptive and future-ready learning environment, where students are equipped to use AI responsibly (Luckin et al., 2016).

For policymakers, the call to action involves establishing and upholding clear standards and guidelines for ethical AI deployment in education. Policymakers should prioritize funding to support equitable access to AI tools, particularly for schools in underserved or resource-limited areas, thus bridging the digital divide and ensuring all students have the opportunity to benefit from AI-enhanced learning (UNESCO, 2021). Additionally, supporting research that examines long-term outcomes of AI-driven education will be crucial in assessing its impact on academic success and retention (Zawacki-Richter et al., 2019). By fostering partnerships between government bodies, educational institutions, and technology developers, policymakers can help build a sustainable and inclusive framework for AI in education.

REFERENCES

Alpaydin, E. (2020). Introduction to Machine Learning (4th ed.). MIT Press.Mitchell, T. M. (1997). *Machine Learning*. McGraw-Hill.Jurafsky, D., & Martin, J. H. (2020). *Speech and Language Processing* (3rd ed.). Pearson.Chen, M., & Zhu, Q. (2019). "Applications of Natural Language Processing in Education: A Review." *Education and Information Technologies*, 24(3), 1695-1716.

Baker, R. S. (2016). Stupid Tutoring Systems: The Current State of Educational Technology. *International Journal of Artificial Intelligence in Education*, *26*(4), 148–164.

Binns, R. (2018). "Fairness in Machine Learning: Lessons from Political Philosophy." *Proceedings of the 2018 Conference on Fairness, Accountability, and Transparency*.

Bobadilla, J., Ortega, F., Serradilla, F., & Hernando, A. (2013). Collaborative Filtering and Recommendation Systems: A Review. *ACM Computing Surveys*, *45*(3), 19.

Chen, C. M., & Hwang, G. J. (2018). "Personalized Learning Environments in Distance Education: A Systematic Review." *Computers & Education*, 126, 1-14.Dziuban, C., Hartman, J., & Moskal, P. (2004). "Blended Learning." *Educause Center for Applied Research*.

Construction and Innovative Exploration of Personalized Learning Systems in the Context of Educational Data Mining. (•••).. . *International Journal of Information and Communication Technology Education*, *20*(1), 1–14. DOI: 10.4018/ijicte.2014010107

Dignum, V. (2019). Responsible Artificial Intelligence: Designing AI for Human Values. *Computer*, *52*(8), 28–36.

DreamBox Learning. (2021). "The Impact of DreamBox Learning on K-12 Student Achievement." McKinsey & Company. (2019). "Georgia State University: Transforming Student Outcomes through Predictive Analytics."

European Commission. (2018). "General Data Protection Regulation (GDPR)." Retrieved from https://ec.europa.eu/info/law/law-topic/data-protection_enO'Neil, C. (2016). *Weapons of Math Destruction: How Big Data Increases Inequality and Threatens Democracy*. Crown Publishing Group.

Fredricks, J. A., Blumenfeld, P. C., & Paris, A. H. (2004). "School Engagement: Potential of the Concept, State of the Evidence." *Review of Educational Research*, 74(1), 59-109. Deterding, S. (2011). "Gamification: Designing for Motivation." *Interactions*, 18(4), 14-17. LinkKapp, K. M. (2012). *Gamification in Training and Education: What, Why, and How.*

Holmes et al. (2019) Zawacki-Richter et al.,(2019), (Luckin et al., 2016), (Zawacki-Richter et al., 2019), (Zawacki-Richter et al., 2019).

Holmes, W., Bialik, M., & Fadel, C. (2019). *Artificial Intelligence in Education: Promises and Implications for Teaching and Learning*. Center for Curriculum Redesign.

Jobin, A., Ienca, M., & Andorno, R. (2019). Artificial Intelligence: The Global Landscape of Ethics Guidelines. *Nature Machine Intelligence*, *1*(9), 389–399. DOI: 10.1038/s42256-019-0088-2

Kapp, K. M. (2012). *Gamification in Training and Education: What*. Why, and How.

Kaur, S., Budhraja, K., Pahuja, A., Nayyar, V., & Saluja, S. (2024). Leveraging Artificial Intelligence in Education: Enhancing Learning Experience. In *Ethical AI and Data Management Strategies in Marketing* (pp. 125-140). IGI Global. DOI: DOI: 10.4018/979-8-3693-6660-8

Kizilcec, R. F., & Schneider, E. F. (2015). Siemens, G. (2013). "Learning Analytics: The Emergence of a New Learning Discipline." *Journal of Educational Technology & Society*, 16(2), 14-20 114 (17) 4348-4353 https://doi.org/DOI: 10.1073/pnas.1611898114

Lamborn, S., Newmann, F., & Wehlage, G. (1992). The significance and sources of student engagement. *Student engagement and achievement in American secondary schools*, 11-39.

List of Cited Literature

Luckin, R. (2017). *Enhancing Learning and Teaching with Technology: What the Research Says*. UCL Institute of Education Press.Kober, N. (2015). *Reaching Students: What Research Says About Effective Instruction in Undergraduate Science and Engineering*. National Academies Press.

Nissenbaum, H. (2010). *Privacy in Context: Technology, Policy, and the Integrity of Social Life*. Stanford University Press.Binns, R. (2018). "Fairness in Machine Learning: Lessons from Political Philosophy." *Proceedings of the 2018 Conference on Fairness, Accountability, and Transparency*.

Pazzani, M. J., & Billsus, D. (2007). "Content-Based Recommendation Systems." In *The Adaptive Web* (pp. 325-341). Springer. DOI: 10.1007/978-3-540-72079-9_10

Siemens, G. (2013). "Learning Analytics: The Emergence of a New Learning Discipline." *Journal of Educational Technology & Society*, 16(2), 14-20. Wang, F., & Wang, Q. (2019). "The Impact of Learning Analytics on Personalized Learning: A Systematic Review. *Journal of Educational Computing Research*, *57*(4), 962–994.

Suresh Babu, C. V., & Adhithya, S. (2023). ChatGPT and Other Generative AI Tools in Education: Transformative Potential and Ethical Considerations. In Keengwe, J. (Ed.), *Creative AI Tools and Ethical Implications in Teaching and Learning* (pp. 135–152). IGI Global., DOI: 10.4018/979-8-3693-0205-7.ch007

Suresh Babu, C. V., Anniyappa, C. S., & Sastha, B. D. (2024). Unraveling the Inner Workings of Massive Language Models: Architecture, Training, and Linguistic Capacities. In B. Gupta (Ed.), Challenges in Large Language Model Development and AI Ethics (pp. 239-279). IGI Global. DOI: 10.4018/979-8-3693-3860-5.ch008

Suresh Babu, C. V., & Auroshaa, A. (2024). Influence of Data Analysis Tools in Teaching and Learning Economics. In Scott, B., & Fox, M. E. (Eds.), *Cases on Economics Education and Tools for Educators* (pp. 229–248). IGI Global., DOI: 10.4018/978-1-6684-7583-6.ch010

Suresh Babu, C. V., & Rohan, B. (2023). Evaluation and Quality Assurance for Rapid E-Learning and Development of Digital Learning Resources. In Santally, M., Rajabalee, Y., & Rajputh, R. (Eds.), *Implementing Rapid E-Learning Through Interactive Materials Development* (pp. 139–170). IGI Global., DOI: 10.4018/978-1-6684-4940-0.ch008

Topping, K. J., & Ehly, S. W. (1998). *Peer-assisted learning: A guide for teachers*. Routledge.McTighe, J., & O'Connor, K. (2005). *Understanding by Design*. ASCD. https://doi.org/DOI: 10.1111/tct.12583

VanLehn, K. (2011). "Educational Software." *Handbook of Human-Computer Interaction*, 3, 978-1008.Kay, J., & Kummerfeld, B. (2016). "Adaptive Learning Technologies: A Review of the Literature." *Journal of Educational Technology & Society*, 19(1), 10-21.Knewton. (2015). "The Rise of Adaptive Learning: How Technology is Personalizing Education." Knewton Report.

Wang, F., & Wang, Q. (2019). The Impact of Learning Analytics on Personalized Learning: A Systematic Review. *Journal of Educational Computing Research*, *57*(4), 962–994.

Woolf, B. P. (2010). *Building Intelligent Interactive Tutors: Student-Centered Strategies for Revolutionizing E-learning*. Morgan Kaufmann.Smith, R. (2013)

Xu, Z. (2024). AI in education: Enhancing learning experiences and student outcomes. *Appl. Comput. Eng*, *51*(1), 104–111. DOI: 10.54254/2755-2721/51/20241187

APPENDIX 1: SUGGESTED READINGS FOR FURTHER EXPLORATION

"Artificial Intelligence in Education: Promises and Implications for Teaching and Learning"

This report by the Stanford Graduate School of Education explores the potential benefits and challenges of using AI in educational contexts, including distance education.

"Artificial Intelligence for Education: A Review"

This article reviews various applications of AI in education, discussing how AI can enhance distance learning through personalized learning paths, assessment tools, and more.

"Adaptive Learning Technologies: A Review of the Literature"

This review provides insights into adaptive learning technologies and their implications for distance education, emphasizing how AI can tailor learning experiences to individual students' needs.

"The Role of Artificial Intelligence in Distance Education: A Systematic Review"

This systematic review analyzes various studies on the impact of AI in distance education, highlighting key findings and future research directions.

"Ethical Implications of AI in Education"

This paper discusses the ethical considerations of implementing AI in educational settings, including issues of equity, privacy, and bias, which are particularly relevant for distance education.

"Using Artificial Intelligence to Enhance Online Learning: A Case Study"

This case study explores how a specific institution integrated AI tools into their online learning programs, detailing the outcomes and lessons learned.

"AI-Powered Learning Analytics in Distance Education"

This article examines the use of AI in learning analytics, discussing how data-driven insights can improve student engagement and success in distance education environments.

"The Future of Education: AI, Learning, and Society"

This book offers a broader perspective on the intersection of AI and education, including discussions on distance learning innovations and implications for educational policy.

"Blended Learning: A Disruptive Innovation?"

This paper explores the integration of online and traditional learning environments, focusing on how AI can facilitate blended learning models in distance education.

"Personalized Learning: A Guide for Engaging Students with Technology"

This guide discusses how technology, including AI, can be used to create personalized learning experiences, particularly in online education.

APPENDIX 2: ADDITIONAL RESOURCES

Additional Resources

- **Online Courses and Webinars:**
  - o **Coursera and edX**: Platforms offering courses on AI in education, including implementation strategies and case studies.
  - o **edWeb.net**: A professional learning community with webinars focused on the use of technology and AI in education.
- **Professional Organizations:**
  - o **International Society for Technology in Education (ISTE)**: Offers resources and networking opportunities for educators interested in integrating technology into their teaching.
  - o **Association for Educational Communications and Technology (AECT)**: Focuses on research and practice in the field of educational technology, including AI applications.
- **Research Journals:**
  - o **Journal of Educational Technology & Society**: Publishes research on the intersection of technology and education.
  - o **Computers & Education**: Features articles on the use of technology, including AI, in educational settings.
- **Books:**
  - o **"Artificial Intelligence in Education: Promises and Implications" by Wayne Holmes et al.**: Discusses the impact of AI on education and how it can transform learning experiences.
  - o **"Designing AI for Education" by Michelle K. Dyer and others**: Offers insights into designing effective AI tools for educational contexts.

Tools and Technologies for AI in Education

- **Learning Management Systems (LMS):**
  - o **Moodle**: An open-source LMS that can integrate AI tools for personalized learning and assessment.
  - o **Canvas**: Offers features powered by AI for student engagement analytics and adaptive learning pathways.
- **AI-Powered Tutoring Systems:**
  - o **Squirrel AI**: An adaptive learning platform that uses AI to provide personalized tutoring and learning experiences.

- **Knewton**: Offers adaptive learning technologies that analyze student performance and suggest personalized content.

- **Assessment and Feedback Tools:**
  - **Turnitin**: Uses AI to provide plagiarism detection and feedback on writing assignments.
  - **Gradescope**: An AI-driven tool that automates grading for various types of assessments and provides analytics on student performance.
- **Learning Analytics Tools:**
  - **Tableau**: A data visualization tool that can be used to analyze learning data and improve course design based on student performance.
  - **Brightspace Insights**: Provides learning analytics tools to help educators monitor student engagement and performance in real-time.
- **Communication and Collaboration Tools:**
  - **Slack and Microsoft Teams**: Platforms that facilitate communication and collaboration among students and educators, with AI features to enhance productivity.
  - **Zoom**: While primarily a video conferencing tool, it offers features like AI-powered transcription and engagement analytics for virtual classrooms.
- **Content Creation Tools:**
  - **Canva**: An online design tool that allows educators to create engaging content and visuals for online courses, with AI-powered design suggestions.
  - **Lumen5**: A video creation platform that uses AI to transform text content into engaging videos for educational purposes.

Chapter 5

Creating Engaging and Personalized Learning Experiences in Distance Education: AI and Learning Analytics

Palanivel Rathinasabapathi Velmurugan
https://orcid.org/0009-0005-0247-0713
Berlin School of Business and Innovation, Germany

R. Swadhi
https://orcid.org/0000-0002-0395-9060
Academy of Maritime Education and Training, India

Krati R. Varshney
Saraswathi Institute of Medical Sciences, Hapur, India

Jimmy Carter Regins
https://orcid.org/0009-0005-2669-3727
Bishop Heber College, India

K. Gayathri
https://orcid.org/0000-0003-0398-0094
Academy of Maritime Education and Training, India

ABSTRACT

This chapter examines how artificial intelligence (AI) and learning analytics are revolutionizing distance education by enhancing personalization and engagement.

DOI: 10.4018/979-8-3693-7195-4.ch005

AI-driven adaptive learning systems adjust content and pace based on individual student needs, while learning analytics offer real-time insights into learner behavior, helping to tailor instruction and support. These technologies boost interaction through tools like virtual assistants, gamification, and interactive simulations, which foster motivation and active participation. Predictive analytics further identify students at risk of falling behind, enabling timely interventions to improve success rates and retention. While the advantages are clear, challenges such as data privacy, potential biases, and over-dependence on technology must be addressed. The chapter also presents case studies demonstrating successful AI applications in K-12 and higher education. As AI continues to advance, it will play a crucial role in reshaping online learning, promoting equity and supporting lifelong education opportunities.

INTRODUCTION

Distance education, also known as online learning or e-learning, refers to an educational model where learners and instructors are separated by time and space, leveraging technology to bridge the gap (Moore & Kearsley, 2012). Its evolution has been driven by technological advancements, beginning with correspondence courses in the 19th century and expanding into digital platforms in the 21st century. Today, it is a critical component of the educational landscape, providing accessible learning opportunities to diverse populations, including working professionals, students in remote areas, and lifelong learners. The significance of distance education has grown exponentially, especially in the wake of the COVID-19 pandemic, which highlighted the need for scalable, flexible, and resilient learning models. According to the World Economic Forum (2020), more than 1.2 billion children were affected by school closures globally, prompting a rapid shift to online education. This transformation, while beneficial, has introduced challenges such as ensuring learner engagement, retention, and personalization. The ability to retain students in a virtual environment is a pressing issue, as dropout rates in online courses are typically higher than in traditional settings (Grau-Valldosera & Minguillón, 2014). Moreover, the lack of face-to-face interaction and the one-size-fits-all content delivery model often result in decreased student engagement (Henrie et al., 2015). To address these challenges, personalized learning and scalable solutions have become essential. Personalization in online learning refers to tailoring educational content, pace, and resources to meet individual learner needs. This approach improves engagement and outcomes by catering to different learning styles, preferences, and prior knowledge (Kumar & Sharma, 2021). Furthermore, scalability delivering quality education to a growing number of learners has become crucial as institutions worldwide look to expand their online offerings.

Role of Technology in Distance Education

The integration of technology in education has been transformative, particularly in distance learning. Digital tools such as learning management systems (LMS), video conferencing platforms, and mobile applications have made it possible to deliver educational content to learners anywhere in the world. These technologies enable asynchronous and synchronous learning, giving students flexibility in when and how they engage with course material (Anderson & Dron, 2011). The shift from traditional classroom settings to technology-enhanced environments has also paved the way for a more interactive and engaging learning experience, incorporating multimedia resources, online discussions, and real-time feedback mechanisms (Picciano, 2017). Among the various technologies reshaping education, Artificial Intelligence (AI) and Learning Analytics are two of the most impactful. AI, the simulation of human intelligence by machines, is increasingly being used in education to create intelligent tutoring systems, adaptive learning platforms, and automated grading systems (Holmes et al., 2019). AI's ability to process large volumes of data enables it to deliver personalized content to learners, offering customized feedback and guidance based on individual progress. This adaptability is especially important in distance education, where the lack of direct interaction with instructors can leave some students feeling isolated or unsupported. Learning Analytics, on the other hand, refers to the collection, analysis, and reporting of data related to learners' interactions with educational content. It provides insights into student behavior, helping educators and institutions identify at-risk students, optimize learning pathways, and enhance overall instructional design (Siemens, 2013). By leveraging learning analytics, educators can monitor student engagement levels, predict academic performance, and implement timely interventions to support learners in their educational journey (Gašević et al., 2015). These technologies are playing a pivotal role in addressing the key challenges of engagement, retention, and personalization in distance education.

Purpose and Scope of the Chapter

The purpose of this chapter is to examine how AI and learning analytics can enhance engagement and personalization in distance education. In recent years, these technologies have shown great potential in addressing the limitations of traditional online learning models by providing more tailored and interactive learning experiences (Woolf et al., 2020). While the role of AI and learning analytics in education is still evolving, their applications are already transforming how educational content is delivered and experienced. This chapter will explore the following areas: (1) how AI-driven systems can personalize learning experiences for diverse student populations, (2) how learning analytics can track and improve student engagement, and

(3) the implications of these technologies for educators, students, and institutions. It will also discuss the ethical considerations surrounding data privacy, algorithmic bias, and equitable access to AI tools in education. For educators, understanding how to integrate AI and learning analytics into their teaching practices is crucial for creating more effective and engaging learning environments. These tools provide instructors with real-time insights into student progress, allowing for more timely and targeted interventions (Ferguson et al., 2016). Furthermore, AI can automate routine tasks such as grading and content delivery, enabling educators to focus on higher-level instructional activities, such as mentoring and course design.

For students, AI and learning analytics offer the possibility of more personalized learning pathways, where content is adapted to their individual needs and preferences. This personalization can lead to increased motivation, better academic performance, and a more positive learning experience (Luckin et al., 2016). Additionally, learning analytics can provide students with insights into their learning habits, helping them take more ownership of their education and make informed decisions about their study strategies. For institutions, the adoption of AI and learning analytics can lead to improved student outcomes, higher retention rates, and more efficient use of resources. By identifying trends and patterns in student data, institutions can better allocate resources to support at-risk students, optimize course offerings, and improve overall institutional performance (Ifenthaler & Yau, 2020). However, the implementation of these technologies must be done carefully, considering the ethical and privacy implications of collecting and analyzing student data. AI and learning analytics hold significant promise for creating engaging and personalized learning experiences in distance education. This chapter aims to provide a comprehensive overview of these technologies, their applications, and their impact on the future of education.

Conceptual Framework

Artificial Intelligence (AI) and learning analytics are increasingly central to modern educational frameworks, particularly in distance education. AI refers to the development of computer systems capable of performing tasks that typically require human intelligence, such as decision-making, pattern recognition, and language understanding (Russell & Norvig, 2020). In education, AI is applied in various capacities, including intelligent tutoring systems, automated grading, adaptive learning environments, and virtual teaching assistants. These AI-driven systems allow for real-time assessments of student progress, enabling educators to provide timely interventions and adjust learning paths based on individual student needs (Holmes et al., 2019). Learning analytics, on the other hand, refers to the collection, measurement, analysis, and reporting of data about learners and their contexts, for the purpose of understanding and optimizing learning experiences (Siemens, 2013). It focuses on identifying patterns in learner data, such as engagement levels, academic performance, and interaction with course materials, to inform data-driven decision-making. Learning analytics can be categorized into three primary types: descriptive analytics (what happened), predictive analytics (what could happen), and prescriptive analytics (what should happen) (Gašević et al., 2015). These types of analytics empower educators to make informed decisions about instructional design, identify at-risk students, and personalize learning experiences to enhance educational outcomes. In the context of distance education, AI and learning analytics serve as complementary technologies. While AI can automate and personalize learning processes, learning analytics offers the insights necessary to monitor and optimize the effectiveness of these AI-driven interventions. Together, they hold the potential to revolutionize online learning by creating more adaptive, student-centered learning environments (Woolf et al., 2020).

Personalized Learning in Distance Education

Personalized learning is crucial in distance education because it tailors the learning experience to meet the individual needs of students, improving both engagement and academic outcomes. In a traditional classroom, instructors can interact with students directly and offer real-time adjustments to teaching methods or course content. However, in a distance learning setting, such interactions are limited, and a one-size-fits-all approach can result in disengagement or ineffective learning. Personalized learning addresses this gap by leveraging technology to adapt the learning environment to the unique needs of each student (Kumar & Sharma, 2021). AI-driven adaptive learning systems are particularly valuable in distance education. These systems analyze a student's performance and learning patterns to adjust the difficulty, content, and pacing of instruction. For example, if a student consistently struggles with a particular concept, the system can provide additional resources, such as tutorials or practice exercises, to help the student grasp the material (Holmes et al., 2019). Similarly, if a student demonstrates mastery of certain topics, the system can introduce more advanced material to keep them engaged and challenged. Individualized feedback is another critical aspect of personalized learning. AI systems can provide immediate feedback on assignments, quizzes, and other assessments, helping students understand their mistakes and guiding them toward the correct solutions. This is especially beneficial in distance education, where students may not have the opportunity for face-to-face interaction with instructors (Zawacki-Richter et al., 2019). The continuous feedback loop provided by AI systems ensures that students receive the support they need to progress through their learning journey, even in an asynchronous online environment. Personalized learning also extends to the customization of content. AI systems can curate learning materials based on a student's preferences, prior knowledge, and learning style, thereby creating a more engaging and effective educational experience. For instance, some students may prefer video-based content, while others may learn more effectively through text-based materials or interactive simulations. By offering a range of content types, AI ensures that students receive information in the format that is most conducive to their learning (Gašević et al., 2015).

Engagement in Distance Learning

Engagement is a critical factor in the success of distance learning. In a virtual environment, students are physically separated from their peers and instructors, which can lead to feelings of isolation and disengagement. Therefore, creating engaging learning experiences is essential to keeping students motivated and on track (Henrie et al., 2015). AI and learning analytics can play a pivotal role in enhancing engagement by facilitating interactive and personalized learning experiences that cater to the specific needs and preferences of students.

Several key factors influence student engagement in online learning environments, including interactivity, collaboration, and motivation. Interactivity refers to the level of active participation that students have with the learning material, their peers, and instructors. AI technologies can enhance interactivity by incorporating features such as interactive simulations, quizzes, and real-time feedback mechanisms, which encourage students to actively engage with the course content (Ifenthaler & Yau, 2020). For example, AI-powered chatbots can simulate conversations with students, guiding them through complex topics and answering their questions in real time. Collaboration is another important component of engagement in distance education. Although students in online courses may be physically separated, technology can facilitate collaborative learning through virtual discussion boards, group projects, and peer-to-peer interactions. AI can enhance these collaborative experiences by analyzing student interactions and forming groups based on complementary skills or learning styles. This ensures that group work is both effective and engaging, helping students feel more connected to their peers (Gašević et al., 2015). Motivation is closely tied to personalization in distance education. When students feel that the learning experience is tailored to their individual needs, they are more likely to remain motivated and engaged (Luckin et al., 2016). AI-driven adaptive learning systems can boost motivation by presenting challenges and rewards that are customized to each student's progress. For example, gamified learning environments, powered by AI, can provide students with incentives such as badges, points, or progression to higher levels as they complete tasks and achieve learning objectives (Zawacki-Richter et al., 2019). Moreover, learning analytics plays a crucial role in tracking student engagement. By analyzing data related to student participation, such as log-in frequency, time spent on tasks, and interaction with course materials, learning analytics can identify students who are at risk of disengagement or dropping out. Educators can then intervene early, providing personalized support and resources to re-engage these students (Siemens, 2013). This proactive approach to student retention is essential in distance education, where the lack of face-to-face interaction can make it difficult to detect disengagement until it is too late.

THEORETICAL FRAMEWORK

Educational Theories Supporting AI and Learning Analytics

The integration of AI and learning analytics into distance education is grounded in several established educational theories, each offering insights into how these technologies can support and enhance learning. Constructivism is a learning theory that posits that knowledge is constructed through active engagement with content rather than passive absorption (Piaget, 1971). AI aligns with this theory by fostering personalized, active learning environments that adapt to individual students' needs. In a constructivist AI-powered classroom, students engage with interactive simulations, virtual labs, or AI-driven platforms that tailor content based on their progress and learning styles. For instance, AI can provide real-time feedback, prompt learners to reflect on their understanding, and adjust the difficulty of tasks based on a learner's performance (Holmes et al., 2019). This dynamic approach encourages deeper learning, as students construct knowledge through problem-solving and exploration. Connectivism, another pertinent theory in this context, views learning as the process of creating connections between individuals and information sources within a network (Siemens, 2005). In the digital age, where information is abundant and constantly evolving, AI acts as a bridge, enabling students to connect with various learning resources, peers, and instructors through intelligent tutoring systems, virtual learning environments, and discussion forums. AI supports networked learning by personalizing resources, suggesting relevant content, and fostering collaboration among students. AI's ability to process vast amounts of data allows it to identify patterns in learning behaviors and suggest the best resources or peer networks for each student, thereby optimizing knowledge-sharing and collaboration. Behaviorism, a theory focused on observable behaviors and reinforcement, finds relevance in the use of learning analytics. Learning analytics allows educators to monitor student behaviors, such as their engagement levels, completion rates, and interaction with course materials, and apply interventions accordingly. According to Skinner's behaviorist principles (1953), behavior is shaped by reinforcement; thus, AI and learning analytics can be used to reinforce positive learning behaviors through personalized feedback and reward systems, such as badges, gamified elements, and real-time performance updates (Luckin et al., 2016). Learning analytics can identify patterns in students' behaviors and suggest interventions, such as providing additional resources or adjusting assignments, to keep learners on track.

AI-Based Theoretical Models in Distance Learning

In addition to grounding AI and learning analytics within educational theories, specific theoretical models have emerged to integrate AI into distance learning, enhancing educational outcomes. Bloom's Taxonomy is a hierarchical model that classifies educational goals into six levels, from basic knowledge acquisition to higher-order thinking skills like analysis, synthesis, and evaluation (Bloom, 1956). AI can support adaptive learning systems aligned with Bloom's Taxonomy by tailoring educational experiences to help students progress through these levels. For example, an AI system may assess a student's current level of understanding through quizzes and exercises, then provide personalized learning paths that scaffold learning objectives from lower-order to higher-order thinking skills. AI-based systems can also generate questions or challenges that promote critical thinking, thus helping students engage in higher-order learning (Holmes et al., 2019). The Zone of Proximal Development (ZPD), a concept introduced by Vygotsky (1978), describes the difference between what a learner can do independently and what they can achieve with guidance. AI-powered tutoring systems can replicate the role of a human instructor by offering scalable, personalized support within the ZPD. For instance, AI systems can identify when a student is struggling with a concept and provide targeted prompts, hints, or additional explanations to guide the learner through the task. This personalized scaffolding helps students progress beyond their current abilities, mirroring the support traditionally offered by a teacher or more knowledgeable peer (Luckin et al., 2016).

Models of Learning Analytics

Learning analytics, which focuses on the use of data to improve teaching and learning, can be implemented through various models that provide insights into learner behaviors and support personalized education. The Learning Analytics Model (LAM) is a widely accepted framework that categorizes analytics into three types: descriptive, predictive, and prescriptive analytics (Siemens, 2013). Descriptive analytics provides an overview of what has happened by analyzing past learner data, such as quiz scores and time spent on tasks. Predictive analytics, on the other hand, forecasts future performance, identifying at-risk students and recommending interventions based on historical trends. Finally, prescriptive analytics offers actionable insights on what should happen next to improve outcomes, such as suggesting personalized learning resources or adjusting course pacing. This model allows institutions to harness the power of data for improving retention rates, academic success, and learner engagement. Another critical model is the Engagement Analytics Framework, which focuses on measuring and enhancing student engagement through data (Henrie et al., 2015). Engagement analytics track how frequently students interact with course materials, participate in discussions, and complete assignments. By analyzing these behaviors, AI and learning analytics platforms can identify patterns of disengagement early, allowing educators to intervene before students fall behind. For example, if a student's engagement metrics drop, the system might send personalized nudges, offer additional resources, or suggest participation in peer-led study groups. This framework emphasizes the proactive role that AI and learning analytics can play in sustaining student motivation and preventing attrition in distance education. AI and learning analytics can be effectively applied using a variety of theoretical models and frameworks, each addressing key aspects of personalized learning and engagement in distance education. By leveraging constructivist principles, connectivism, and behaviorism, as well as AI-driven models like Bloom's Taxonomy and ZPD, educational institutions can foster more engaging, adaptive, and successful learning environments. Moreover, the application of learning analytics models such as LAM and the Engagement Analytics Framework ensures that data-driven decision-making is at the heart of educational innovation.

RESEARCH METHODOLOGY

The research methodologies employed in exploring the role of AI and learning analytics in distance education encompass a variety of approaches, including both qualitative and quantitative designs. A mixed-methods approach is particularly beneficial, allowing researchers to triangulate data and gain a comprehensive understanding of how AI and learning analytics can enhance personalized learning experiences and engagement among students. Quantitative methods, such as surveys and experiments, provide empirical evidence of the effectiveness of AI-driven interventions on student outcomes, while qualitative methods, including interviews and case studies, offer deeper insights into individual learner experiences and perceptions (Creswell & Creswell, 2018). Qualitative methods are essential for understanding the complexities of personalization and engagement in distance education. Through in-depth interviews and focus groups, researchers can gather rich, contextual data on how students interact with AI systems and how these technologies influence their learning experiences. For instance, studies may explore students' perceptions of

AI-driven feedback mechanisms, their feelings of agency in personalized learning environments, and the factors that contribute to their engagement in online courses. Thematic analysis of qualitative data enables researchers to identify recurring patterns and themes, providing a nuanced understanding of the interplay between AI, learning analytics, and learner engagement (Braun & Clarke, 2006). Additionally, case studies of institutions that have successfully implemented AI and learning analytics can serve as valuable sources of data. By examining real-world applications, researchers can analyze the specific strategies employed, the challenges encountered, and the overall impact on student engagement and learning outcomes. This approach not only contributes to the academic discourse on AI in education but also provides practical insights for educators and policymakers aiming to adopt similar technologies in their institutions.

Data Sources

The examination of AI and learning analytics in distance education draws from a diverse array of data sources. A comprehensive review of existing literature is fundamental to understanding the current state of research in this field. This includes scholarly articles, conference papers, and systematic reviews that outline the theoretical underpinnings of AI and learning analytics and their applications in educational settings. Recent studies highlight various AI tools and learning analytics platforms that have been implemented in distance education, showcasing their effectiveness in fostering personalized learning experiences and improving student engagement (Zawacki-Richter et al., 2019). Real-world case studies of educational institutions that have integrated AI and learning analytics into their distance education programs provide further valuable data. These case studies offer insights into the practical challenges and successes encountered during implementation, allowing researchers to assess the impact of these technologies on teaching and learning processes. For example, examining how a specific institution has utilized AI to analyze student data and tailor educational content can reveal best practices and potential pitfalls that can inform future applications (García-Peñalvo et al., 2020). In addition to academic literature and case studies, publicly available datasets from educational institutions and organizations involved in AI and learning analytics research can be invaluable. These datasets often include anonymized student data, engagement metrics, and assessment results that can be analyzed to identify trends and correlations, contributing to a more robust understanding of how AI influences learning outcomes in distance education.

Ethical Considerations

As the use of AI and learning analytics in education grows, it is crucial to address ethical considerations related to data privacy and security. The collection and analysis of student data raise significant concerns about how this information is stored, shared, and utilized. Educators and institutions must ensure compliance with regulations, such as the General Data Protection Regulation (GDPR) in Europe and the Family Educational Rights and Privacy Act (FERPA) in the United States, which mandate strict guidelines for protecting student privacy (Huang et al., 2020). Establishing transparent data practices and obtaining informed consent from students are essential steps in fostering trust and ensuring that individuals feel secure when engaging with AI technologies. Moreover, reducing bias in AI algorithms is vital to ensuring equitable access to education. AI systems can inadvertently perpetuate existing biases if not carefully designed and monitored (O'Neil, 2016). For instance, biased data used to train AI models can lead to unfair recommendations or assessments, disproportionately affecting marginalized student groups. To mitigate these risks, it is imperative to employ diverse and representative datasets, continually assess algorithms for fairness, and involve stakeholders from various backgrounds in the development and evaluation of AI applications in education. This commitment to equity and inclusivity will help create a more just and effective educational environment for all learners.

SOLUTIONS AND RECOMMENDATIONS

Strategies for Enhancing Personalization

In the evolving landscape of distance education, enhancing personalization through adaptive learning technologies is critical. Implementing such technologies enables the delivery of customized content tailored to the individual learning needs of students. Adaptive learning systems analyze learners' interactions, performance data, and preferences to create personalized learning paths. These systems can adjust the difficulty of tasks, recommend resources, and provide feedback based on real-time assessments (Kerr & McCormick, 2019). For instance, platforms like Smart Sparrow and DreamBox Learning utilize adaptive algorithms to modify content in response to student performance, ensuring that learners engage with materials that are appropriately challenging and relevant to their interests.

Utilizing predictive analytics further supports personalized learning by offering timely interventions and support. Predictive analytics leverages historical data to identify patterns and forecast student outcomes, enabling educators to intervene proactively when students may be at risk of disengagement or underperformance. For example, Learning Management Systems (LMS) equipped with predictive analytics can highlight students who have not logged in recently or those who are struggling with specific concepts, allowing educators to reach out and provide targeted support (Wang et al., 2020). By employing these strategies, institutions can foster a more responsive educational environment that meets the diverse needs of learners.

Increasing Learner Engagement

Increasing learner engagement in distance education is essential for promoting motivation and enhancing learning outcomes. One effective strategy involves incorporating AI-driven tools such as gamification, simulations, and interactive environments into the curriculum. Gamification integrates game-like elements—such as points, badges, and leaderboards—into educational activities to create a more engaging learning experience. Research indicates that gamification can significantly improve student motivation and engagement by making learning more enjoyable and rewarding (Deterding et al., 2011). Platforms like Kahoot! and Quizlet allow instructors to create interactive quizzes and games that promote active participation and enhance knowledge retention. Simulations and virtual environments also play a crucial role in increasing learner engagement. By immersing students in realistic scenarios, these tools facilitate experiential learning, allowing learners to apply theoretical knowledge in practice. For instance, medical and nursing students can benefit from virtual patient simulations, providing a safe space to practice clinical skills and decision-making without the risk of harming real patients (Le et al., 2020). These immersive experiences not only engage students but also enhance their understanding and retention of complex concepts.

Leveraging Natural Language Processing (NLP) can further enhance learner engagement by providing real-time feedback and interaction. NLP enables the development of conversational agents or chatbots that can answer student queries, provide additional resources, and offer personalized feedback on assignments. Tools like IBM's Watson Assistant and Google's Dialogflow can be integrated into online courses to facilitate student interactions and enhance engagement. By enabling immediate responses to student inquiries, these AI-driven systems create a more interactive and supportive learning environment, helping students feel more connected to their educational experience (Hwang et al., 2021).

Designing Ethical and Inclusive AI Systems

As the implementation of AI and learning analytics in education grows, it is imperative to address ethical considerations and ensure that these systems are designed inclusively. Reducing bias in AI-based educational systems is a fundamental aspect of ethical design. Bias can arise from the data used to train algorithms, leading to inequitable outcomes for marginalized student populations. Institutions must employ diverse and representative datasets during the development of AI systems and continuously monitor algorithms for fairness (Holstein et al., 2019). Additionally, incorporating input from a diverse group of stakeholders, including students, educators, and community representatives, can help identify potential biases and inform more equitable AI solutions. Promoting transparency and ethical AI use in educational settings is equally vital. Educational institutions should establish clear guidelines and policies regarding the use of AI and learning analytics. This includes ensuring that students are informed about how their data is collected, used, and protected, as well as the decision-making processes behind AI-driven recommendations. Creating transparent systems fosters trust among students and educators, encouraging a culture of collaboration and ethical practice (García et al., 2020). Furthermore, institutions should engage in regular audits of their AI systems to assess their impact on student outcomes and make necessary adjustments to ensure fairness and equity.

Faculty Development and Support

The successful integration of AI and learning analytics in distance education requires robust faculty development and support. Training educators in effectively using these technologies is essential to maximizing their potential benefits. Professional development programs should focus on equipping educators with the skills to interpret data analytics, adapt their teaching strategies accordingly, and leverage AI tools to enhance learning outcomes. Workshops, webinars, and collaborative learning communities can provide educators with ongoing support and resources to navigate the complexities of AI and learning analytics in their teaching practice (Smith & McKinnon, 2021). Fostering a data-driven culture for teaching and learning is also critical. Institutions should encourage faculty members to embrace data analytics as a tool for informed decision-making. By providing access to relevant data and training educators on how to analyze and interpret this information, institutions can empower faculty to make data-informed adjustments to their instructional practices. This approach not only enhances the overall quality of education but also encourages a continuous cycle of improvement in teaching and learning (Sclater, 2017). Moreover, collaborative initiatives that promote the sharing of best practices among educators can lead to innovative uses of AI and learning analytics. Establishing communities of practice where faculty can share their experiences, successes, and challenges can foster an environment of collective learning and innovation, ultimately enhancing the educational experience for all learners.

FUTURE RESEARCH DIRECTIONS

The intersection of artificial intelligence (AI) and education continues to expand, presenting exciting opportunities for enhancing learning experiences and outcomes. As the field evolves, several areas merit further investigation, including innovations in AI for education, the expanded use of learning analytics, addressing challenges and barriers, and the role of AI in lifelong learning. Each of these domains has the potential to significantly impact how educators, students, and institutions interact with educational technologies.

Innovations in AI for Education

One of the most promising innovations in AI for education is **Emotion AI**, which refers to the capability of AI systems to detect and respond to human emotions. This emerging field leverages natural language processing, computer vision, and affective computing to analyze students' emotional states through various inputs, such as facial expressions, voice intonation, and written responses (Calvo & D'Mello, 2010). Emotion AI can enhance learning experiences by providing educators with insights into students' emotional engagement and well-being, allowing for timely interventions and support. Future research could explore the effectiveness of Emotion AI in online and blended learning environments, focusing on its impact on student engagement and motivation. Moreover, AI advancements are paving the way for more sophisticated assessments of complex cognitive and creative skills. Traditional assessment methods often fall short in measuring higher-order thinking, problem-solving abilities, and creativity. AI-powered tools can offer dynamic assessments that adapt in real time based on student performance, enabling educators to gauge deeper learning outcomes (Pérez et al., 2021). Future studies should investigate the development and implementation of AI-driven assessment models that capture a broader spectrum of student capabilities, providing insights into how these assessments can inform instructional practices and support individualized learning paths.

Expanding the Use of Learning Analytics

The integration of learning analytics in education has gained momentum, yet its full potential remains untapped. Future research should focus on the integration of social and behavioral **analytics** to develop a more comprehensive understanding of learner behavior. While traditional learning analytics primarily rely on academic performance data, social analytics can provide insights into learners' interactions and collaborations, while behavioral analytics can capture non-cognitive factors such as persistence and motivation (Gordon et al., 2021). By combining these data sources, educators can gain a holistic view of student engagement and success, leading to more informed decision-making and targeted interventions. Additionally, using analytics for adaptive assessment and personalized feedback represents a crucial area for research. Adaptive assessments, powered by AI and learning analytics, can adjust the complexity and nature of assessment tasks based on real-time student responses. This approach not only enhances the relevance of assessments but also allows for immediate feedback tailored to individual learning needs (Hwang et al., 2021). Future studies could explore how adaptive assessments can be implemented across various disciplines and educational contexts, examining their effects on student performance and motivation.

Addressing Challenges and Barriers

Despite the promising potential of AI and learning analytics, several challenges and barriers must be addressed. One of the most pressing issues is data privacy and security in AI-driven education. With the increasing reliance on data for personalized learning, institutions must implement robust measures to protect sensitive student information and ensure compliance with data protection regulations (Pardo & Siemens, 2014). Future research should focus on developing frameworks and best practices for maintaining data privacy while leveraging the benefits of AI and learning analytics. This could include exploring decentralized data storage solutions, transparent data usage policies, and ethical guidelines for data collection and analysis. Another significant challenge lies in **access and equity** in the global adoption of AI for education. Disparities in access to technology and digital resources can exacerbate existing inequalities, particularly in underrepresented and underserved communities (Hodges et al., 2020). Future studies should investigate strategies to bridge the digital divide and promote equitable access to AI-driven educational tools. This could involve exploring partnerships between educational institutions and technology companies, as well as developing community-based initiatives to enhance digital literacy and access in marginalized populations.

AI's Role in Lifelong Learning

As the job market evolves and the demand for continuous skills development increases, AI is poised to play a pivotal role in lifelong learning. Future research should explore how AI-driven personalized pathways can support individuals in their lifelong learning journeys, professional development, and upskilling efforts. AI can facilitate personalized learning experiences by recommending relevant courses, resources, and learning opportunities based on individuals' career goals and skills gaps (Zawacki-Richter et al., 2019). Investigating the effectiveness of these personalized pathways can provide valuable insights into how AI can empower learners to take charge of their education throughout their lives. Moreover, AI can serve as a support tool for career navigation and personalized learning journeys. AI-driven platforms can offer tailored career advice, suggesting skill development opportunities aligned with current job market trends and individual aspirations. Future research should examine the role of AI in enhancing career guidance services and supporting learners in making informed decisions about their professional paths. This could involve exploring the integration of AI with existing career services and examining the outcomes of AI-supported career navigation on student success and satisfaction.

SUMMARY OF KEY FINDINGS

AI and learning analytics have emerged as powerful tools that can significantly enhance personalization and engagement in distance education. Through adaptive learning technologies, educators can tailor instructional content to meet the unique needs of each learner, fostering a more individualized learning experience (Kukulska-Hulme, 2020). These technologies can analyze vast amounts of data to identify patterns in student behavior, allowing for real-time feedback and timely interventions. Such personalized approaches not only enhance academic performance but also increase student motivation and satisfaction (D'Mello & Graesser, 2015). Furthermore, learning analytics can inform instructional design by providing educators with insights into student engagement and learning outcomes, facilitating data-driven decision-making that enhances the overall quality of distance education (Siemens, 2013).

Implications for Educators and Institutions

The adoption of AI technologies in education is no longer optional; it is essential for creating future-ready educational environments. Educators are encouraged to embrace these technologies as they offer unprecedented opportunities for innovation and improvement in teaching and learning (Holmes et al., 2021). Institutions must invest in training and professional development for faculty members to effectively leverage AI and learning analytics in their teaching practices. This investment not only enhances educators' capacity to personalize learning experiences but also ensures that they remain competitive in an increasingly digital education landscape. Moreover, it is critical to prioritize ethical and inclusive AI practices in distance learning. As AI systems can perpetuate biases present in training data, institutions must implement measures to ensure fairness, transparency, and inclusivity in AI applications (O'Neil, 2016). Educators should actively engage in discussions about the ethical implications of using AI in education and strive to create environments that respect student privacy and promote equitable access to learning resources. The responsible implementation of AI technologies can help mitigate the risks associated with bias and discrimination, fostering a more inclusive educational experience for all learners.

CONCLUSION

The integration of artificial intelligence (AI) and learning analytics into distance education marks a significant evolution in the design and delivery of educational experiences. This chapter has highlighted how these technologies contribute to enhancing personalization and engagement, fundamentally transforming the landscape of distance learning. As educational institutions strive to meet the diverse needs of learners, the deployment of AI and learning analytics offers innovative solutions that are crucial for fostering effective learning environments. AI's potential to tailor educational experiences to individual learner profiles cannot be overstated. By utilizing adaptive learning technologies, educators can provide personalized content that aligns with each student's unique abilities, preferences, and learning styles. This customization fosters deeper engagement, as students feel more connected to the material and motivated to participate actively in their learning journeys. The ability to analyze vast amounts of data through learning analytics further empowers educators to make informed decisions, identify at-risk students, and implement timely interventions, thereby enhancing overall educational outcomes. As distance education continues to grow and evolve, the role of AI and learning analytics becomes increasingly critical. These technologies not only enhance student learning experiences but also support lifelong learning initiatives. In a rapidly changing job market, where adaptability and continuous skill development are paramount, AI-driven educational pathways offer learners tailored opportunities for professional growth and career advancement. This approach ensures that education remains relevant and responsive to the demands of the workforce, preparing students for success in a dynamic and technology-driven world. However, the integration of AI in education also presents challenges that must be addressed to ensure equitable access and ethical implementation. Data privacy concerns, algorithmic bias, and the need for transparency in AI applications are critical considerations that educators and institutions must navigate. By prioritizing ethical practices and fostering a culture of inclusivity, stakeholders can harness the full potential of AI and learning analytics, creating environments where all learners can thrive. The future of distance education is bright, with AI and learning analytics poised to drive innovation and enhance educational experiences. As educational institutions embrace these technologies, they must also commit to ethical and responsible practices that prioritize student well-being and success. The ongoing exploration of AI's impact on education will continue to inform strategies and practices, ensuring that learners are equipped with the skills and knowledge necessary to excel in the 21st century. By leveraging the transformative power of AI and learning analytics, we can create dynamic, inclusive, and engaging learning environments that prepare students for the challenges and opportunities of the future.

REFERENCES

Anderson, T., & Dron, J. (2011). Three generations of distance education pedagogy. *International Review of Research in Open and Distance Learning*, *12*(3), 80–97. DOI: 10.19173/irrodl.v12i3.890

Bloom, B. S. (1956). *Taxonomy of educational objectives: The classification of educational goals*. Longman.

Braun, V., & Clarke, V. (2006). Using thematic analysis in psychology. *Qualitative Research in Psychology*, *3*(2), 77–101. DOI: 10.1191/1478088706qp063oa

Calvo, R. A., & D'Mello, S. K. (2010). Affect detection: An interdisciplinary review of the literature. *IEEE Transactions on Affective Computing*, *1*(1), 18–37. DOI: 10.1109/T-AFFC.2010.1

Creswell, J. W., & Creswell, J. D. (2018). *Research design: Qualitative, quantitative, and mixed methods approaches* (5th ed.). SAGE Publications.

D'Mello, S. K., & Graesser, A. C. (2015). Feeling, thinking, and computing: A review of the affective computing literature. *International Journal of Artificial Intelligence in Education*, *25*(1), 1–13. DOI: 10.1007/s40593-014-0028-0

Deterding, S., Dixon, D., Khaled, R., & Nacke, L. (2011). From game design elements to gamefulness: defining" gamification." In Proceedings of the 15th international academic MindTrek conference: Envisioning future media environments (pp. 9-15). DOI: 10.1145/2181037.2181040

Ferguson, R., Shum, S. B., & McAndrew, P. (2016). Learning analytics to identify exploratory dialogue within synchronous text chat. *Learning Analytics Review*, *6*, 1–21. DOI: 10.18608/jla.2016.32

García, I., Ayllón, F., & López, C. (2020). The ethical and social implications of AI in education: A systematic review. *Education and Information Technologies*, *25*(4), 3135–3156. DOI: 10.1007/s10639-020-10332-8

García-Peñalvo, F. J., Cruz-Benito, J., & Rodríguez-Conde, M. J. (2020). Educational innovation and learning analytics. *Journal of Universal Computer Science*, *26*(4), 476–486. DOI: 10.3217/jucs-026-04-0476

Gašević, D., Dawson, S., & Siemens, G. (2015). Let's not forget: Learning analytics are about learning. *TechTrends*, *59*(1), 64–71. DOI: 10.1007/s11528-014-0822-x

Gordon, R., Vang, C., & O'Neill, R. (2021). The power of social and behavioral analytics in education. *Journal of Learning Analytics*, *8*(2), 19–31. DOI: 10.18608/jla.2021.82.3

Grau-Valldosera, J., & Minguillón, J. (2014). Rethinking dropout in online higher education: The case of the Universitat Oberta de Catalunya. *International Review of Research in Open and Distance Learning*, *15*(1), 290–308. DOI: 10.19173/irrodl.v15i1.1628

Henrie, C. R., Halverson, L. R., & Graham, C. R. (2015). Measuring student engagement in technology-mediated learning: A review. *Computers & Education*, *90*, 36–53. DOI: 10.1016/j.compedu.2015.09.005

Hodges, C., Moore, S., Lockee, B., Trust, T., & Bond, A. (2020). The difference between emergency remote teaching and online learning. *EDUCAUSE Review*, *27*(2). https://er.educause.edu/articles/2020/3/the-difference-between-emergency-remote-teaching-and-online-learning

Holmes, W., Bialik, M., & Fadel, C. (2021). Artificial Intelligence in Education: Promises and Implications for Teaching and Learning. Center for Curriculum Redesign. https://curriculumredesign.org/wp-content/uploads/AI-in-Education-Report-2021.pdf

Holstein, K., Wortman, J., Daumé, H.III, & Dudik, M. (2019). Improving fairness in machine learning systems: A survey. *SIGKDD Explorations*, *21*(2), 18–20. DOI: 10.1145/3361689.3361691

Huang, Y., Xu, H., & Ma, X. (2020). Data privacy and security in learning analytics: A systematic review. *Educational Technology Research and Development*, *68*(3), 1643–1669. DOI: 10.1007/s11423-020-09706-3

Hwang, G. J., Wu, P. H., & Chen, C. H. (2021). AI-based personalized learning: A systematic review and meta-analysis. *Computers & Education*, *175*, 104356. DOI: 10.1016/j.compedu.2021.104356

Ifenthaler, D., & Yau, J. Y. (2020). Utilising learning analytics to support study success in higher education: A systematic review. *Educational Technology Research and Development*, *68*(4), 1829–1851. DOI: 10.1007/s11423-020-09788-z

Kerr, D., & McCormick, R. (2019). Adaptive learning technologies in distance education: A review of the literature. *Educational Technology Research and Development*, *67*(6), 1237–1265. DOI: 10.1007/s11423-019-09680-4

Kukulska-Hulme, A. (2020). Will student learning be different in the future? *Distance Education*, *41*(3), 285–293. DOI: 10.1080/01587919.2020.1776633

Kumar, K. L., & Sharma, S. (2021). Personalized learning: The potential of AI to drive engagement and success in online education. *Journal of Educational Technology & Society*, *24*(3), 23–35.

Le, D. N., Hoang, V. Q., & Hwang, G. J. (2020). Effects of virtual patient simulation on learning outcomes in nursing education: A systematic review and meta-analysis. *Nurse Education Today*, *90*, 104465. DOI: 10.1016/j.nedt.2020.104465

Luckin, R., Holmes, W., Griffiths, M., & Forcier, L. B. (2016). *Intelligence unleashed: An argument for AI in education*. Pearson.

Moore, M. G., & Kearsley, G. (2012). *Distance education: A systems view of online learning* (3rd ed.). Wadsworth Publishing.

O'Neil, C. (2016). *Weapons of Math Destruction: How Big Data Increases Inequality and Threatens Democracy*. Crown Publishing Group.

Pardo, A., & Siemens, G. (2014). Ethical and privacy considerations in learning analytics. *Proceedings of the Fourth International Conference on Learning Analytics and Knowledge*, 1-5. DOI: 10.1145/2567574.2567585

Pérez, F. J., Pérez, P. A., & García, J. E. (2021). AI-driven assessment: A new approach for complex cognitive skills. *Computers & Education*, *167*, 104179. DOI: 10.1016/j.compedu.2021.104179

Piaget, J. (1971). *The construction of reality in the child*. Ballantine Books.

Picciano, A. G. (2017). Theories and frameworks for online education: Seeking an integrated model. *Online Learning: the Official Journal of the Online Learning Consortium*, *21*(3), 166–190. DOI: 10.24059/olj.v21i3.1225

Russell, S., & Norvig, P. (2020). *Artificial intelligence: A modern approach* (4th ed.). Pearson.

Sclater, N. (2017). Learning analytics: The current state of play in higher education. Jisc Report. https://www.jisc.ac.uk/reports/learning-analytics-the-current-state-of-play-in-higher-education

Siemens, G. (2005). Connectivism: A learning theory for the digital age. *International Journal of Instructional Technology and Distance Learning*, *2*(1), 3–10.

Siemens, G. (2013). Learning analytics: The emergence of a discipline. *The American Behavioral Scientist*, *57*(10), 1409–1410. DOI: 10.1177/0002764213498851

Skinner, B. F. (1953). *Science and human behavior*. Macmillan.

Smith, D. M., & McKinnon, D. H. (2021). Faculty development in online education: A systematic review of the literature. *International Journal of Online Pedagogy and Course Design*, *11*(4), 1–24. DOI: 10.4018/IJOPCD.20211001.oa4

Vygotsky, L. S. (1978). *Mind in society: The development of higher psychological processes*. Harvard University Press.

Wang, Y., Wang, Y., & Wang, Y. (2020). Predictive analytics in education: A systematic review. *International Journal of Educational Technology in Higher Education*, *17*(1), 1–24. DOI: 10.1186/s41239-020-00219-x

World Economic Forum. (2020). The COVID-19 pandemic has changed education forever. This is how. https://www.weforum.org

Zawacki-Richter, O., Marín, V. I., Bond, M., & Gouverneur, F. (2019). Systematic review of research on artificial intelligence applications in higher education–where are the educators? *International Journal of Educational Technology in Higher Education*, *16*(1), 1–27. DOI: 10.1186/s41239-019-0171-0

Zawacki-Richter, O., Marinsky, V., & Dhanjal, K. (2019). The role of AI in lifelong learning. *International Journal of Educational Technology in Higher Education*, *16*(1), 1–15. DOI: 10.1186/s41239-019-0171-7

KEY TERMS AND DEFINITIONS

Artificial Intelligence (AI): Artificial Intelligence refers to the capability of machines to perform tasks typically requiring human intelligence. This includes various functions such as learning from experience, reasoning, problem-solving, understanding natural language, and making decisions. In education, AI can personalize learning experiences, automate administrative tasks, and provide insights into student performance.

Learning Analytics: Learning analytics involves the systematic collection, analysis, and reporting of data concerning student learning processes. The aim is to understand and enhance learning and teaching by utilizing insights drawn from data. This can include information about student interactions, assessment results, and engagement metrics. Effective learning analytics can help educators make informed decisions to improve curriculum design and instructional strategies.

Personalized Learning: Personalized learning is an educational approach that seeks to customize learning experiences to meet the diverse needs, preferences, and abilities of individual learners. This method recognizes that students have varying backgrounds, interests, and learning styles, allowing for tailored educational pathways. By focusing on the unique needs of each student, personalized learning aims to enhance motivation, engagement, and academic achievement.

Gamification: Gamification refers to the application of game design elements in non-game contexts, particularly in education. By incorporating features such as points, badges, leaderboards, and challenges, gamification aims to boost student engagement and motivation. It transforms traditional learning activities into interactive and enjoyable experiences, encouraging students to participate more actively and persist in their learning endeavors.

Adaptive Learning: Adaptive learning is an instructional method that employs AI to modify the presentation of educational content based on each learner's performance, preferences, and needs. This approach allows for real-time adjustments, ensuring that learners receive appropriate challenges and support tailored to their individual learning paths. By continually assessing student progress, adaptive learning systems aim to optimize the learning experience and improve outcomes.

Natural Language Processing (NLP): Natural Language Processing is a field of AI that focuses on enabling computers to understand, interpret, and generate human language in a meaningful way. In education, NLP can facilitate various applications, including automated feedback on written assignments, chatbots for student support, and tools for analyzing student discussions. By bridging the gap between human communication and machine understanding, NLP enhances interactive learning experiences.

Predictive Analytics: Predictive analytics involves utilizing historical data, statistical algorithms, and machine learning techniques to forecast future events or behaviors. In the educational context, predictive analytics can identify at-risk students, anticipate learning outcomes, and inform interventions aimed at improving student success. By analyzing trends and patterns, educational institutions can make data-driven decisions that enhance teaching and learning effectiveness.

Chapter 6
Personalised Learning Experiences in Distance Learning

Alvaro Marcos Antonio de Araujo Pistono
https://orcid.org/0000-0001-6863-0453
Universidade de Trás-os-Montes e Alto Douro, Portugal

ABSTRACT

This chapter examines the impact of digital transformation on education, focusing on how advanced technologies like Experience API (xAPI), Artificial Intelligence (AI), and serious games are reshaping distance learning. The xAPI is highlighted for its ability to capture detailed learning data, enhance learning analytics, and enable the creation of personalised reports and tracking of student progress. The integration of AI, including Machine Learning and NLP, is explored in the context of e-learning, showcasing its role in personalisation, real-time feedback, and intelligent tutoring systems. The chapter also delves into serious games, presenting their benefits for student engagement and motivation. The Framework for Adaptive Serious Games (F4ASG) is discussed, demonstrating how Learning Analytics and AI can enhance engagement and learning effectiveness. Finally, the chapter explores the integration of these technologies, providing practical insights, examples, and strategies for creating adaptive learning experiences in distance education.

DOI: 10.4018/979-8-3693-7195-4.ch006

INTRODUCTION

The rapid advancement of digital technologies has significantly transformed various sectors, and education is no exception. The convergence of Learning Analytics (LA), Artificial Intelligence (AI), and Distance Learning (DL) represents a pivotal shift in how educational experiences are designed, delivered, and assessed.

Dawson & Siemens (2014) state that:

"Learning analytics uses the data associated with a learner's interactions with content, other learners, and the educational institution to make decisions and evaluations about teaching practices, personalised content, and needed interventions for learner success."

Broadly, Artificial Intelligence is defined by IBM as a "technology that enables computers and machines to simulate human intelligence and problem-solving capabilities" (What is Artificial Intelligence (AI)?, 2023). In this text, AI will refer to specific applications such as large language models and machine learning.

As defined by the Association for Talent Development (ATD):

"Distance learning is an educational delivery in which the instructor and students are separated by time, location, or both. Distance learning can be synchronous or asynchronous" (Talent Development Glossary Terms, n.d.).

This chapter delves into the intricate interplay of these technologies, offering a comprehensive guide to leveraging them for enhanced educational outcomes.

The impact of digital transformation on education is profound, enhancing accessibility and flexibility through online learning platforms. These platforms break down geographical barriers, allowing students worldwide to access high-quality education. With the advent of digital tools, education is no longer confined to the traditional classroom. Flexible learning models such as blended learning and flipped classrooms enable students to learn at their own pace and on their own schedule.

Adaptive learning technologies use data to adjust the learning path and pace according to the individual needs of each student, ensuring that learners receive the support they need to succeed, thereby improving learning outcomes. By collecting and analysing student performance and engagement data, educators can gain insights into how students learn best and tailor their instruction accordingly.

Digital transformation has introduced various interactive tools such as virtual labs, simulations, and gamified learning platforms that make learning more engaging and enjoyable. Online tools facilitate collaboration among students, allowing them to work together on projects, participate in discussions, and share resources regardless of their physical location.

Key technologies driving digital transformation include the Experience API (xAPI), a specification set that describes communication about learner activity and experiences between technologies (Experience API (xAPI) Standard, n.d.), allows for the collection of detailed data on learning activities from various sources, providing a comprehensive view of the learning process. xAPI's flexibility ensures that it can work seamlessly with different learning management systems and educational platforms, enhancing the ability to track and analyse learning across diverse environments.

Artificial Intelligence also plays a significant role, with machine learning algorithms analysing vast amounts of educational data to identify patterns and predict outcomes, aiding in developing personalised learning experiences. Natural Language Processing (NLP) enables AI systems to understand and respond to student inquiries in real time, providing instant feedback and support. Computer vision technology allows for the automatic grading of assignments and the monitoring of student engagement during online classes.

Learning Analytics (LA) involves the use of data to inform educational decisions, from curriculum design to instructional strategies, ensuring that they are based on evidence rather than intuition. With LA, educators can monitor student progress in real time, identifying those who may need additional support and adjusting their teaching methods accordingly.

Serious games use game mechanics to enhance learning experiences, making them more engaging and motivating for students. These games often focus on developing specific skills such as problem-solving, critical thinking, and collaboration through immersive and interactive scenarios.

The digital transformation in education is an ongoing process that continues to evolve with technological advancements. The future of education lies in the seamless integration of these technologies to create learning environments that are not only effective but also adaptive to the needs of each student. By leveraging the power of xAPI, AI, LA, and serious games, educators can create a dynamic and responsive educational ecosystem that prepares students for the challenges of the modern world.

First, this chapter will explore the Experience API (xAPI), a powerful tool for capturing detailed learning activity data: "Combined with learning analytics, xAPI promises to revolutionise the way education and training are conducted, managed, and measured" (Experience API (xAPI) Standard, n.d.).

Following this, the role of Learning Analytics in interpreting this data to inform educational practices will be examined. The discussion will then move to Artificial Intelligence, highlighting its transformative educational potential.

Additionally, the application of serious games – games with a purpose beyond entertainment (Pistono et al., 2024) – as a strategy to boost student engagement and motivation will be explored.

Finally, integrating these technologies to create a holistic and adaptive educational ecosystem will be addressed.

The digital transformation in education refers to the adoption of digital technologies to enhance teaching and learning processes. This shift has been accelerated by the proliferation of internet access and the development of new educational tools. Technologies such as learning management systems (LMS), mobile learning apps, and interactive digital content have made learning more accessible and flexible.

The digital age has brought about unprecedented changes across various sectors, and education is at the forefront of this transformation. Digital transformation in education refers to the integration of digital technologies into all aspects of teaching, learning, and administration, fundamentally altering how educational content is delivered, consumed, and assessed. This shift is not just about adopting new tools; it is about reimagining the educational experience to meet the evolving needs of learners in the 21st century.

Mukul & Büyüközkan (2023) highlight:

"Technological developments not only affect educational institutions at general and specific levels, but also sets of new skills that this new life and business ecosystem require. It is the new education system combined with independent lifelong learning that will engender these skills."

By the end of this chapter, readers will have a deeper understanding of how to harness these technologies to meet the diverse needs of students in distance learning environments. The insights, examples, and best practices provided will equip educators and developers with the tools necessary to navigate and capitalise on the innovations shaping the future of education. In conclusion, digital transformation is redefining education by making it more accessible, personalised, and engaging. The adoption of advanced technologies such as xAPI, AI, and LA, along with innovative approaches like serious games, is paving the way for a new era of learning. As educators and institutions continue to embrace these changes, they will be better equipped to meet the diverse needs of their students and foster a culture of continuous improvement and innovation in education.

E-LEARNING TRACK

There are numerous opportunities for continuous learning beyond traditional education or training methods. These opportunities have existed for a long time and need to be refined, recognised as valid forms of learning, promoted, and supported across all initiatives.

The diversity in the workforce is ever-increasing, leading to varied ways in which people learn, seek information, and communicate. Technological evolution has influenced how content is consumed and distributed.

Table 1 outlines three significant phases in the technological evolution of education, with a particular focus on distance learning.

Table 1. Technology-assisted education in distance learning

Phase	Technology application
Stand-alone technologies	• Multimedia CDs were followed by Web-Based Training (WBT) courses, which included content presentations, animations, exercises, e-mail, forums, chat, tutors and monitors, often all in the same course. • However, these courses were labour-intensive and expensive.
SCORM	• SCORM - Sharable Content Object Reference Model (SCORM®. n.d.) is a way of communicating (interoperating) between courses and management systems. • With SCORM, a course works in all management systems that also support SCORM. • SCORM has significantly boosted the use of e-learning, leading to the development of many courses. • It has made content production more agile and cost-effective, with the aim of creating courses that can be used in any system and reused with other courses. • SCORM has long been the most widely used "standard" for e-learning courses and continues to be very important.
Nowadays	• However, SCORM has limitations, and recent technological advances have revealed several learning activities that it does not accommodate • There are technologies that support the new educational expectations of personalised learning (Mukul & Büyüközkan, 2023).

This table illustrates the technologies used in distance learning education and training scenarios, specifically e-learning, over the last few decades. It starts with expensive, labour-intensive methods and goes through SCORM, which stands for Sharable Content Object Reference Model (SCORM®. n.d.), which facilitated the widespread adoption of e-learning and culminated in the emerging paradigm of Education 4.0.

In e-learning courses, the information usually collected includes:

- Whether a course has been accessed.
- Who accessed the course.
- Whether it was completed (access to all content).
- Whether the exercises were done correctly or not.
- How long a learner acessed the content.
- How far each learner progressed in the course, identifying the last content viewed. This allows learners to resume the course from where they left off.

SCORM addresses all these points, providing this information in its simplest form. Although these details are often sufficient, they do not fully capture all of the learners' experiences. Consequently, measuring learning based on this set of information is inadequate.

The Experience API - xAPI (Experience API (xAPI) Standard, n.d.), also known as the Tin Can API, is a standard that enables the collection and tracking of online and offline learning experiences. Unlike traditional learning management systems (LMS), which capture data mainly within the confines of their environment, xAPI allows for more comprehensive and flexible data capture, encompassing a wide range of learning activities.

xAPI and SCORM are compared in Table 2, where each technology's set of activities and applications is evidenced (SCORM vs xAPI., 2012).

Table 2. SCORM and xAPI comparative table

Activity	Covered by
• Completion • Spent time • Pass or fail track • Report a single score	• SCORM • xAPI
• Report multiple scores • Detailed test results • Keep complete control over the content • Mobile apps activities • Serious games • Simulations • Informal learning • Real-world performance • Offline learning • Interactive learning • Adaptive learning • Blended learning • Long-term learning • Team-based learning	• xAPI

In addition to the range of activities listed in **Table 2**, xAPI offers significant features that enhance the application of learning tracking and analysis:

- No LMS required.
- No internet browser is required.
- No cross-domain limitation.
- Platform transition (i.e. computer to mobile).

Thus, xAPI provided a more appropriate approach to learning activities. It is not only a recording but also an analysis of participants' data, providing conclusions and adaptations that enhance the results of learning initiatives.

LEARNING ANALYTICS AND xAPI

As Mukul and Büyüközkan (2023) point out, education today is much more than formal education on school benches or in training sessions:

> *"Education 4.0 is a new experience-based education system that uses technology and meets the expectations of today's world within the framework of personalized education needs." (Mukul & Büyüközkan, 2023)*

As shown in Table 1, SCORM has significantly advanced e-learning. The widespread adoption of SCORM in professional training is mainly due to its purposes:

- Accessibility, guaranteed by its web-based learning objects.
- Interoperability, because instructional material developed for one system can also be used in other systems.
- Durability, because a learning object continues to work when the technology changes.
- Reusability, which means that the same instructional materials can be incorporated into various applications.

Although it is still widely used and many systems and contents have already been developed, SCORM is no longer sufficient to represent all the learning activities that exist in education and professional training.

In 2013, ADL - Advanced Distributed Learning, the same organisation responsible for the SCORM specifications, suggested a new set of specifications in the form of APIs: xAPI (Experience API (xAPI) Standard, n.d.; xAPI-Spec: The xAPI Specification describes communication about learner activity and experiences between technologies, n.d.), originated from the maturing of the Tin Can project at the same institution.

Recognising the relevance of xAPI in learning environments, xAPI 2.0 became the open source standard IEEE 9274.1.1-2023 (xAPI officially Becomes a Published IEEE Standard, n.d.).

The basic principle of these specifications is to send "*I did this*" statements, representing their three main elements (actor, verb and object), to unstructured data repositories, from where this data is read and interpreted by reporting and analysis applications, as described in Table 3.

Table 3. xAPI's core elements

xAPI element	Description of element's function
Activity Provider	Any action on a computer, tablet, smartphone or another device, even offline, for future synchronisation.
Learning Record Store – LRS	Structured and unstructured data in data repositories.
Report Tool	Reporting and data analysis software commonly incorporated into commercial LRSs.

Figure 1 shows the relationship between these three xAPI elements.

Figure 1. xAPI infrastructure

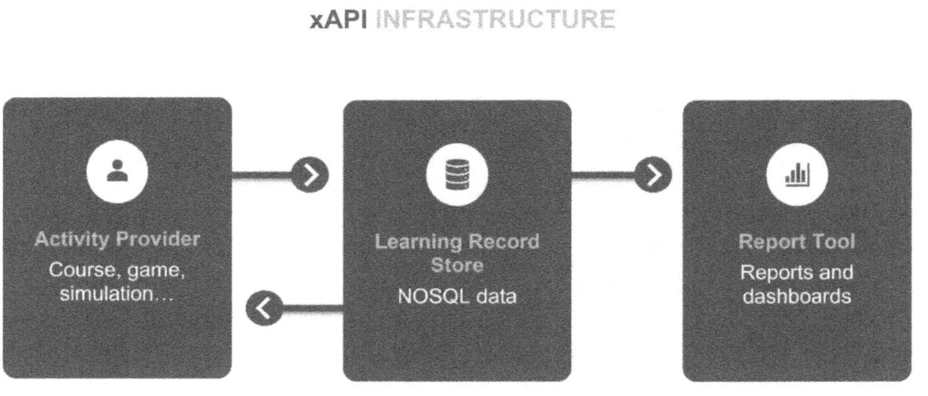

By using the xAPI specifications, it is possible to:

- Record various interactions with their individual characteristics (context, performance, etc.).
- Record data in various formats.
- Fully control the content, not just time counting and exercise results.
- Use multiple domains, which is a SCORM limitation.

Unlike its predecessor, SCORM, xAPI is not limited to LMS, web browsers, computers, or Internet access. That is, for a learning experience to be recorded according to the xAPI specifications, it is not necessary to access an LMS. The experience can be conducted in environments other than Internet browsers, nor is it even necessary to have a computer or Internet access, as activities can be carried out on mobile devices, for example, offline (to be later synchronised with an LRS).

Thus, with xAPI, it is possible to record and analyse various types of activities, such as games and adaptive activities. In other words, in an adaptive Serious Game, xAPI would be suitable for recording data, analysing results and adapting activities.

People learn continuously in various ways, and xAPI offers a flexible method for recording their experiences, such as watching a video or participating in a workgroup activity. Other examples include content consumed and learnt via mobile devices, social networks, various forums, and serious games. Consequently, SCORM currently proves insufficient to capture these activities, as shown in Table 2.

In the xAPI model, being connected to an LMS or involved in an e-learning course is unnecessary. All activities can be recorded, analysed, and compared with other situations and with students. Even offline activities can be recorded in the xAPI model, and when Internet access is available, the activity will be recorded.

Learning Analytics (LA) involves collecting, analysing and interpreting data about students and their contexts in order to improve learning outcomes and optimise learning environments. Using xAPI with learning analytics tools can be useful in the way educational data is collected and analysed, providing deeper insights into the learning process, as shown in Table 4.

Table 4. Examples of logging and analysis using xAPI

Feature	Samples
Data Capture and Storage	• Detailed Learning Records: xAPI can capture granular data about a learner's interactions, such as clicks, views, completions, and scores. • Contextual Data: xAPI captures not just what the learner did but also the context in which the learning activity occurred. This includes information about the tools used, the learning environment, and the conditions under which the learning took place.
Flexibility and Interoperability	• Beyond the LMS: xAPI's flexibility allows it to track learning experiences outside traditional LMS environments. This includes mobile learning, simulations, games, group activities, and even offline experiences. • Integration with Other Systems: xAPI can seamlessly integrate with various educational technologies and platforms, providing a holistic view of a learner's activities across different environments.

Khalil & Slade (2022), in their systematic review of learning analysis frameworks, mention that artefacts of this type:

> *"... provide overviews of who decides what is created and implemented, and which groups and individuals may be impacted by the use of learning analytics, and in what ways." (Khalil & Slade, 2022)*

Examples of practical applications of xAPI and how it could be used in Learning Analytics are shown in Table 5.

Table 5. xAPI applications in learning analytics

Application	Examples
Tracking formal and informal learning	• Monitor both formal learning (e.g., online courses and assessments) and informal learning (e.g., social learning, experiential learning).
Group activities	• xAPI's flexibility allows it to capture group activities, collaborative projects, and even offline learning experiences, such as workshops and field trips.
Learning data analysis	• The data collected by xAPI can be integrated with learning analytics tools to provide deeper insights into learner behaviour, engagement and performance.
Serious Games and gamification	• In addition to traditional exercises, using xAPI makes it possible to track different interactions, such as the paths chosen and performance in challenges, in order to record students' progress and needs.

As shown in this table, xAPI allows educators/instructors to adapt their interventions and support to meet the needs of each learner, enabling more personalised support and better learning outcomes.

The role of xAPI in learning analytics is transformative, offering comprehensive data collection and powerful integration capabilities. xAPI's ability to capture granular data about learner interactions provides a rich dataset for analysis, detailing not only what learners did but also how, when, and in what context they did it. This includes real-time data collection, enabling educators to monitor learner progress and engagement as it happens and intervene promptly when necessary.

By integrating xAPI data with learning analytics tools, educators can conduct holistic analyses of learner behaviour and performance. This integration allows for identifying trends, patterns, and correlations that can inform instructional strategies. Additionally, learning analytics tools can use xAPI data to generate personalised reports for learners, highlighting their strengths and areas for improvement, thus empowering them to take control of their own learning journey.

Using xAPI, therefore, it is possible to track and analyse activities that go beyond e-learning courses, such as:

- Simulation.
- Competition.
- Informal learning.
- Social learning.
- Reinforcement.
- Performance support.

Simulations allow students to experience situations where they need to expose themselves to risks or situations that cannot be easily reproduced (due to high costs, for example), allowing them to practise several times before facing real scenarios. Training individuals who need to operate in high-risk or high-cost environments, such as firefighting, emergency evacuation at a nuclear power plant or the disposal of explosive ordnance. Other examples of simulation include financial simulations, planning scenarios, negotiations, and customer service.

In some circumstances, simulations can be used to practise procedures and monitor participants' reactions, such as the sequence of movements, word choices, route selections, times involved, etc. In extreme cases, monitoring participants' heart rate and breathing can be considered.

Stimulating competition between individuals can be beneficial in highly competitive environments, such as sales teams. Different competitions, groupings, and rankings can be considered. For a group trained online or in person, a challenge or competition can be launched in which performances are scored, creating a ranking in which all participants are listed.

In these examples, a Serious Game could be applied as a safe environment for students to seek better learning outcomes (Pistono et al., 2024).

In the xAPI model, for example, there is the possibility of identifying which videos are being accessed the most, which parts of these videos students spend the most time on, which parts are frequently watched again or paused, as well as knowing that students have accessed the videos, as SCORM can record.

Other situations in which learning takes place and can be recorded and then analysed using xAPI are:

- Informal learning: The exchange of information between individuals is an invaluable source of learning. This learning can be documented and utilised by others. Individuals experienced in specific subjects can dynamically contribute to the knowledge of others, and both information and individuals can be categorised according to their relevance in each situation.
- Learning reinforcement: After training, much of what has been learnt is quickly forgotten. Therefore, a reinforcement strategy is key to retaining knowledge and linking it to daily performance. This process can also be monitored to generate data to analyse the effectiveness of the training.
- Performance support: Another opportunity to record activities is when individuals are carrying out tasks, which is called on-the-job training or performance support.

A good example of activities aligned with Education 4.0 is the use of Serious Games, such as "*Encontrando Tempo*" (Pistono et al., 2024). In this game about time management, the student/player evolves as they solve challenges in missions and move on to the next level when they pass pedagogical milestones, in an adaptive game, a game in which missions adapt completion time, difficulty and feedback.

All activities are tracked and sent to an xAPI LRS. The game can then be analysed and rebalanced.

A mission in the game "*Encontrando Tempo*" is exemplified in Figure 2.

Figure 2. "Encontrando Tempo" game mission

Also, to exemplify the use of a serious game, Figure 3 shows a level of challenge in the same game.

Figure 3. "Encontrando Tempo" level challenge

Pistono (2023) cites that:

"Although the flexibility of xAPI is favourable for recording learning activities in various formats, its use and interoperability can be difficult precisely because of this flexibility. In order to facilitate the use and dissemination of xAPI, profiles have been created for different learning experiences (ADL xAPI Profile Server, n.d.)." (Pistono, 2023)

Serrano-Laguna et al. (2017) presented the Serious Games xAPI Profile, which can be applied to record all interactions that take place in a game (xAPI Serious Games profile: A Serious Games Profile for the Experience API (xAPI), n.d.).

The benefits of xAPI are numerous and transformative for the educational landscape. By capturing data from a broad spectrum of learning activities, xAPI offers a holistic view of the student journey, allowing educators to understand how diverse experiences contribute to learning outcomes.

This comprehensive data collection supports improved decision-making, as educators can analyse learning patterns, identify gaps and adjust their instructional strategies accordingly.

Analysing xAPI data to identify patterns of engagement and disengagement can increase student engagement. This helps educators understand student motivation and design effective interventions. Learning analytics tools can use this data to create adaptive learning experiences tailored to individual needs. In addition, xAPI data can support at-risk students by developing early warning systems to identify those who need help and allowing educators to create targeted interventions to increase their chances of success.

In addition, the detailed insights gained through xAPI facilitate enhanced personalisation, allowing for the creation of customised learning paths that meet each student's unique needs and preferences. In addition, xAPI enables real-time feedback, providing students with immediate guidance based on their activities and helping them stay on track while promptly addressing any emerging issues.

SERIOUS GAMES IN EDUCATION AND TRAINING

Serious games, generically defined, are games with serious purposes other than entertainment. They are games designed for purposes beyond entertainment, such as education, training, and skill development. They leverage game mechanics to create engaging and immersive learning experiences, motivating students to learn through play.

Djaouti, Alvarez, & Jessel (2011) consider that some games originally developed for entertainment can be used as Serious Games, what they call serious gaming.

Although sometimes playing and learning seem contradictory, as cited by Huynh-Kim-Bang, Wisdom, and Labat (2010), these two activities can be brought together in Serious Games by exploiting the individual characteristics of each (game and instruction) for the best results. For example, taking advantage of the engagement potential of games to increase students' hours of dedication to study subjects and linking the challenges of games to those of problem-solving learning (Pistono, 2023).

O'Brien and Toms (2008) cite long, complex, and difficult activities as similarities between the learning process and the act of playing. Additionally, within learning activities, an interactive process challenges learners and establishes rules for them to acquire knowledge and skills.

Serious Games have been used to achieve various learning outcomes, such as knowledge and skill acquisition, attitude change, motivation, and improved communication (Wouters, van der Spek, & van Oostendorp, 2009).

Mayer (2014) concludes that the main contribution of game research is the union of cognitive and motivational domains:

"A major theoretical contribution of game research is to integrate both cognitive and motivational processes in a theory of learning with games. As theories become better specified, they can suggest specific research predictions for empirical testing."(Mayer, 2014, p.341)

Serious games provide an interactive learning environment that captures students' attention, making learning both fun and engaging. The incorporation of challenges, rewards, and progression fosters intrinsic motivation, encouraging students to persist and achieve their learning goals.

Additionally, serious games help develop critical thinking and problem-solving skills by requiring players to solve complex problems and make decisions. They also promote the development of collaboration and communication skills through teamwork and social interaction.

To ensure adaptive learning opportunities for the students, a Serious Game can also be adaptive.

Pistono, Santos, & Baptista (2021), in a systematic review of the literature on adaptable Serious Games applied to vocational training, found that all game elements are potentially adaptable. These elements range from scenarios to game mechanics, with an emphasis on intelligent agents (such as NPCs), with the elements most used in online adaptations, i.e. during gameplay (Lopes & Bidarra, 2011).

Regarding the use of artificial intelligence in the adaptation of Serious Games, Streicher & Smeddinck (2016) mentioned that the main focus was on dynamically adjusting the difficulty and adjusting the mechanics and content of the game.

Artificial intelligence techniques, such as intelligent tutoring, could be used in Serious Games to adapt them to the players, increase their motivation and engagement, and obtain better results. Or models, such as MPL - Multi-layer perceptron optimisation, could help predict the need for and adaptation of Serious Games according to the evolution and actions of the players (Pistono, 2023).

Many are studies about Serious Games in several areas. One of the areas in which they are widely used is science education, as described in the systematic literature review conducted by Kara (2021), which points out that these games have been used since elementary school.

Pistono (2023) cites that:

> *"In professional training, they have been used in various contexts for more than two decades in varied training courses, such as compliance or related to specific procedures." (Pistono, 2023, p.49)*

FRAMEWORK FOR ADAPTIVE SERIOUS GAMES: F_4ASG

To facilitate the application of Serious Games in learning initiatives and seek enhanced learning outcomes, Pistono (2023) proposed the Framework for Adaptive Serious Games - F_4ASG for both development and evaluation purposes.

Figure 4 illustrates the F_4ASG, which was developed from a systematic literature review, focus groups, expert interviews, and the field application of the "*Encontrando Tempo*" game, created using this framework.

Figure 4. Framework for adaptive serious games: F_4ASG

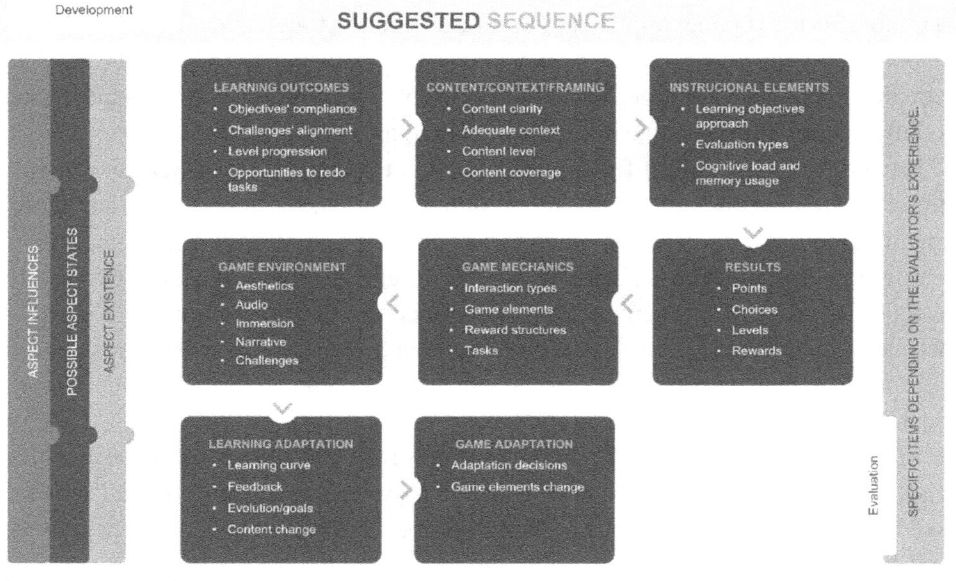

In this framework, there are four dimensions relating to learning and four to game fields. The learning dimensions include learning outcomes, content/context/framework, instructional elements, and adaptation of learning. The game dimensions encompass results, game mechanics, game environment, and game adaptation. This framework integrates all the components observed in a Serious Game and introduces two dimensions into each field, focusing on results and adaptation.

Each dimension is subdivided into aspects, such as the approach to learning objectives or the aesthetics of the game. At the most granular level, items are identified as elements of the artefact. For each aspect, the framework specifies whether it exists or should be considered, its possible states, and its influences.

As an example of applying this framework in developing the "*Encontrando Tempo*" game, the process began with the learning outcomes dimension and followed the recommended sequence through content/context/framing. The first three steps were:

- Establishing a reference for work activities, specifically the EQF - European Qualification Framework.
- Defining the corresponding learning objectives.
- Identifying the content associated with these objectives.

Subsequently, other elements of the Serious Game were developed according to the framework: Narrative, interaction types, content coverage, level objectives, points, achievements, preparatory practice, difficulty level changes, navigation, missions, and challenges (Pistono, 2023), as shown in Table 6.

Table 6. "Encontrando Tempo" game specifications

Characteristic	Description
Content	Basics of time management
Delivery format	Web
Technologies	HTML5 and xAPI
Narrative	The general narrative of the game is that the player must retrieve some time capsules that have gone missing. As a new employee in the organisation, in the position of Time Hunter, the player has to accomplish some missions to help the Time Hunters succeed.
Main game mechanic	Board game with challenges.
Other game mechanics	Drag and drop matching items, hangman game, word search, and crosswords.
Adaptations	According to the player's performance in each mission, the difficulty level is altered, up or down. It is reflected in the feedback format, the visual clues, and the time available for completing the missions.
Rewards	Points, collectable items, bonus points for mission performance and stars for success in challenges.
Game results	Points achieved, missions performed on each difficulty level, levels completed, challenges succeeded, items accumulated and time spent playing the game.
Learning outcomes	Learning objectives successfully demonstrated in the missions and challenges (pedagogical milestones).
Data logs	Start and end time of each activity, performance in each mission, number of attempts and earned items (points, collectables and stars).

Pistono (2023) applied the "*Encontrando Tempo*" game using xAPI to record and analyse participants' performance. In a within-subjects design, a group of 51 professionals engaged in five activities, as shown in Table 7 and Figure 5.

Table 7. "Encontrando Tempo" game experiment activities

Position	Activity	Description
1	Demographic data acquisition	Initial form for players' data acquisition.
2	Pre-test	Learning assessment based on the learning outcomes and learning objectives listed in the design of Serious Game "Encontrando Tempo".
3	Serious Game "Encontrando Tempo"	Serious Game developed using the Framework for Adaptive Serious Games – F4ASG.
4	Post-test	Same as the pre-test.
5	Reaction assessment	Reaction assessment based on previously defined subjects: • Experience with the Serious Game in general. • Content approach. • Use of audio-visual elements. • Mechanics used in the game. • Forms of interaction.

Figure 5. "Encontrando Tempo" experiment gamified environment

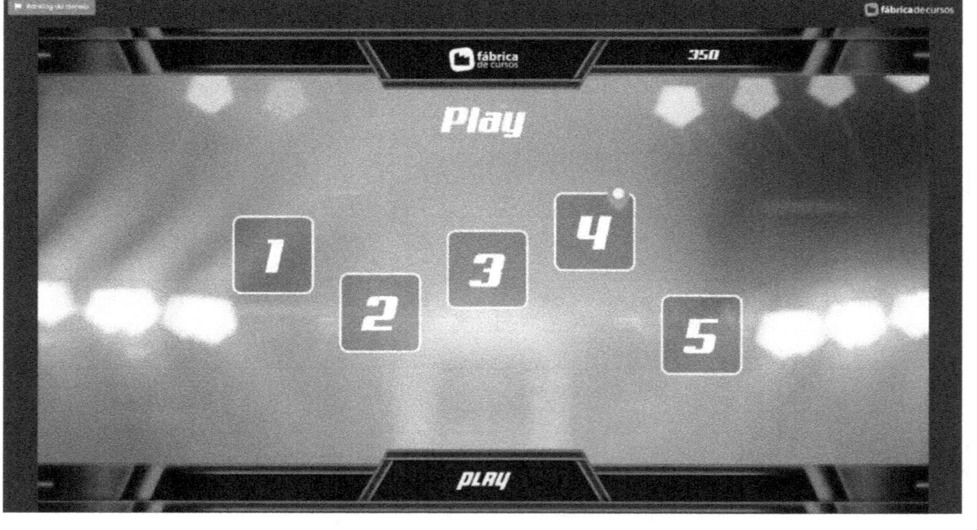

All the data collected can be valuable for analysing learning, from the initial collection of demographic information to the evaluation of reaction. It can also be used to adapt the learning experience.

ARTIFICIAL INTELLIGENCE IN PERSONALISED LEARNING

With the use of artificial intelligence, both the adaptation and analysis of learning can be improved. AI can suggest new challenges or generate dashboards that allow managers and teachers to monitor the progress of activities effectively.

Artificial intelligence can improve the development of such artefacts and their adaptation to each group or individual.

Artificial intelligence has become a transformative force in education, harnessing technologies such as machine learning, natural language processing (NLP) and computer vision to create intelligent systems that enhance learning and teaching. These technologies offer personalised learning experiences, automate administrative tasks and provide real-time feedback, significantly improving educational outcomes (Popenici & Kerr, 2017).

Machine learning algorithms are used for predictive analysis to forecast student results and provide personalised content recommendations. For example, NLP enables the development of intelligent tutoring systems and the automated assessment of written assignments, offering instant feedback and support (Zawacki-Richter et al., 2019).

Combining AI with serious games increases the ability to collect and analyse data on student behaviour, performance and preferences. This data-driven approach allows for more precise and effective personalisation of learning experiences. AI algorithms can dynamically adjust game scenarios and challenges based on real-time data, ensuring that students remain engaged and challenged throughout the learning journey.

Using F_4ASG, for example, AI can be a powerful tool for enhancing the personalised student experience by identifying, classifying, and grouping each student's characteristics to analyse their progress and learning preferences.

Ouyang & Zhang (2024) state that:

"AI techniques have introduced promising methods for implementing learning analytics in CSCL, which offers the potential to improve both instruction and learning through real-time, personalized feedback."

This statement underscores the potential of AI in computer-supported collaborative learning (CSCL). AI can be utilised in collaborative learning contexts, with xAPI serving as a means to implement and enhance personalised learning experiences.

CONCLUSION

The integration of advanced technologies such as xAPI, AI, serious games, and learning analytics represents a significant step forward in the evolution of education. These technologies offer powerful tools for creating personalised, engaging and effective learning experiences that meet the diverse needs of modern students.

Throughout this chapter, we explore the features and benefits of each technology, discuss their practical applications and examine how they can be integrated to create a cohesive educational ecosystem. By harnessing these innovations, educators can enhance their instructional strategies, support student success and foster a culture of continuous improvement and innovation.

As the educational landscape continues to evolve, it's crucial to stay abreast of technological advances and adopt new approaches. Understanding and harnessing the potential of these technologies ensures that educators and institutions are well-equipped to face the challenges and opportunities of the 21st century.

In conclusion, the future of education lies in the seamless integration of advanced technologies to create adaptive, data-driven learning environments. By combining the strengths of xAPI, AI, serious games and learning analytics, it is possible to develop a dynamic and responsive educational ecosystem that empowers students and prepares them for the complexities of the modern world.

REFERENCES

Dawson, S., & Siemens, G. (2014). Analytics to literacies: The development of a learning analytics framework for multiliteracies assessment. *International Review of Research in Open and Distance Learning*, *15*(4). Advance online publication. DOI: 10.19173/irrodl.v15i4.1878

Djaouti, D., Alvarez, J., & Jessel, J.-P. (2011). Classifying Serious Games: The G/P/S Model. In Handbook of Research on Improving Learning and Motivation through Educational Games: Multidisciplinary Approaches (pp. 118–136). IGI Global. DOI: 10.4018/978-1-60960-495-0.ch006

Experience, A. P. I. (xAPI) Standard. (n.d.). ADL Initiative. Retrieved July 15, 2024, from https://adlnet.gov/projects/xapi/

Huynh-Kim-Bang, B., Wisdom, J., & Labat, J.-M. (2010). Design patterns in Serious Games: A blue print for combining fun and learning. Project SE-SG, 1–18. https://seriousgames.lip6.fr/DesignPatterns/designPatternsForSeriousGames.pdf

Kara, N. (2021). A Systematic Review of the Use of Serious Games in Science Education. *Contemporary Educational Technology*, *13*(2), ep295. https://www.cedtech.net/article/asystematic-review-of-the-use-of-serious-games-in-science-education-9608

Khalil, M., Prinsloo, P., & Slade, S. (2022). A Comparison of Learning Analytics Frameworks: a Systematic Review. *LAK22: 12th International Learning Analytics and Knowledge Conference*, 152–163. DOI: 10.1145/3506860.3506878

Lopes, R., & Bidarra, R. (2011). Adaptivity Challenges in Games and Simulations: A Survey. *IEEE Transactions on Computational Intelligence and AI in Games*, *3*(2), 85–99. DOI: 10.1109/TCIAIG.2011.2152841

Mayer, R. E. (2014). Computer games for learning: An evidence-based approach. MIT Press. https://www.google.com/books?hl=pt-BR&lr=&id=VckIBAAAQBAJ&oi=fnd&pg=PR7&dq=Mayer+2014+game+review&ots=5xIU86Tf9F&sig=5dQmaQfr4NlEcBWIl8YNHmJgnHc

Mukul, E., & Büyüközkan, G. (2023). Digital transformation in education: A systematic review of education 4.0. *Technological Forecasting and Social Change*, *194*, 122664. DOI: 10.1016/j.techfore.2023.122664

O'Brien, H. L., & Toms, E. G. (2008). What is user engagement? A conceptual framework for defining user engagement with technology. Journal of the American Society for Information Science. *Journal of the American Society for Information Science and Technology*, *59*(6), 938–955. DOI: 10.1002/asi.20801

Ouyang, F., & Zhang, L. (2024). AI-driven learning analytics applications and tools in computer-supported collaborative learning: A systematic review. *Educational Research Review*, *44*, 100616. DOI: 10.1016/j.edurev.2024.100616

Pistono, A. M. A. de A. (2023). Influence of adaptability of Serious Games on learning outcomes and the application of knowledge and skills in professional training. https://hdl.handle.net/10348/12187

Pistono, A. M. A. de A., dos Santos, A. M. P., Baptista, R. J. V., & Mamede, H. S. (2024). Framework for adaptive serious games. Computer Applications in Engineering Education, n/a(n/a), e22731. DOI: 10.1002/cae.22731

Pistono, A. M. A. A., Santos, A. M. P., & Baptista, R. J. V. (2021). A Review of Adaptable Serious Games Applied to Professional Training. *Journal of Digital Media & Interaction*, *4*(11), 60–85. DOI: 10.34624/jdmi.v4i11.26419

Popenici, S. A. D., & Kerr, S. (2017). Exploring the impact of artificial intelligence on teaching and learning in higher education. *Research and Practice in Technology Enhanced Learning*, *12*(1), 22. DOI: 10.1186/s41039-017-0062-8 PMID: 30595727

SCORM®. (n.d.). ADL Initiative. Retrieved May 2, 2020, from https://www.adlnet.gov/projects/scorm/

SCORM vs xAPI. (2012, July 24). xAPI.com. https://xapi.com/scorm-vs-the-experience-api-xapi/

Serrano-Laguna, Á., Martínez-Ortiz, I., Haag, J., Regan, D., Johnson, A., & Fernández-Manjón, B. (2017). Applying standards to systematize learning analytics in serious games. *Computer Standards & Interfaces*, *50*, 116–123. DOI: 10.1016/j.csi.2016.09.014

Streicher, A., & Smeddinck, J. D. (2016). Personalized and Adaptive Serious Games. In R. Dörner, S. Göbel, M. Kickmeier-Rust, M. Masuch, & K. Zweig (Eds.), Entertainment Computing and Serious Games: International GI-Dagstuhl Seminar 15283, Dagstuhl Castle, Germany, July 5-10, 2015, Revised Selected Papers (pp. 332-377). Springer International Publishing. DOI: 10.1007/978-3-319-46152-6_14

Talent Development Glossary Terms. (n.d.). Retrieved July 15, 2024, from https://www.td.org/talent-development-glossary-terms

What is Artificial Intelligence (AI)? (2023, August 25). https://www.ibm.com/topics/artificial-intelligence

Wouters, P., van der Spek, E. D., & van Oostendorp, H. (2009). Current Practices in Serious Game Research: A Review from a Learning Outcomes Perspective. In Games-Based Learning Advancements for Multi-Sensory Human-Computer Interfaces: Techniques and Effective Practices (pp. 232–250). IGI Global. DOI: 10.4018/978-1-60566-360-9.ch014

xAPI officially Becomes a Published IEEE Standard. (n.d.). ADL Initiative. Retrieved July 9, 2024, from https://adlnet.gov/news/2023/11/22/xAPI-Officially-Becomes-a-Published-IEEE-Standard/

xAPI Serious Games profile: A Serious Games Profile for the Experience API (xAPI). (n.d.). Retrieved December 12, 2021, from https://adlnet.gov/news/2016/12/09/a-serious-games-profile-for-xapi/

xAPI-Spec: The xAPI Specification describes communication about learner activity and experiences between technologies. (n.d.). Github. Retrieved November 25, 2022, from https://github.com/adlnet/xAPI-Spec

Zawacki-Richter, O., Marín, V. I., Bond, M., & Gouverneur, F. (2019). Systematic review of research on artificial intelligence applications in higher education – where are the educators? *International Journal of Educational Technology in Higher Education*, *16*(1), 39. Advance online publication. DOI: 10.1186/s41239-019-0171-0

Chapter 7
AI-Driven Personalized Learning-Enhancing Student Engagement and Outcomes

Muhammad Usman Tariq
https://orcid.org/0000-0002-7605-3040
Abu Dhabi University, UAE & University College Cork, Ireland

ABSTRACT

This chapter dives into the extraordinary capability of artificial intelligence driven customized learning in upgrading understudy commitment and results, especially inside the setting of distance training. The chapter begins by outlining the significance of personalized learning in fostering individualized educational experiences and addressing the diverse requirements of students. It investigates key parts and advantages of customized getting the hang of, outlining how simulated intelligence innovations, for example, AI, versatile calculations, and regular language handling customize and upgrade the educational experience. The section likewise features different computer-based intelligence driven apparatuses, including versatile learning stages and smart coaching frameworks, that altogether add to understudy inspiration and interest. It also looks at how AI can simplify grading and assessment, provide real-time feedback, and overcome obstacles when implementing AI in education.

DOI: 10.4018/979-8-3693-7195-4.ch007

1. INTRODUCTION

Personalized learning has ended up a basic component in cutting edge instruction, particularly within the setting of separate learning. The rise of innovation has empowered a move from conventional, one-size-fits-all educating strategies to more custom-made, individualized learning encounters. Personalized learning in distance instruction is fundamental since it addresses the differing needs, inclinations, and learning styles of students, subsequently improving engagement and making strides instructive results. By leveraging Artificial Intelligence (AI) and other progressed innovations, teachers can make learning situations that adjust to the special needs of each student, guaranteeing that they get the fitting level of challenge and back (Rekha et al., 2024).

One of the key preferences of personalized learning in separate education is its capacity to supply adaptability unlike conventional classroom settings, where students must follow to a fixed schedule and pace, personalized learning permits understudies to memorize at their possess pace and on their claim plan. This adaptability is particularly beneficial for grown-up learners, working experts, and understudies with other obligations, because it empowers them to balance their considers with their other commitments (Ayeni et al., 2024).

In addition, personalized learning can offer assistance to shut the accomplishment crevice by giving support to students who may battle with certain subjects, whereas permitting students to advance more rapidly (Katiyar et al., 2024). The significance of personalized learning in separate instruction is to assist students by the expanding utilize of AI-driven innovations. AI can analyse endless sums of information to distinguish designs and patterns in students' behaviour, learning inclinations, and execution. This data can at that point be utilized to form personalized learning plans that are custom-made to wants of each person understudy. For example, AI can suggest particular learning assets, such as recordings, articles, or intuitively works out, that are best suited to a student's learning fashion (Ellikkal and Rajamohan, 2024).

Furthermore, AI can provide real-time criticism, permitting students to track their progress and make alterations as required. This level of personalization not only improves their learning but also makes a difference in students' inspiration and engagement (Dandachi, 2024). Another noteworthy advantage of personalized learning in remove instruction is the capacity to cultivate self-directed learning. Personalized learning energizes students to take ownership of their instruction by permitting them to set their possess learning objectives and select the assets and exercises that best meet their needs. This approach not as it were engaging understudies but moreover makes a difference to create vital aptitudes such as basic considering, problem-solving, and time management (Almusaed et al., 2023). Besides, personalized learning can offer assistance to make a more comprehensive learning environment by giving support for students with different needs, such as those with inabilities or learning contrasts (Baba et al., 2024). This chapter points to explore the part of personalized learning in remove instruction, with a specific center on the integration of AI and other progressed innovations.

The chapter will start by looking at the current state of remove instruction and the challenges that students and educators face in this environment. It will further investigate the different ways in which personalized learning can address these challenges, counting the use of AI to form customized learning experiences, the significance of adaptability and self-directed learning, and the part of personalized learning in advancing inclusivity and equity in instruction (Castro et al., 2024). The chapter will briefly investigate the diverse AI-driven personalized learning frameworks that have been created and actualized in later a long time. This will incorporate a talk of the different highlights and capabilities of these frameworks, as well as their affect on students engagement, accomplishment, and in general learning outcomes (Kanchon et al., 2024).

Thus, the chapter will explore the potential future advancements in AI and personalized learning, and how these progressions seem assist change separate instruction. Moreover, the chapter will talk about the moral contemplations and challenges related with the utilize of AI in personalized learning. This will incorporate an examination of issues such as information protection, algorithmic inclination, and the potential for AI to worsen existing imbalances in instruction (Mahmoud and Sørensen, 2024). The chapter will also give suggestions for teachers and policymakers on how to guarantee that AI-driven personalized learning frameworks are implemented in a way that's reasonable, straightforward, and advantageous for all students.

At last, the chapter will conclude with a talk of the implications of personalized learning for the longer term of remove instruction. This will incorporate an investigation of the potential benefits and challenges of personalized learning, as well as the ways in which educators and educate can best bolster understudies in this advancing instructive scene (Waterways and Holland, 2022). The chapter will also highlight the significance of continuous investigate and advancement in personalized learning, and the require for ceaseless collaboration between teachers, analysts, and innovation designers to ensure that personalized learning frameworks are viable, impartial, and accessible for all learners (Maghsudi et al , 2021).

Thus, this chapter gave a comprehensive outline of the part of personalized learning in separate instruction, with a center on the integration of AI and other progressed technologies. Through a nitty gritty examination of current hones, challenges, and future bearings, the chapter provides importance suggestions to teachers, policymakers, and analysts working within the field of separate instruction. By highlighting the significance of personalized learning and the potential of AI to enhance the educational encounter, this chapter looks for to contribute to the progressing improvement and improvement of separate instruction for learners around the world.

2. BACKGROUND/LITERATURE

Understanding Personalized Learning

Personalized learning is an individualized educational process of learning that is based on the needs, interests and aspiration of every student. While the traditional learning models tend to stick to a strict curriculum and duration, personalized learning on the other hand aims to achieve more flexibility. Recognizing the factor that every student is different, this approach factors in prior learning, modality, preferences, and learning rate to present a tailored education to one student or a class (Ellikkal & Rajamohan, 2024). Learner control or learner autonomy has been identified as one of the features that form the basis of PL.

In a personalized learning environment, there is more freedom for the student and the student has more say in his or her learning. They are able to select the resource, activities and project which they wish to undertake based on their interest and learning acquisition. This enhances students' participation in their learning processes since they are in a position to direct it themselves and this leads to increased motivation to learn among students (Almusaed et al., 2023). For instance, a fine example is a student in environmental science is likely to opt for projects dealing with climate change, whereas a student in computing and technology is likely to undertake projects in coding and application development among other activities.

The fourth aspect that is an element of differentiation is data and technology to assist in learning facilitation. AI also holds the main position in personalized learning because it is able to assess the data of the students and choose the appropriate patterns and preferences for learning. This makes it possible for the trainers to develop and implement student-cantered learning plans which consider each learner (Katiyar et al., 2024). For instance, AI-based systems can monitor the student's performance in real-time and can suggest particular materials or approaches that may help the student to overcome difficulties or focus on particular topics in which he or she shows strength.

Another characteristic of personalised learning is the possibility of flexible learning paths. In traditional systems of learning, the learners are put through a system that can only grant knowledge based on standard curriculum and at a set speed. But personalization makes it possible for a student to acquire content whenever he or she feels more comfortable. Students can learn at their own pace meaning that one can spend many lessons trying to understand a certain topic that he or she did not understand the previous lesson. This is advantageous especially in distance learning since students are faced with different levels of constraint in terms of resource and support (Rekha et al., 2024). For instance, a website providing an online learning environment may provide a set of modules that can be mastered individually; such approach enables students to concentrate upon those issues, which they find interesting or difficult or whichever needs additional mastering.

Therefore, other elements of learners' individualization also include assessment of work and feedback. Thus, this shows the constant formative evaluation of learning in personalized learning environment since the student is given feedback on daily basis. This feedback is not only general, which is an indication of passing or failing, but the evaluators provide detailed explanations of the learner's strengths and the aspects that need to be worked on. Automated tools in particular may give immediate formative feedback on assignment submissions, quizzes, and interactive exercises, which allow the student to learn their misconceptions (Ayeni et al., 2024). For instance, the language learning application that can help a student improve his or her pronunciation can utilize AI to assess the student's pronunciation and offer detailed instructions on how to correct it.

Thus, personalized learning is very effective in stressing the need to foster a friendly environment in which learners can work together. Personalized learning is normally considered with elements of individual learning and, at the same time, it pays attention to the process of social learning and group collaboration. This means students ought to be able to relate to fellow students, exchange ideas and be able to collaborate in their group assignments. This maintains the spirit of teamwork among the students meaning that such interventions are useful in creating a group or communal feel of the students hence improving their performance especially in the online learning environment as noted by Baba et al. in their 2024 accounting article.

With respect to this context, learners stand to benefit from Personalized learning in a number of ways concerning their engagement and results. As the educational process is adjusted to students' concerns and interests, effective motivational factor appears to be the result of PBL implementation. Another advantage of this system of learning is that it helps in the engagement of students. When students are permitted to learn under conditions that appeals to them, then one can vouch for active participation amongst students. Thus, this increased engagement results in enhanced understanding and learners' better attitudes toward it (Rivers & Holland, 2022). For instance, a music lover will pay attention in a mathematics lesson more so if the teacher uses musical acronyms to explain a concept.

This was argued to be another advantage of personalized learning since it opens academia to higher levels of learning performance. Individual approach to the learning makes it possible for the learners to advance through the materials at their own pace without developing gaps in the knowledge that they should possess.

It achieves this as it does not create the gaps of knowledge that are evident in the traditional class where every student is supposed to learn in the same class and at the same pace. Therefore, students who engage themselves in personalised learning activities have been exposed to good grades in comparison with other students (Mahmoud & Sørensen, 2024). For example, research which aimed at identifying the effectiveness of personalized learning in mathematics, it was concluded that student using personalized approach were more effective in tests than the students given traditional approach.

For one knowledge with everyday utility is also attained through personal experiences, critical thinking and problem-solving abilities are also enhanced as is self-regulation. Since the students have to play an active role in the learning process while being involved in the personalized learning, they are active participants in the learning process. This autonomy makes them to learn unimportant life skills that will assist them in their academic and working lives (Maghsudi et al., 2021). For instance, a student who will put his/her own learning objectives and time-tables is likely to master organizational and time management skills for overall life apart from learning.

Besides the academic value, personalised learning also promotes students' social and emotional aspects. In developing capacity to learn, OSS creates a culture of learning thus promoting togetherness that is important for student success. This sense of belonging is important especially for distance learning students most of whom will feel stranded or have no other learners most of the time (Dandachi, 2024). Since the students are grouped according to ability, students and teachers are able to build good rapport with each other as well as students with other students through partnership. For instance, an online course may comprise of a discussion forum and/or a group assignment where students can interact with each other as well as share their experiences.

In addition, it also important in closing down the achievement gap as well as ensuring students who may have a tendency of lagging behind to be given the necessary support that they need. Due to this, personalized learning guarantees that all students can be successful regardless of the previous academic performance and the background they come from (Castro et al., 2024). For example, a personalized learning plan may offer extra information or individual lessons for a learner who is having difficulty in a certain topic to bring her or him on par with fellow learners.

Last but not the least; personalized learning enables students for more learning for life based on the development of the growth pattern. In the schools where students are empowered and assisted to be responsible for their own learning, they develop positive attitude towards schooling and develop perceptive that they can do it. This disposition is critical in fostering lifelong learning since it makes the students to always search for more knowledge and skills for their entire lives (Kanchon et al., 2024).

For instance, students who have come through successful learning environments such as personalized learning environment are likely to adopt education or professional development in the future.

Therefore, as modified from the original definition, personalized learning is a strong educational model that has a lot of advantages in student learning. That is why, through adjusting to the pace, the content delivery method, the content type, or the goal of each learner, personalized learning enhances the level of interest, motivation, and learning support of the learning process. As the application of AI and other advanced technologies in education rises, LPP has a vast chance to revolutionize the educational process and equip all learners with the right tools with which to face a constantly developing world.

3. ROLE OF AI IN PERSONALIZED LEARNING

The use of artificial intelligence can therefore be seen as central for the development of PLEs as it applies the use of different technologies that facilitate the achievement of the goal in the education industry for individual learners. Technologies like Machine learning, Adaptive algorithms and Natural language processing embrace this change to ensure that educators create learning experiences that will meet the needs of each learner (Almusaed et al., 2023). They apply these technologies in part and parcel of learning solutions to extract huge data on students' performance, learning style and behaviour to foster content development.

Artificial intelligence has a subcategory known as machine learning where the systems come with an ability to learn from data and gain adequate experience of a task in the process of performing the task and enhancing the efficiencies of the task with time through self-learning rather than being programmed. As for adaptive learning, machine learning schemes make use of information obtained during students' activities with digital learning environments to perceive trends and forecast the further learning behaviour of students (Katiyar et al., 2024). This information is used to guide the specific learning resources, learning activities and learning assessments for the student, which fulfills the student's requirements. For instance, an LMS created through AI might find out that a particular learner is weak in some forms of math problems, and will later adapt the level of challenge, or provide extra practice questions appropriate for that particular learner.

Another proven artificial intelligence technique in applied personalization is adaptive algorithms. These algorithms modify the field content and the speed of learning in a way that results from analysis of students' performance and participation. In this context, through dynamic observation of the process through which the students engage with the material that is provided for learning, it becomes possible to adjust the flow of the materials that are presented so as to challenge all the students adequately and/or support those who may need it (Maghsudi et al., 2021). For example, it could pose more challenging questions to a particular student who preforms well in the test while giving a particular student extra time to solve a particular problem.

Another application of NLP is also in personalized e-learning in which the field of intelligent tutoring systems and language learning have applied NLP. NLP compels AI systems to translate and reason like human beings respond and communicate. This capability ensures establishment of communication platforms in which the students can learn with responses in tutorials, making it conversational (Baba et al., 2024). For instance, an NLP-based language learning application can dialogue with the student, correct the grammatical errors as well as pronunciation and also present vocabulary lessons in relative to the student's learning level.

AI fosters intelligent learning based on utilization of advance artificial intelligence, intelligent algorithms, and Natural language processing that helps in enhancing learning to individual students basing on a student's characteristics and learning abilities. Machine learning is then used in this process of determining the students' educational skills, their difficulties, and individually developed ways of learning through analysis of patterns derived from students' interactions with learning platforms (Ellikkal & Rajamohan, 2024). Knowledge of these patterns helps an intelligent system to suggest certain content, activities and assessments to improve the student's learning environment. Other aspects such as adaptive algorithms enhance the learning process since it adapts according to the learners' feedback in real-time.

At different stages in the learning curve, these algorithms update the student behaviour and the learning process to fit the student's needs given the new levels of difficulty (Rekha et al., 2024). For instance, if a student is good at let's say mathematics, the algorithm might help the student have updated content to practice the next level of mathematics while helping the student do more exercises in areas the student finds challenging.

Natural language processing improves the approaches to learning personalization as it allows an AI system to engage the learner more like a human being does. In NLP, pro-active tutoring, the use of natural language processing, to dialogically and knowledgeably axiomatically interact and question and answer with students in multilingual learning environments in order to respond and correct effectively to their dialectic and answers accordingly (Dandachi, 2024). This interaction not only enhances the learning process by making it more interesting but also provides an opportunity to provide constant formative assessments which enable the teacher to modify the students' learning in order to meet their learning needs as and when they arise.

Therefore, machine learning, adaptive algorithms, and NLP are some of the AI technologies that are crucial for the customization of learning experience. It's thus possible for educators to employ these technologies to design individual learning plans that are sensitive to each student's needs and academic interests thus increasing their productivity and efficiency. In the future AI, use in personalized learning is definitely set further its abilities to enhance the learning process of students and supporting them in their learning process is set to grow.

4. TECHNIQUES FOR ENHANCING STUDENT ENGAGEMENT

It can be said that with the help of artificial intelligence (AI) of learners' students' engagement can be improved through motivation and participation in activities. One such technique includes Artificial Intelligence driven gamification where the system incorporates the aspects of point, badges, and leaderboard into the learning process (Ellikkal & Rajamohan, 2024). By changing instructive substance into intuitive and cutthroat encounters, computer-based intelligence driven gamification can make learning more agreeable and propelling for understudies. For instance, a man-made intelligence-controlled stage could grant focuses for finishing tasks on time or dominating new abilities, empowering understudies to remain connected with and take a stab at consistent improvement.

Another methodology includes customized learning ways, where simulated intelligence adjusts the educational plan in view of individual understudy progress and inclinations. This approach guarantees that understudies are neither exhausted by satisfied that is too simple nor overpowered by material that is excessively troublesome (Rekha et al., 2024). By fitting the growth opportunity to every understudy's remarkable necessity, computer-based intelligence keeps up with their advantage and inspiration. An AI system might, for instance, determine a student's preferred method of learning, such as visual or auditory, and then present the material in a way that matches this preference, making the learning experience more engaging and efficient. Through real-time feedback mechanisms, AI can also increase student participation. Because it enables students to comprehend their errors and make prompt corrections, immediate feedback is essential for keeping students engaged (Maghsudi et al., 2021).

Computer based intelligence-controlled devices can examine students' reactions continuously and give moment, customized input, assisting students with remaining focused and supporting their learning. In addition to keeping students engaged, this immediate feedback loop helps them gain a deeper comprehension of the material. The usefulness of artificial intelligence (AI) in educational settings is demonstrated by the successful implementation of a number of AI-driven tools to increase student engagement. One notable illustration is "Carnegie Learning," an AI-based tutoring system that uses machine learning algorithms to tailor math instruction to each student. The framework adjusts the trouble level and kind of issues in light of every student's presentation, guaranteeing that they remain tested however not baffled. Students are more likely to remain motivated when the learning material is appropriately challenging, which is why this personalized approach has resulted in improved academic outcomes and increased student engagement (Katiyar et al., 2024).

"Duolingo," a language learning platform that uses AI to create personalized learning experiences, is another illustration. Adaptive algorithms and natural language processing are used in Duolingo to tailor lessons to the user's learning style and progress. The application's gamified components, for example, streak counts and accomplishment identifications, further improve commitment by rousing clients to consistently rehearse. Duolingo's progress in keeping up with elevated degrees of client commitment features the capability of artificial intelligence driven devices to make learning more intelligent and agreeable (Baba et al., 2024).

In the domain of advanced education, artificial intelligence driven conversation stages like "Packback" have additionally shown guarantee in expanding students commitment. Packback utilizes computer-based intelligence to energize more significant and inside and out conversations among students by giving continuous input on the nature of their commitments. The stage investigates students posts for decisive reasoning, innovation, and profundity, directing understudies to work on their reactions and connect all the more nicely with the material.

According to Dandachi (2024), this has resulted in richer class discussions and increased student participation. Taking everything into account, computer-based intelligence offers various techniques for upgrading students' commitment, from gamification and customized learning ways to ongoing criticism. The effectiveness of these strategies in motivating students and increasing their participation in educational activities is demonstrated by case studies of AI-driven tools like Carnegie Learning, Duolingo, and Packback. As computer-based intelligence keeps on advancing, it will probably assume a significantly larger part in encouraging understudy commitment and working on instructive results.

5. ADAPTIVE LEARNING PLATFORMS

Versatile learning stages are changing training by offering customized opportunities for growth custom-made to individual students needs. Based on the learner's strengths and weaknesses, these platforms use cutting-edge algorithms and data analytics to evaluate a student's performance in real time and adjust the content, pace, and instructional strategies accordingly. This unique methodology guarantees that every student gets the right degree of challenge, consequently upgrading learning results and improving commitment (Rekha et al., 2024).

One of the essential functionalities of versatile learning stages is their capacity to constantly screen student progress and change the learning way likewise. For instance, the system can provide additional resources, practice problems, or alternative explanations to a student who is having trouble grasping a particular concept before moving on to the next topic. On the other hand, the platform can accelerate the learning process by introducing more advanced topics to students who have demonstrated proficiency in a particular area, thereby preventing boredom and maintaining motivation (Maghsudi et al., 2021).

One more critical advantage of versatile learning stages is their ability to help different learning styles and inclinations. By dissecting information on how student connect with the material, these stages can introduce content in different configurations — like recordings, intelligent reenactments, or text-put together clarifications — depending with respect to what turns out best for the student. Students are more likely to engage with content that aligns with their preferred learning style as a result of this personalized approach, which not only makes learning more efficient but also more enjoyable (Ellikkal & Rajamohan, 2024).

Additionally, educators can benefit from adaptive learning platforms' scalability, particularly in the context of distance education. These platforms are able to handle a large number of students while still providing individualized instruction, which is something that traditional teaching methods would be nearly impossible to accomplish. In online education settings, where instructors may have limited opportunities to interact with each student individually, this scalability is especially useful. Adaptive learning platforms make it possible for all students, regardless of class size or location, to receive the support they need to succeed by automating the personalization process (Katiyar et al., 2024). A few versatile learning frameworks have been effectively carried out in distance schooling, displaying the capability of these advances to further develop learning results. One conspicuous model is "ALEKS" (Evaluation and Learning in Information Spaces), a versatile learning stage utilized basically in math and science schooling. ALEKS evaluates a student's knowledge and identifies comprehension gaps, adjusting the learning environment accordingly. By consistently adjusting to the student's advancement, ALEKS guarantees that student center around the areas where they need the most assistance, prompting more productive learning and better scholarly execution (Baba et al., 2024).

"Knewton," which powers personalized learning for a wide range of subjects, is yet another effective adaptive learning system. Knewton creates a comprehensive profile of each student's strengths and weaknesses by utilizing data from student interactions with educational material. After that, this profile is used to personalize the learning experience so that the right content is presented at the right time to help students succeed. In distance schooling conditions, Knewton has been especially viable in supporting understudies who might battle with self-guided advancing by furnishing them with an organized and customized way to follow (Dandachi, 2024). "Shrewd Sparrow" is another outstanding versatile learning stage, especially in advanced education. It enables educators to develop individualized adaptive courses that respond immediately to student performance. The platform of Smart Sparrow is designed to be adaptable and customisable, allowing instructors to create engaging and adaptive learning experiences. This framework has been utilized effectively in different disciplines, including clinical schooling, where it assists understudies with dominating complex ideas by adjusting the trouble and focal point of the substance in light of their singular requirements (Rekha et al., 2024).

Thus, versatile learning stages offer huge advantages concerning customized training, adaptability, and further developed learning results. The effectiveness of these platforms in distance education is demonstrated by examples like ALEKS, Knewton, and Smart Sparrow, which provide individualized support tailored to each learner's needs. As the reception of versatile learning advancements keeps on developing, they are probably going to assume an undeniably significant part in moulding the eventual fate of schooling.

6. INTELLIGENT TUTORING SYSTEMS

Intelligent Tutoring Systems (ITS) are a significant development in educational technology because they provide individualized, real-time instruction that is comparable to that of a human tutor. These systems make use of artificial intelligence (AI) to evaluate a student's comprehension of a subject, spot knowledge gaps, and provide individualized feedback and instruction based on the needs of each student. By giving this degree of personalization, ITSs upgrade the opportunity for growth and work on instructive results (Cen et al., 2024).

One of the critical elements of ITSs is their capacity to adjust to every student learning speed and style. ITSs analyse data from student interactions, such as responses to questions and approaches to problem-solving, to develop a comprehensive understanding of the learner's strengths and weaknesses, in contrast to traditional classroom settings, where instruction is frequently generalized. In view of this examination, the framework progressively changes the trouble of assignments, offers designated clues, and even adjusts the grouping of points to more likely line up with the understudy's learning way. This guarantees that student stay connected with and tested, yet not overpowered, which is basic for supporting inspiration and advancing further figuring (Mayer and Russo, 2021).

The effect of ITSs on learning is significant, especially in distance training where students might need prompt admittance to human educators. ITSs fill this hole by giving ceaseless, individualized help, empowering students to deal with complex subjects at their speed while getting moment criticism and direction. Research has shown that understudies involving ITSs frequently beat their friends in customary learning conditions, as the customized guidance assists them with dominating ideas all the more successfully and holding data longer (Anderson et al., 2024). By making high-quality tutoring accessible to all students, regardless of location or socioeconomic status, ITSs also contribute to education equity. This is especially important in distance education, where students may not access the same resources or opportunities as in traditional classrooms. ITSs democratize admittance to customized picking up, guaranteeing that all students have the help they need to succeed (Kumar and Rich, 2024).

The effectiveness of ITSs in improving student learning has been demonstrated by several AI-driven tutoring systems. One striking model is the "Mental Guide," created via Carnegie Realizing, which centres around science schooling. Students are guided step-by-step through the process of solving math problems by a Cognitive Tutor, which makes use of AI to model the thought processes of skilled human tutors. The system provides individualized feedback and adjusts to the learning pace of the student, assisting them in developing a deeper comprehension of mathematical concepts. Reviews have shown that understudies who utilize Mental Coach accomplish higher grades and foster better critical thinking abilities than those in customary learning conditions (Anderson et al., 2024).

Another example is the ITS "AutoTutor," which was made to make science and reading more understandable. AutoTutor draws in student in a conversational style, clarifying pressing issues and giving clarifications that are custom-fitted to the student reactions. This system mimics a real-life tutoring session by utilizing natural language processing (NLP) to comprehend student input and provide pertinent feedback. AutoTutor has demonstrated the potential of ITSs to enhance learning in a wide range of subjects by enhancing students' reading comprehension and critical thinking skills (Graesser et al., 2024).

An ITS called "ASSISTments" is used in middle and high school mathematics to give students immediate feedback on their work and point them in the right direction if they have trouble with a particular problem. What makes ASSISTments extraordinary is its joining with homeroom guidance; instructors can utilize the information created by the framework to distinguish regions where students need extra assistance and change their showing procedures likewise. It has been demonstrated that this combination of AI-driven tutoring and human instruction significantly boosts student performance, particularly in difficult subjects like algebra (Heffernan & Heffernan, 2024).

Thus, intelligent tutoring systems transform education by providing personalized, adaptive instruction that boosts student engagement and learning outcomes. Contextual investigations of frameworks like Mental Guide, AutoTutor, and ASSISTments outline the capability of simulated intelligence-driven coaching to work on scholarly execution across different subjects and instructive settings. As innovation keeps on advancing, ITSs are probably going to assume an undeniably significant role in providing open, great training for all understudies, especially in distance learning conditions.

7. AUTOMATED GRADING AND ASSESSMENT TOOLS

Utilizing artificial intelligence, Intelligent Tutoring Systems (ITS) are potent instruments that provide students with individualized instruction and feedback. These frameworks reproduce the experience of having an individual guide by changing the trouble and sort of satisfied in light of the student's exhibition. As understudies work through illustrations, the ITS keeps tabs on their development, distinguishes regions where they battle, and offers designated help to work on understanding. This customized approach assists understudies with learning at their own speed and guarantees they get the particular direction they need to dominate complex subjects (Cen et al., 2024). ITSs fundamentally affect training, particularly in distance realizing, where students might not have quick admittance to an educator. By giving customized guidance and prompt criticism, ITSs assist with overcoming any issues among understudies and instructors, making learning more open and powerful. For example, frameworks like “Mental Guide” and “AutoTutor” have been displayed to upgrade understudy execution and commitment by offering modified opportunities for growth that customary homeroom settings frequently can't give (Anderson et al., 2024).

Additionally, education's grading and assessment procedures have been transformed by artificial intelligence (AI). Computerized reviewing instruments, controlled by artificial intelligence, can assess students work rapidly and reliably, saving instructors' opportunity to zero in on educating and customized help. These apparatuses are especially helpful in huge classes or online courses where physically evaluating tasks would be tedious and inclined to irregularities. From grading multiple-choice questions to evaluating essays and even complex problem-solving exercises, AI-driven assessment tools can handle a wide range of tasks. For instance, frameworks like "Gradescope" use man-made intelligence to grade composed replies, permitting educators to evaluate students work all the more productively.

This paces up the evaluating system as well as guarantees that all students are reviewed by similar models, decreasing the potential for human inclination (Heffernan and Heffernan, 2024). In addition, computer-based intelligence can dissect designs in understudy reactions to give bits of knowledge into their comprehension and learning progress. This information can assist teachers with recognizing normal areas of trouble, permitting them to change their guidance to address these difficulties. Subsequently, artificial intelligence driven reviewing and appraisal instruments smooth out the evaluating system as well as add to more educated and successful showing methodologies (Kumar and Rich, 2024).

The utilization of simulated intelligence in evaluating and appraisal offers a few advantages, especially regarding effectiveness and consistency. For large-scale educational settings, automated grading systems are ideal because they can process a large volume of student work in a fraction of the time required by a human grader. This speed takes into account faster input to students, which is essential for their learning and improvement. Furthermore, man-made intelligence frameworks apply reviewing models reliably across all students, limiting the gamble of predisposition and guaranteeing reasonableness in evaluation (Mayer and Russo, 2021). However, AI-driven assessment strategies come with their own set of difficulties.

One main pressing issue is the exactness of these frameworks, particularly while evaluating more abstract tasks like articles. While simulated intelligence can assess specific parts of composing, for example, language and design, it might battle with more nuanced components like inventiveness, tone, and argumentation. This brings up issues about the decency and unwavering quality of artificial intelligence in evaluating mind boggling, unassuming undertakings (Graesser et al., 2024). Another test is the potential for over-dependence on computer-based intelligence devices, which could prompt a decrease in basic human oversight. While man-made intelligence can productively grade many sorts of tasks, it is fundamental that teachers stay associated with the appraisal cycle to guarantee that all parts of students execution are precisely assessed. In addition, there is a concern that students might modify their work in a way that they believe will please an AI system, which could hinder creativity and more in-depth critical thinking (Anderson et al., 2024).

Thus, AI-driven grading and assessment tools are valuable assets in modern education, particularly in large-scale or distance learning settings, due to their efficiency and consistency advantages. However, these tools also come with problems, especially when it comes to making sure that assessments are accurate and fair. As man-made intelligence innovation keeps on advancing, it will mean quite a bit to adjust the advantages of mechanization with the requirement for human judgment and oversight to guarantee that instructive evaluations stay extensive and impartial.

8. REAL-TIME FEEDBACK MECHANISMS

Feedback is very important at any point of learning particularly in blended learning environments. If students are provided with feedback in the shortest time possible, they are in a position to work on their shortcomings and can work their weakness and this can also give them an idea as to how they should develop their skills. This gives students a feeling that whatever they are doing will yield some fruits and this also provides them with constructive criticism which is important for growth. Hence, students will be more motivated to study. Since distance education often implies students' independent work, feedback is critical as it provides learners with orientation and makes them feel that they are not alone on this learning path (Hattie and Timperley, 2024).

In customized learning, criticism isn't just about remedying blunders; it's additionally about directing students through their learning ways. It makes the learning experience more efficient and tailored to each student's needs by providing specific information about their strengths and weaknesses. For instance, if a student is having trouble understanding a particular math concept, they might get immediate feedback that not only points out the error but also suggests additional resources or other ways to better understand the concept.

According to Mayer & Russo (2002), this method ensures that each student's pace and learning style are respected and that learning is ongoing and adaptable. Artificial intelligence has enormously improved the capacity to give constant criticism in instructive settings. Artificial intelligence-controlled devices can investigate understudy execution as they complete undertakings and proposition moment criticism custom fitted to their particular necessities. With the help of these tools, you can spot patterns in a student's behavior, such as areas where they frequently make mistakes or hesitate, and respond with specific guidance or more opportunities for practice. According to Graesser et al. (2024), this type of immediate, individualized feedback aids students in correcting errors on the spot and reinforces their learning before misconceptions can take root.

One illustration of a computer-based intelligence application giving ongoing criticism is "Grammarly," a broadly utilized instrument that assists understudies with working on their composition. As students' type, Grammarly breaks down their text for sentence structure, accentuation, and style issues, giving thoughts for amendments and improvements continuously. Instead of waiting for teacher feedback, which may arrive days or even weeks later, this allows students to learn and apply correct writing techniques immediately (Heffernan & Heffernan, 2024). Another model is "ALEKS" (Appraisal and Learning in Information Spaces), a simulated intelligence driven stage that gives ongoing criticism in math and science training. ALEKS consistently surveys understudy information as they deal with through issues, offering moment criticism on their responses and adjusting the trouble of resulting questions in view of their exhibition.

According to Cent et al. (2024), this ensures that students are always working at a level that is appropriate for them and challenges them just enough to encourage learning without causing frustration. These artificial intelligence applications give moment criticism as well as assist students with building trust in their capacities. Students are encouraged to experiment with novel ideas and take risks because they know they will receive support in the event that they make mistakes because they receive prompt, constructive feedback on their work. This cultivates a more powerful and intuitive learning climate, where students are effectively taken part in their schooling and roused to accomplish their best (Anderson et al., 2024).

All in all, ideal criticism is a foundation of compelling customized picking up, assisting understudies with remaining focused, right mix-ups, and develop how they might interpret the material. Man-made intelligence-controlled devices that give ongoing input assume a basic part in this cycle, offering prompt, customized direction that improves understudy learning and commitment. It is likely that these technologies will become even more integral to personalized education as they continue to develop, assisting students in realizing their full potential.

9. CASE STUDIES OF PERSONALIZED LEARNING IN ACTION

Many learning environments and courses have adopted AI- based learner-centred approach with encouraging trends of students' interest and performance. One such case in point is the Arizona State University (ASU) which has incorporated adaptive learning technologies in its first level mathematics courses. As for customized and adaptive learning- technology, ASU employs AI based platforms like "ALEKS" and "Knewton." These platforms allow testing students' knowledge in real-time and adapt the content based on the topics that are difficult for them. This has helped earn better outcome of the students in terms of their retention and pass rates in such a class (Graesser et al., p 2024).

Another case is the AltSchools – schools located in the United States of America which empowers the utilization of an artificial intelligence algorithm to develop individual learning processes for every learner. At AltSchool, student performance and behaviour data are recorded across different classes and for the teachers to later guide them and give them detailed feedback to facilitate proper alignment of instruction and activities for the individual learner. Such an approach puts emphasis on using statistical techniques that would enable the teachers know how each learner can be taught in the best way possible.

The effectiveness of the concepts transferred in schools is increased by the fact that at AltSchools learning environment is personalized, which allows students to progress at the rate convenient for them and reach their academic objectives in the shortest time possible (Heffernan & Heffernan, 2024).

Therefore, the success of these programs presents several key lessons and best practice that can improve the implementation of AI based personalized learning in other educational contexts. First, it is necessary to emphasize the general need for data as the crucial factor of the modern world. Authentic concept of personalized learning depends on amping both the accumulation and processing of student information to enable accurate modification of students' learning experiences on continual basis. Entities concerned need to develop effective means of handling the data and also ensure that the instructors are equipped on how to understand the data and how to use it (Mayer & Russo, 2021).

Another very important ideology is in modality flexibility in teaching or delivery methods that are used. As for the use of AI in creating personalized learning platforms, it is crucial to note that it should be integrated with a flexible curriculum where changes can be made depending on the student's progress AI driven approaches are most effective. A major expectation is that educators should be ready to adapt to different kinds of lesson plans and time schedules which has to be adopted in regards to the customized suggestions given by the AI systems. This flexibility helps ensuring that the technology brings positive impact on the learning process and not negative impacts (Anderson et al., 2024).

However, it also important to note that the educator will always be needed in AI enabled personalisation of learning. The use of AI can benefit students by offering personalized information as well as changing content to meet the needs of individual learners However, it is the teacher who can help in the interpretation of the data and put the information in context and it is always the teacher who can keep the students interested and motivated. AI should not be considered by educators as competing against the facilitation that human being can provide to students (Cen et al., 2024).

Thus, it could be argued that the usage of AI systems should be made clear to the students and the parents as to how we are using AI in delivery of personalized learning. It is crucial to convince the stakeholders regarding the objectives of personalized learning and the use of AI in the process, as well as the method of data gathering and their further application. I found that engaging all the parties into the process enhances learning within institutions and makes it efficient and welcoming to learners (Hattie & Timperley, 2024). Therefore, the opportunities of AI in personalized learning are proved by the development of such schools as Arizona State University and AltSchool. Therefore, based on the principles such as data, flexibility, engagement of educators, and openness, other institutions can also foster and adopt the personalized learning that is effective in engagement of students and improvement of the performance. Of course, the experiences from these pioneers that have used these technologies will provide a lot of lessons that will prove very useful as the technologies progress.

10. CHALLENGES AND ETHICAL CONSIDERATIONS

The use of enhanced AI-enhanced learning system entails a variety of factors that institutions need to consider in the implementation process. The major issue depends on the high costs of developing and maintaining artificial intelligence technologies. Schools and Universities may require assistance in acquiring the initial capital required to undertake the acquisition of the platforms as well as other issues such as upgrading, staff training, and technical support (Anderson et al., 2024). Furthermore, adoption of these technologies can pose difficulty when incorporated into current education systems. This means, that it is necessary to abandon the traditional approach to learning that may be a problem for teachers who might be reluctant to change or who do not possess appropriate skills to operate AI (Graesser et al., 2024).

The possibility that AI-driven systems will amplify existing biases is another obstacle. The data used to train AI algorithms is only as impartial as the data themselves. In the event that the information reflects cultural imbalances, the artificial intelligence framework could propagate these predispositions, prompting unjustifiable results for specific gatherings of understudies (Cen et al., 2024). For instance, there may be a digital divide as a result of an AI system's inability to accurately assess or assist students from diverse backgrounds when it relies primarily on data from students in wealthy areas.

The utilization of artificial intelligence in customized learning raises critical moral issues, especially concerning information security. For AI systems to work well, a lot of student data—such as academic performance, behaviour, and even personal information—is needed. If it is not handled correctly, this data collection may be risky. (Mayer & Russo, 2021) There is a concern that sensitive information could be misused, resulting in privacy breaches.

Additionally, the gamble of information is being imparted to outsiders without the educated assent regarding understudies and their families, which could prompt unapproved utilization of individual data. The possibility that AI will reduce the importance of human judgment in education is another ethical issue. Although AI can provide individualized learning paths, it may not fully comprehend the specific requirements of each student. Over-dependence on simulated intelligence could prompt a decrease in the unique interaction among teachers and students, which is imperative for an all-encompassing instructive experience (Heffernan and Heffernan, 2024).

To address these difficulties and moral worries, instructive establishments ought to embrace best practices for the dependable utilization of computer-based intelligence in customized learning. First, openness is essential. Schools' ought to obviously convey to understudies and their families how man-made intelligence frameworks work, what information is gathered, and the way in which it will be utilized. According to Heather & Timperley (2024), transparency fosters trust and ensures that all stakeholders are aware of the potential benefits and risks. Privacy of data ought to be a top priority.

Organizations should serious areas of strength for execute insurance measures, for example, encryption and customary security reviews, to protect students' data. They ought to likewise guarantee that information assortment is negligible and applicable just to the instructive objectives, and that understudies and guardians have the choice to quit information assortment in the event that they decide (Anderson et al., 2024). Engaging educators in the AI implementation process is yet another best practice. Instructors ought to get sufficient preparation on the most proficient method to utilize computer-based intelligence devices successfully and comprehend how these apparatuses can supplement their educating. Educators can use AI to improve learning outcomes while maintaining their essential role of guiding and mentoring students (Graesser et al., 2024).

Last but not least, institutions ought to regularly examine and update their AI systems to address any potential biases. This includes ceaselessly observing the presentation of computer-based intelligence calculations and making changes as important to guarantee that they serve all understudies fairly (Cen et al., 2024). All in all, while simulated intelligence driven customized learning offers critical advantages, it likewise presents difficulties and moral contemplations that should be painstakingly made due. By focusing on straightforwardness, information protection, instructor association, and progressing observing, instructive organizations can bridle the force of computer-based intelligence capably and successfully, guaranteeing that all understudies benefit from customized growth opportunities.

11. FUTURE TRENDS AND INNOVATIONS

Among the trends, it is possible to list the active implementation of adaptive learning technologies. These systems employ the use of Artificial Intelligence where the program runs a student's performance over time and adjusts both content and delivery speed to fit this learners' needs better (Anderson et al., 2024). For example, if a student is not able to solve a particular problem, the AI can adapt and offer supplementary documents or explanations so that the student will understand completely the topic at hand before proceeding to the next one.

One trend refers to the incorporation of artificial intelligence based virtual tutors. Such virtual assistants are advancing to be more realistic, providing real time assistance to the students whenever they want it. Unlike a live tutor, student does not have wait for him to be around and explain, answer questions and even solve a certain problem at his own time. This constant availability can greatly improve the learning experience especially in cases where the students may not be able to readily consult the instructors as may be the case in distance learning (Graesser et al., 2024).

The following is also increasingly used in the field of personalized learning; Full name processing; Natural Language Processing (NLP). NLP enables the machine to interact with the students fluently by enabling it to comprehend human language. For instance, teachers are now able to determine the extent of the student's understanding just by analysing his or her written work, and even offer feedback to help the student enhance his or her writing performance and content mastery (Mayer & Russo, 2021). This trend is especially apparent in language acquisition and all courses that entail the need to apply interpersonal communication skills.

In the future, there are great prospects for developing personalized learning in distance education as artificial intelligence is expected to be even more involved. One of them is that the individual learning trails controlled by artificial intelligence will become a norm in an online class. New generations of learning algorithms can make a much better and more effective learning plan based on a student's learning preferences and even his or her state of mind. This may enhance learning productivity because to the Equalizer each student gets the necessary help for efficient learning (Heffernan & Heffernan, 2024).

Another prediction that can be made is the growth of learning environments, based on artificial intelligence. Since VR and AR technologies could be powered by AI, these could make studying highly involving and immersive education. Picture learning where students can go to Antique Egypt, come to Greece, or even watch a doctor as he or she accomplishes a surgery. They could enrich the learning process and make it more stimulating – especially for the distance learners – so that the latter would not feel isolated from the topic at hand (Cen et al., 2024).

Computer based intelligence driven evaluations are likewise expected to advance, moving past conventional testing strategies. A student's interactions with the learning material may enable future AI systems to continuously assess their skills and knowledge, provide real-time feedback, and adjust the curriculum as necessary. This could prompt more powerful and responsive school systems that address the issues of individual students (Hattie and Timperley, 2024). At last, there is the potential for artificial intelligence to upgrade cooperative learning in distance schooling. Computer based intelligence can work with bunch work by coordinating students with comparable interests or corresponding abilities and giving devices to assist them with teaming up, regardless of whether they are situated in various areas in the world. This could help students develop needed teamwork skills, which are increasingly valued in today's global economy, and enrich learning experiences (Anderson et al., 2024).

Thus, AI is expected to drive significant innovations, which bodes well for the future of personalized learning in distance education. These upcoming trends—adaptive learning technologies, immersive environments, and advanced assessments—promise to make learning more individualized, engaging, and efficient for students worldwide. As artificial intelligence keeps on developing, it will without a doubt assume a vital part in forming the fate of training.

12. CONCLUSION

In this chapter, we looked at how AI-driven personalized learning plays a big role in distance education, focusing on how it can change student engagement and outcomes. The excursion started with a comprehension of the significance of customized learning, especially with regards to separate training where students frequently pass up the customized consideration they could get in conventional study hall settings. Customized learning tailors the instructive experience to individual necessities, empowering understudies to learn at their own speed and as per their novel learning styles (Anderson et al., 2024).

In distance education, where the physical distance between students and instructors can occasionally lead to feelings of isolation, this strategy is critical. We then, at that point, dove into the definition and key parts of customized getting the hang of, featuring how it benefits understudy commitment and results. By zeroing in on individual learning ways, customized learning keeps students more connected as well as assists them with accomplishing better scholarly outcomes. By applying data-driven insights to real-time adaptation and refinement of educational material, the incorporation of AI into personalized learning amplifies these advantages. This capacity takes into consideration a more responsive and adaptable learning climate, where understudies get support customized to their nearby requirements (Graesser et al., 2024).

The job of simulated intelligence in customized learning was inspected exhaustively, covering how innovations, for example, AI, versatile calculations, and normal language handling add to making a more individualized growth opportunity. Simulated intelligence's capacity to dissect huge measures of information empowers it to customize learning on a scale that would be outside the realm of possibilities for human educators alone. According to Heffernan & Heffernan (2024), AI can, for instance, identify patterns in a student's behaviour or performance and suggest specific resources or activities to address their weaknesses. This upgrade learning effectiveness as well as keeps up with students inspiration by keeping them tested at this point upheld. We likewise talked about different methods for improving understudy commitment through artificial intelligence, including methodologies for expanding inspiration and interest.

Case studies of AI-driven tools like adaptive learning platforms and intelligent tutoring systems gave concrete examples of how these technologies are working well in distance education. These apparatuses show the way that simulated intelligence can establish more intuitive and connecting with learning conditions, which are essential for keeping up with understudy interest and advancing further learning (Mayer and Russo, 2021). The conversation on versatile learning stages and canny coaching frameworks featured the usefulness and advantages of these artificial intelligence-controlled arrangements. These frameworks offer customized content as well as change the growing experience continuously, guaranteeing that students stay on target. Automated grading and assessment tools were also looked at, showing how AI can speed up the evaluation process and provide timely feedback that is crucial to continuous improvement (Cen et al., 2024).

In taking into account the fate of computer-based intelligence driven customized learning, we recognized arising patterns and developments that can change distance schooling. These trends, from advanced AI-driven assessments to immersive learning environments, point to a future in which education will become even more tailored to each student's needs, resulting in improved learning outcomes for a wide range of student populations (Hattie & Timperley, 2024). All in all, artificial intelligence driven customized learning addresses a useful asset for improving students' commitment and results in distance schooling. By utilizing artificial intelligence advances, teachers can make more customized, responsive, and compelling learning conditions that take special care of the different requirements of students. As these advances keep on developing, they hold the possibility to change training in manners that were beforehand unfathomable, making learning more open, drawing in, and fruitful for all understudies. AI will undoubtedly play a significant role in shaping the learning experiences of the future, making the education industry s future exciting.

REFERENCES

Agarwal, M. B., & Lahoti, Y. (2023). Transforming education: The impact and potential of artificial intelligence in personalized learning environments. *Journal for ReAttach Therapy and Developmental Diversities*, *6*(1), 1754–1761.

Alenezi, A. (2023). Teacher perspectives on AI-driven gamification: Impact on student motivation, engagement, and learning outcomes.

Almusaed, A., Almssad, A., Yitmen, I., & Homod, R. Z. (2023). Enhancing student engagement: Harnessing "AIED"'s power in hybrid education—A review analysis. *Education Sciences, 13*(7), 632.78.

Ayeni, O. O., Al Hamad, N. M., Chisom, O. N., Osawaru, B., & Adewusi, O. E. (2024). AI in education: A review of personalized learning and educational technology. *GSC Advanced Research and Reviews*, *18*(2), 261–271.

Baba, K., Faddouli, E., & Cheimanoff, N. (2024). Mobile-optimized AI-driven personalized learning: A case study at Mohammed VI Polytechnic University. *International Journal of Interactive Mobile Technologies*, *18*(4).

Barrera Castro, G. P., Chiappe, A., Becerra Rodríguez, D. F., & Gonzalo Sepulveda, F. (2024). Harnessing AI for education 4.0: Drivers of personalized learning. *Electronic Journal of e-Learning*, *22*(5), 01–14. DOI: 10.34190/ejel.22.5.3467

Bin Salem, I. (2024). Integrating artificial intelligence in personalized learning: A future-oriented approach to enhance student engagement and achievement. *International Journal of Post Axial: Futuristic Teaching and Learning*, 111-119.

Biswas, R. A., & Molla, A. (2024). Impact of artificial intelligence on personalized learning. In *Artificial intelligence in education* (p. 302).

Castro, G. P. B., Chiappe, A., Rodríguez, D. F. B., & Sepulveda, F. G. (2024). Harnessing AI for education 4.0: Drivers of personalized learning. *Electronic Journal of e-Learning, 22*(5), 01-14.

Dandachi, I. E. (2024). AI-powered personalized learning: Toward sustainable education. In *Navigating the intersection of business, sustainability and technology* (pp. 109–118). Springer Nature Singapore.

Ellikkal, A., & Rajamohan, S. (2024). *AI-enabled personalized learning: Empowering management students for improving engagement and academic performance.* Vilakshan-XIMB Journal of Management.

Kanchon, M. K. H., Sadman, M., Nabila, K. F., Tarannum, R., & Khan, R. (2024). Enhancing personalized learning: AI-driven identification of learning styles and content modification strategies. *International Journal of Cognitive Computing in Engineering*, *5*, 269–276. DOI: 10.1016/j.ijcce.2024.06.002

Katiyar, N., Awasthi, M. V. K., Pratap, R., Mishra, M. K., Shukla, M. N., & Tiwari, M. (2024). AI-driven personalized learning systems: Enhancing educational effectiveness. *Educational Administration: Theory and Practice*, *30*(5), 11514–11524.

Maghsudi, S., Lan, A., Xu, J., & van Der Schaar, M. (2021). Personalized education in the artificial intelligence era: What to expect next. *IEEE Signal Processing Magazine*, *38*(3), 37–50. DOI: 10.1109/MSP.2021.3055032

Mahmoud, C. F., & Sørensen, J. T. (2024). Artificial intelligence in personalized learning with a focus on current developments and future prospects. *Research and Advances in Education*, *3*(8), 25–31. DOI: 10.56397/RAE.2024.08.04

Nursalim, A., Judijanto, L., & Asfahani, A. (2022). Educational revolution through the application of AI in the digital era. *Journal of Artificial Intelligence and Development*, *1*(1), 31–40.

Omar, Z. F., Mior Harun, M. H., Mohd Ishar, N. I., Mustapha, N. A., & Ismail, Z. (2024). Enhancing professional development and training through AI for personalized learning: A framework to engaging learners. *International Journal of e-Learning and Higher Education (IJELHE), 19*(3), 115-138.

Praveen, J. V. S. (2024). Understanding the potential impact of AI-powered classroom management on student engagement, and overall learning outcomes. *Global Journal of Business and Integral Security*, *1*(2).

Rasheed, Z., Ghwanmeh, S., & Abualkishik, A. Z. (2023). Harnessing artificial intelligence for personalized learning: A systematic review. *Data and Metadata*, *2*, 146–146. DOI: 10.56294/dm2023146

Rekha, K., Gopal, K., Satheeskumar, D., Anand, U. A., Doss, D. S. S., & Elayaperumal, S. (2024, May). AI-powered personalized learning system design: Student engagement and performance tracking system. In *2024 4th International Conference on Advance Computing and Innovative Technologies in Engineering (ICACITE)* (pp. 1125-1130). IEEE.

Rivers, C., & Holland, A. (2022). Management education and artificial intelligence: Toward personalized learning. In *The future of management education* (pp. 184–204). Routledge.

Rizvi, S. (2023). Revolutionizing student engagement: Artificial intelligence's impact on specialized learning motivation. *International Journal of Advanced Engineering Research and Science, 10*(09), 27–31. DOI: 10.22161/ijaers.109.4

Ruksana, T. P. (2024). AI-driven pedagogy: Unveiling ChatGPT's influence in education. *Journal of Applied Science, Engineering, Technology and Management, 2*(01), 09-14.

Saaida, M. B. (2023). AI-driven transformations in higher education: Opportunities and challenges. *International Journal of Educational Research and Studies, 5*(1), 29–36.

Swargiary, K. (2024). *The impact of AI-driven personalized learning on mathematics achievement and student engagement in rural vs. urban schools in Karnataka*. Google.

Vashishth, T. K., Sharma, V., Sharma, K. K., Kumar, B., Panwar, R., & Chaudhary, S. (2024). AI-driven learning analytics for personalized feedback and assessment in higher education. In *Using traditional design methods to enhance AI-driven decision making* (pp. 206–230). IGI Global. DOI: 10.4018/979-8-3693-0639-0.ch009

Widono, S., Saddhono, K., Nurhasanah, F., Nugraheni, A. S. C., & Legowo, B. (2024, May). A strategic design of personalized based learning system for improving the experience of outcome based education. In *2024 4th International Conference on Advance Computing and Innovative Technologies in Engineering (ICACITE)* (pp. 1149-1154). IEEE. DOI: 10.1109/ICACITE60783.2024.10616811

Yekollu, R. K., Bhimraj Ghuge, T., Sunil Biradar, S., Haldikar, S. V., & Farook Mohideen Abdul Kader, O. (2024, February). AI-driven personalized learning paths: Enhancing education through adaptive systems. In *International Conference on Smart Data Intelligence* (pp. 507-517). Springer Nature Singapore. DOI: 10.1007/978-981-97-3191-6_38

ADDITIONAL READING

Tariq, M. U. (2025). Revitalizing Pedagogy: Integrating Indigenous Knowledge and Practices Into Higher Education Disciplines. In Kgari-Masondo, M. (Ed.), *Indigenous Teaching Disciplines and Perspectives for Higher Education* (pp. 379–400). IGI Global Scientific Publishing., https://doi.org/10.4018/979-8-3693-9296-6.ch018

Tariq, M. U. (2025). Bridging Cultures and Languages: Innovative Literacy Strategies for Inclusive and Engaged Classrooms. In Tussey, J., & Haas, L. (Eds.), *Supporting Cultural Differences Through Literacy Education* (pp. 257–282). IGI Global Scientific Publishing., https://doi.org/10.4018/979-8-3693-9271-3.ch010

Tariq, M. U. (2025). Community-Led Tourism and Social Equity: A Regenerative Approach to Sustainable Development. In Sousa, B., Arantes, L., & Bhartiya, S. (Eds.), *Regenerative Tourism for Social Development* (pp. 339–360). IGI Global Scientific Publishing., https://doi.org/10.4018/979-8-3373-0235-5.ch014

Tariq, M. U. (2025). Innovative Business Models: Integrating Social, Economic, and Environmental Goals in Rural Manufacturing. In Prabhakar, A., Yu, P., & Erokhin, V. (Eds.), *Rural Social Entrepreneurship Development: Network-Based Manufacturing System Model* (pp. 147–174). IGI Global Scientific Publishing., https://doi.org/10.4018/979-8-3693-7515-0.ch005

Tariq, M. U. (2025). Revolutionizing Communication: EEG-Based Brain-Computer Interface for Speech and Mood Detection. In Prabhakar, A., Yu, P., & Erokhin, V. (Eds.), *Rural Social Entrepreneurship Development: Network-Based Manufacturing System Model* (pp. 237–264). IGI Global Scientific Publishing., https://doi.org/10.4018/979-8-3693-7515-0.ch008

Tariq, M. U. (2025). AI and Work-Life Balance: Transforming Employee Wellbeing in the Modern Workplace. In Ahmed, E., Babar, A., Samad, A., Ahmed, R., & Beydoun, G. (Eds.), *Strengthening Human Relations in Organizations With AI* (pp. 85–110). IGI Global Scientific Publishing., https://doi.org/10.4018/979-8-3693-6507-6.ch004

Tariq, M. U. (2025). AI and the Ethical Crossroads: Navigating Privacy, Personhood, and Autonomy in the Digital Age. In Chakraborty, S. (Ed.), *Human Values, Ethics, and Dignity in the Age of Artificial Intelligence* (pp. 49–72). IGI Global Scientific Publishing., https://doi.org/10.4018/979-8-3693-9035-1.ch003

Chapter 8

Leveraging AI and Learning Analytics for Enhanced Distance Learning: Transformation in Education

Venice J. Arockia
https://orcid.org/0009-0008-9743-4791
DMI-St.Eugene University, Zambia

R. Vettriselvan
https://orcid.org/0000-0002-1324-136X
Academy of Maritime Education and Training, India

Deepa Rajesh
Academy of Maritime Education and Training, India

Palanivel Rathinasabapathi Rathinasabapathi Velmurugan
https://orcid.org/0000-0002-0395-9060
Berlin School of Business and Innovation, Germany

Chinyama Cheelo
DMI-St.Eugene University, Zambia

ABSTRACT

This chapter delves into how AI and learning analytics are reshaping distance learning by enabling a more personalized, adaptive, and data-informed educational experience. AI-driven tools allow educators to analyze student behavior, engage-

DOI: 10.4018/979-8-3693-7195-4.ch008

ment, and performance, facilitating timely support and targeted interventions that enhance learning outcomes. Learning analytics helps predict challenges, enabling proactive measures that keep students on track, while also providing insights into diverse learning needs. Through AI, online education becomes more interactive and efficient, as automation handles routine tasks and customizes content to suit individual progress and preferences. This approach not only improves the efficacy of distance learning but also drives a shift in traditional educational methods toward a more inclusive and responsive framework. As educational institutions adopt these technologies, understanding their capabilities and limitations becomes essential for effectively advancing digital learning and supporting diverse learner success.

INTRODUCTION

Artificial intelligence (AI) and learning analytics are rapidly transforming the educational landscape by providing tools and methods to create personalized and data-driven learning experiences. AI in education encompasses a range of applications, including intelligent tutoring systems, automated grading, and adaptive learning platforms that respond to students' individual learning paths (Luckin et al., 2016). Learning analytics, closely related to AI, involves the collection, analysis, and interpretation of data about learners and their contexts to improve learning experiences (Siemens & Long, 2011). When combined, AI and learning analytics enable educators to identify patterns in student engagement and outcomes, guiding interventions that can lead to improved academic success (Gašević et al., 2015).

Historically, educational practices have relied on a generalized approach, often overlooking the diverse needs and capabilities of individual learners. With AI and learning analytics, educational systems are moving toward personalized learning models that support different learning paces, styles, and abilities. AI-driven tools analyze vast amounts of data from learning management systems (LMS), including clickstream data, quiz performance, and time-on-task metrics, to provide insights that inform real-time adjustments in teaching and curriculum (Baker & Siemens, 2014). These innovations foster adaptive learning, where content dynamically adjusts to a learner's needs, promoting student engagement and satisfaction (Dziuban et al., 2018).

The Rise of Distance Learning and the Push for Data-Driven Education

The recent surge in online and distance learning has accelerated the adoption of AI and learning analytics across educational institutions. Distance learning, defined as the delivery of education to students who are not physically present in a traditional classroom, grew substantially during the COVID-19 pandemic (Adedoyin & Soykan, 2020). This shift highlighted the need for advanced tools to support student engagement and academic success in remote settings, where face-to-face interaction is limited. Traditional online courses, often characterized by high attrition rates and limited interactivity, presented challenges that educational institutions sought to address through technological innovation. Data-driven education has become a focal point in the move toward more effective distance learning. By integrating AI and learning analytics, institutions can better understand the unique challenges and learning behaviors associated with online education (Gašević et al., 2015). Data collected from digital interactions enables educators to monitor progress, anticipate obstacles, and make informed decisions to enhance learning outcomes (Pardo et al., 2019). For instance, early warning systems can identify at-risk students based on behavioral indicators, allowing educators to intervene before academic performance declines (Arnold & Pistilli, 2012). This capacity to personalize and monitor online learning processes represents a significant advancement in addressing the demands of a growing and diverse learner population.

Significance of Integrating AI and Analytics in Learning Systems

The integration of AI and learning analytics into educational systems is essential to achieving a more inclusive and efficient distance learning environment. By embedding these technologies, institutions can transcend the limitations of traditional teaching models, providing data-informed, responsive education tailored to each student's needs. AI can automate routine tasks, such as grading and content recommendation, freeing instructors to focus on higher-order teaching responsibilities (Holmes et al., 2019). Through analytics, educational institutions gain actionable insights into student behaviors, learning outcomes, and course effectiveness, supporting continuous improvement in curriculum design and instructional strategies (Sclater et al., 2016). Furthermore, AI-driven learning analytics can promote equity in education by offering students from diverse backgrounds personalized support that adapts to their unique challenges (Baker, 2019). For example, adaptive learning platforms can provide additional resources to students who struggle with specific concepts, ensuring that they receive the same quality of education as their peers, regardless of their location or socioeconomic background (Norvig & Russell, 2021). As such, the application of AI and learning analytics in distance education not only supports academic success but also fosters an equitable learning environment that is responsive to individual differences and needs.

Problem Statement and Purpose of the Chapter

Despite the potential of distance learning to reach a broader audience, traditional models often fall short in providing the level of personalization and interactivity necessary to sustain student engagement and performance. High dropout rates and limited access to timely feedback have been persistent issues in distance education, where students frequently lack the motivation and support systems present in conventional classrooms (Xu & Jaggars, 2013). Furthermore, the reliance on static content and one-size-fits-all approaches fails to address the diverse needs and learning styles of online students, leading to varying academic outcomes (Means et al., 2014). AI and learning analytics offer promising solutions to these challenges by providing real-time insights into student performance and engagement. These technologies enable a shift from reactive to proactive support in education, where issues are identified and addressed before they impact academic achievement (Siemens, 2013). For instance, predictive models can identify patterns that signal a student's likelihood of disengagement or failure, prompting timely interventions that keep learners on track (Rienties et al., 2018). This chapter aims to explore these advancements and demonstrate how AI and learning analytics can enhance the distance learning experience by overcoming traditional limitations. The purpose of this chapter is to examine the transformative potential of AI and learning analytics in distance learning, with a focus on how these technologies can improve academic outcomes, support personalized learning, and enhance student engagement. By analyzing recent studies and theoretical frameworks, this chapter will provide a comprehensive overview of the role that AI and learning analytics play in creating effective, data-driven educational environments. This exploration will offer insights into best practices, ethical considerations, and future directions for AI in distance learning, equipping educators and institutions with the knowledge needed to implement these tools successfully.

Chapter Objectives and Structure

This chapter is organized into several sections, each addressing key aspects of AI and learning analytics in distance education. Following the introduction, the Conceptual Framework section will define core concepts, including AI, learning analytics, and adaptive learning, providing a foundation for understanding the technologies discussed throughout the chapter. The Theoretical Framework section will explore the educational theories that underpin AI and analytics in learning, drawing on constructivist and connectivist perspectives to explain how these tools support meaningful learning experiences. The Research Methodology section will review the methodologies used in current research on AI and learning analytics in distance education, highlighting common data collection and analysis techniques. The Solutions and Recommendations section will offer practical insights into implementing AI and learning analytics, including best practices and case studies. This will be followed by Future Research Directions, which will identify emerging trends and gaps in the literature, suggesting avenues for further study. Finally, the Conclusion will summarize the chapter's main points and reflect on the implications of AI and learning analytics for the future of distance education. This structured approach will allow readers to understand both the theoretical and practical aspects of AI and learning analytics, gaining a holistic view of how these technologies can transform distance learning.

CONCEPTUAL FRAMEWORK

Artificial Intelligence (AI) refers to the simulation of human intelligence processes by computer systems, enabling them to perform tasks that typically require human cognitive functions, such as understanding natural language, recognizing patterns, and making decisions (Russell & Norvig, 2021). Within the domain of AI, **machine learning** (ML) is a subset that focuses on the development of algorithms that allow computers to learn from and make predictions based on data without explicit programming (Bishop, 2006). Machine learning techniques include supervised learning, unsupervised learning, and reinforcement learning, each of which has specific applications in educational contexts. Deep learning, a further specialization within machine learning, employs artificial neural networks to model complex patterns in large datasets (Goodfellow et al., 2016). Deep learning has gained prominence due to its effectiveness in tasks such as image and speech recognition and natural language processing, making it increasingly relevant in educational technologies that leverage multimedia content and interactive interfaces (Zhang et al., 2018). Learning analytics refers to the collection, analysis, and interpretation of data about learners and their contexts to improve learning experiences and outcomes (Siemens & Long, 2011). It encompasses various methodologies for examining learner behaviors, engagement, and performance to inform instructional strategies and enhance educational effectiveness (Ferguson, 2012). The synergy between AI and learning analytics creates opportunities for more intelligent and responsive educational environments, where systems can adapt to individual learner needs in real time.

Distance learning is defined as an educational process where students engage in learning activities without being physically present in a traditional classroom setting (Moore et al., 2011). The rise of digital technologies has facilitated the growth of distance learning, enabling educational institutions to offer courses and programs that reach learners across geographical boundaries. Digital learning environments, which include online courses, virtual classrooms, and blended learning models, are characterized by their reliance on technology to mediate the learning experience (Garrison & Vaughan, 2008). In a digital learning environment, various multimedia resources, such as videos, interactive simulations, and discussion forums, enhance the learning experience and foster collaboration among learners. The integration of AI and learning analytics into these environments provides educators with tools to monitor student engagement and performance, offering insights that inform instructional design and support (Dziuban et al., 2018). As distance learning continues to evolve, the role of AI and analytics in creating engaging and effective digital learning experiences becomes increasingly significant.

Key Elements of AI and Learning Analytics in Distance Education

AI applications in education have gained traction due to their potential to enhance the learning experience and improve educational outcomes. Adaptive learning systems utilize AI algorithms to customize content delivery based on individual student performance and learning preferences (Knewton, 2018). These systems analyze data from learner interactions and dynamically adjust the difficulty and type of content presented, allowing for personalized learning pathways that cater to diverse learner needs (VanLehn, 2011). Recommendation systems are another key application of AI in education, employing machine learning algorithms to suggest relevant resources and activities to learners based on their interests, behaviors, and performance (Jannach & Adomavicius, 2016). These systems can enhance engagement and motivation by providing personalized learning experiences that align with students' goals and preferences. Additionally, automated assessments powered by AI facilitate efficient and objective evaluation of student performance. AI-driven tools can grade assignments, quizzes, and exams, providing instant feedback to learners (Baker et al., 2019). This automation not only saves educators time but also enables timely interventions for students who may require additional support, thereby fostering a more responsive learning environment. The effectiveness of AI applications in distance education is greatly enhanced by the concepts and methodologies of learning analytics. Data gathering involves collecting quantitative and qualitative data from various sources, including learning management systems (LMS), student interactions, and demographic information (Sclater et al., 2016). This data serves as the foundation for understanding learner behavior and outcomes, allowing educators to make informed decisions. Behavioral analysis is a critical component of learning analytics, focusing on examining how students engage with course materials, participate in discussions, and complete assignments (Winne & Baker, 2013). By analyzing these behaviors, educators can identify patterns that indicate student engagement, motivation, and learning challenges. This information is crucial for developing targeted interventions and improving instructional strategies. Predictive analytics further extends the capabilities of learning analytics by employing statistical algorithms and machine learning techniques to forecast future learner behaviors and outcomes (Papamitsiou & Economides, 2014). For instance, predictive models can identify at-risk students who may be likely to disengage or underperform, enabling timely interventions that enhance retention and success rates (Arnold & Pistilli, 2012). By leveraging predictive analytics, educational institutions can create proactive support systems that anticipate student needs and facilitate academic achievement.

The Interplay Between AI, Learning Analytics, and Student-Centered Education

AI's Role in Personalized Learning, Engagement Tracking, and Content Customization

AI plays a pivotal role in fostering personalized learning experiences that meet the unique needs of individual students. By analyzing data from learning analytics, AI systems can track student engagement and performance, adjusting content delivery and instructional strategies accordingly (Zawacki-Richter et al., 2019). This personalized approach enhances the learning experience by ensuring that students receive appropriate challenges and support, ultimately improving academic outcomes (Baker & Inventado, 2014).

Moreover, AI enables content customization, allowing educators to create tailored learning materials that align with diverse learner preferences and backgrounds. For example, AI-driven systems can automatically generate supplementary resources based on a student's performance and learning style, ensuring that each learner has access to relevant content (Kay & Knaack, 2011). This adaptability is crucial in distance learning environments, where students often face varied challenges and may require different resources to succeed. Relationship Between Data Analytics and Academic Success, Inclusivity, and Accessibility

The integration of data analytics in education not only supports academic success but also promotes inclusivity and accessibility for all learners. By utilizing learning analytics, educators can identify gaps in performance and engagement, enabling them to address inequities in educational access (Czerkawski & Lyman,

2016). For instance, analytics can reveal disparities in performance among different demographic groups, prompting institutions to develop targeted support programs that cater to underrepresented populations (Margaryan et al., 2019). Furthermore, AI and learning analytics can enhance accessibility by providing adaptive technologies that accommodate diverse learning needs. For example, AI-powered tools can offer real-time captions for video lectures, translate materials into multiple languages, or provide alternative formats for learners with disabilities (Al-Azawei et al., 2020). By creating a more inclusive learning environment, AI and analytics empower all students to engage fully in the learning process, regardless of their individual challenges. The conceptual framework outlined in this chapter highlights the core concepts and definitions of AI, learning analytics, and distance education, while emphasizing the key elements that contribute to effective educational practices. The interplay between AI, learning analytics, and student-centered education underscores the potential for these technologies to transform distance learning by fostering personalized, engaging, and inclusive experiences.

THEORETICAL FRAMEWORK

The integration of Artificial Intelligence (AI) in education is heavily influenced by various educational theories, particularly constructivism and connectivism. Constructivist theory posits that learners construct their own understanding and knowledge of the world through experiences and reflecting on those experiences (Brusilovsky & Millán, 2007). In digital and distance education, AI can facilitate this learning process by providing personalized content and adaptive learning paths that cater to individual learners' needs. For instance, intelligent tutoring systems can analyze student interactions and adjust instructional strategies accordingly, fostering deeper engagement and understanding (Murray et al., 2020). Connectivism, on the other hand, emphasizes the role of social and cultural contexts in learning, positing that knowledge is distributed across networks and that learning occurs through interaction with those networks (Siemens, 2005). In distance education, AI technologies can enhance connectivist principles by enabling collaborative learning through social media, discussion forums, and peer assessments. These platforms encourage learners to share knowledge and resources, which enriches the learning experience and promotes a sense of community, even in virtual environments (Garrison & Anderson, 2003).

Adaptive Learning Theory and Theories of Personalized Education

Adaptive learning theory is another critical component that underpins AI applications in education. This theory supports the idea that instruction should be tailored to the unique learning needs of each student, allowing for a more personalized educational experience (Kerr, 2016). Vygotsky's sociocultural theory emphasizes the importance of social interaction in learning, advocating for the notion of the Zone of Proximal Development (ZPD). Vygotsky argued that learners can achieve higher levels of understanding with appropriate guidance and support (Vygotsky, 1978). AI systems can act as these guides by offering real-time feedback and resources that challenge learners just beyond their current capabilities, thus promoting cognitive growth. Similarly, Piaget's theory of cognitive development highlights the stages of learning that children undergo as they interact with their environment (Piaget, 1976). AI can support this development by adapting the complexity of tasks based on a learner's stage, ensuring that content is both accessible and appropriately challenging. By applying these theories, AI-powered educational tools can effectively enhance personalized learning experiences, fostering greater student engagement and retention in distance learning contexts.

Learning Analytics Theories

Learning analytics is a field that leverages data to improve learning outcomes, and several theoretical frameworks guide its implementation. The Learning Analytics Cycle outlines the process of collecting, analyzing, and acting upon data related to learner performance (Siemens, 2013). This cycle begins with data collection, progresses to analysis, and culminates in actionable insights that can be used to enhance teaching and learning practices. By following this cycle, educators can identify trends, make informed decisions, and personalize instruction based on real-time data, thus improving student outcomes (Long & Siemens, 2011). Educational Data Mining (EDM) is another critical framework within learning analytics, focusing on the extraction of knowledge from educational data using data mining techniques (Baker & Siemens, 2014). EDM encompasses various methods, including clustering, classification, and regression analysis, which can reveal patterns in learner behaviors and performance. For example, data mining can help identify factors contributing to student attrition or predict which students may need additional support. By harnessing these insights, educators can tailor interventions that foster student engagement and improve retention rates in distance education settings. Theories related to data-driven decision-making and student engagement also play a vital role in learning analytics. Motivation Theory, particularly Self-

Determination Theory (SDT), posits that individuals are motivated by their need for competence, autonomy, and relatedness (Deci & Ryan, 2000). In educational contexts, understanding student motivation is crucial for designing interventions that promote engagement and success. Learning analytics can provide insights into student behavior, helping educators identify when learners are disengaged or struggling, allowing for timely support that addresses these motivational factors (Delen & Gamage, 2013). Another relevant framework is the Community of Inquiry (CoI) model, which emphasizes the importance of social, cognitive, and teaching presence in creating meaningful learning experiences (Garrison, Anderson, & Archer, 2000). Learning analytics can help facilitate these presences by providing data on student interactions, participation levels, and content engagement. By analyzing this data, educators can identify opportunities for enhancing collaboration and support within digital learning environments.

Linking Theory to Practice: AI and Student Outcomes

Linking theoretical frameworks to practice is essential for understanding how AI and learning analytics impact student outcomes. The TPACK framework (Technological Pedagogical Content Knowledge) emphasizes the integration of technology in teaching practices and highlights the interplay between content knowledge, pedagogical strategies, and technological tools (Mishra & Koehler, 2006). AI tools can support educators in this integration by offering insights into effective instructional strategies that align with both content and student needs. For instance, adaptive learning technologies can analyze student performance data to recommend appropriate pedagogical approaches that enhance learning outcomes (Yuan et al., 2019). Moreover, research has shown that effective use of AI and learning analytics can lead to improved student engagement and retention rates. For example, studies indicate that students who receive timely feedback through AI-driven systems demonstrate higher levels of motivation and satisfaction (Hattie & Timperley, 2007). By understanding the relationship between these theoretical models and practical applications, educators can design distance learning experiences that foster engagement, support retention, and ultimately enhance academic achievement.

The practical application of AI and analytics theories in distance learning settings has shown promising results. Institutions are increasingly adopting AI-driven platforms to facilitate personalized learning experiences and support student engagement (Zawacki-Richter et al., 2019). For example, some universities have implemented chatbots powered by AI to provide instant support and information to students, addressing queries related to course content, deadlines, and administrative processes (Wang et al., 2020). This application not only improves student satisfaction but also allows educators to focus on higher-order instructional tasks. Additionally, learning analytics is being used to inform institutional decision-making. By analyzing data related to student performance and engagement, institutions can identify trends that inform curriculum development, resource allocation, and student support services (Ferguson, 2012). This data-driven approach enables institutions to respond proactively to student needs, creating a more supportive and effective distance learning environment. The theoretical framework presented in this chapter underscores the importance of integrating educational theories with AI and learning analytics to enhance distance education. By leveraging constructivist, connectivist, and adaptive learning theories, educators can create personalized learning experiences that foster engagement and success. Furthermore, frameworks such as the Learning Analytics Cycle and EDM provide valuable insights into data-driven decision-making, allowing institutions to implement effective interventions that support student outcomes.

RESEARCH METHODOLOGY

In the rapidly evolving field of AI and learning analytics, various research methodologies have been employed to investigate the effectiveness and implications of these technologies in educational contexts. A comprehensive overview reveals that studies predominantly utilize qualitative approaches, each offering unique insights into the dynamics of learning environments enhanced by AI. Quantitative methodologies, characterized by structured data collection and statistical analysis, have been widely used to measure the impact of AI interventions on learning outcomes. For example, studies employing controlled experiments often assess the effectiveness of adaptive learning systems by comparing student performance metrics before and after implementation (Mikhael et al., 2022). These studies provide robust statistical evidence regarding the efficacy of AI tools, enabling educators to make informed decisions about their integration into curricula. Conversely, qualitative approaches play a crucial role in understanding the subjective experiences of learners and educators interacting with AI and learning analytics. By employing interviews, focus groups, and case studies, researchers can explore participants' perceptions, challenges, and successes in using AI-enhanced learning platforms (Zawacki-Richter et al., 2019). For instance, qualitative analyses may reveal nuanced insights into how students perceive personalized learning experiences, contributing to a deeper understanding of engagement and motivation in digital learning environments. The analytical techniques employed in studying AI and learning analytics are diverse and tailored to address specific research questions. In recent literature, machine learning techniques, including neural networks **and** decision trees, have gained prominence for their ability to process large datasets and identify complex patterns within educational data (Goodfellow et al., 2016). Neural networks, for instance, are particularly effective in predicting student outcomes based on historical data, enabling educators to intervene proactively when students are at risk of underperforming (Zhang et al., 2020). Decision trees, on the other hand, facilitate the visualization of decision-making processes, allowing researchers to interpret how various factors contribute to learning outcomes in a straightforward manner.

SOLUTIONS AND RECOMMENDATIONS

The integration of AI and learning analytics into distance learning environments can significantly enhance educational outcomes when implemented effectively. Successful case studies provide valuable insights into best practices. For instance, a notable example is the University of Arizona's use of predictive analytics to improve student retention. By analyzing data from learning management systems (LMS) and student demographics, the university identified at-risk students and implemented targeted interventions, resulting in a 10% increase in retention rates (Murray et al., 2020). Such applications highlight the power of data-driven decision-making in educational settings. In addition to case studies, the design of adaptive learning pathways and recommendation systems is critical for personalizing the learning experience. Adaptive learning technologies leverage AI algorithms to analyze student performance in real time and adjust the learning material accordingly (VanLehn, 2018). For instance, platforms like Knewton and Smart Sparrow have successfully developed adaptive learning systems that tailor content delivery based on individual student needs and learning paces. These systems not only enhance student engagement but also foster a more effective learning environment by addressing knowledge gaps promptly. When designing these systems, it is essential to employ user-centered design principles to ensure that the tools are intuitive and accessible for both students and educators. Collaborating with stakeholders including students, instructors, and instructional designers during the development process can help identify user needs and preferences, resulting in tools that genuinely enhance the learning experience (Shute & Rahimi, 2017).

Figure 1. AI applications in education: A conceptual framework

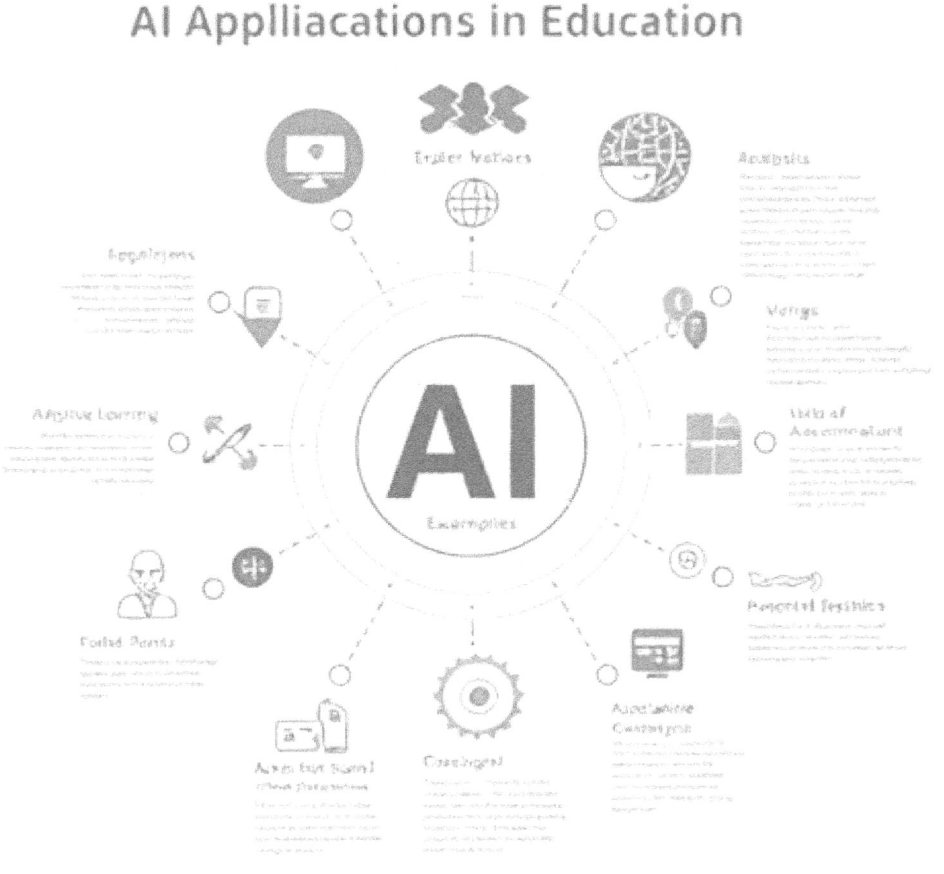

This Figure 1 visually outlines key AI applications in education, including adaptive learning, recommendation systems, and automated assessments. It features a flowchart layout with icons for each application, accompanied by brief descriptions or examples, illustrating their interactions within the learning environment to enhance educational outcomes.

Overcoming Challenges and Risks

Despite the promising potential of AI and learning analytics, challenges related to data privacy, security, and ethical considerations must be addressed to ensure successful implementation. As educational institutions collect vast amounts of data on student behaviors and performance, they must establish robust data governance frameworks to protect sensitive information. The Family Educational Rights and Privacy Act (FERPA) and the General Data Protection Regulation (GDPR) provide essential guidelines for safeguarding student data (Regan & Jesse, 2021). Institutions should prioritize transparency regarding data usage and obtain informed consent from students, ensuring they are aware of how their data will be utilized. Furthermore, managing biases inherent in AI algorithms is critical for equitable educational practices. Bias can manifest in various forms, including the selection of training data and the design of algorithms, potentially leading to unfair treatment of certain student demographics (Barocas et al., 2019). To mitigate these risks, institutions must conduct regular audits of their AI systems and employ diverse datasets that accurately represent the student population. Additionally, fostering a culture of inclusivity and fairness in AI development can help identify and address biases early in the process, resulting in more equitable educational tools. Another challenge lies in ensuring transparency in AI systems. Educators and students should understand how AI tools function, including the criteria used for decision-making and recommendations. Implementing explainable AI (XAI) principles can enhance trust in these technologies, as XAI aims to make AI systems more interpretable and comprehensible (Gilpin et al., 2018). Educators should receive training on interpreting AI-generated insights, allowing them to leverage these tools effectively in their instructional practices.

Figure 2. Learning analytics cycle

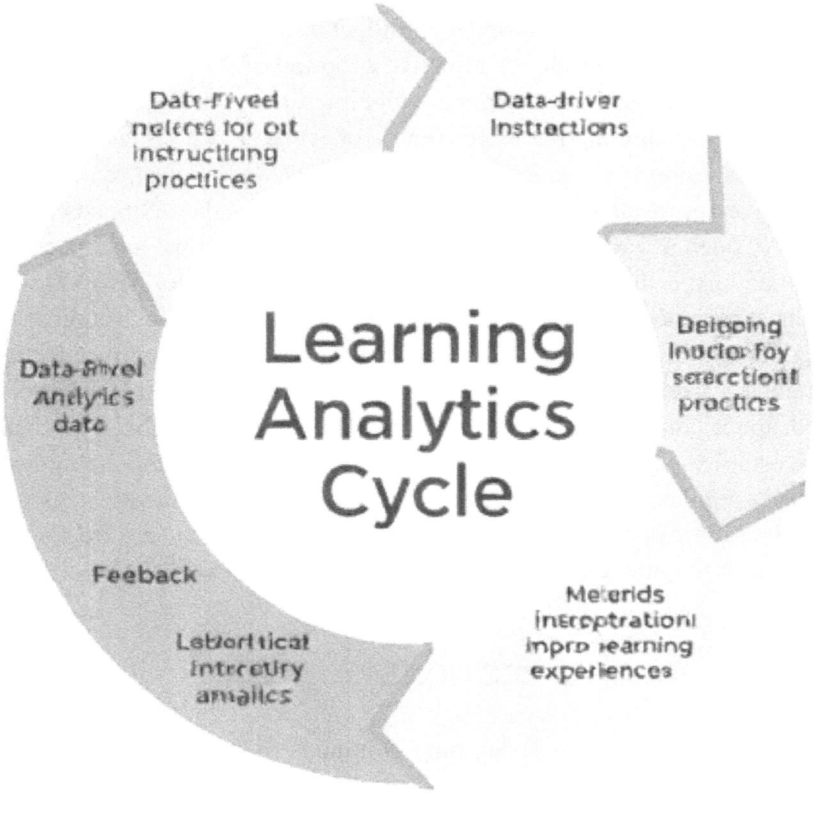

This figure 2 illustrates the Learning Analytics Cycle, highlighting key stages such as data collection, analysis, interpretation, and feedback. Featuring a circular layout with labeled stages and arrows to indicate data flow, it includes annotations that explain the significance of each stage in informing instructional practices and enhancing learning experiences..

Guidelines for Educators and Institutions

To harness the full potential of AI and learning analytics, institutions must provide educators with the necessary training and resources. Developing comprehensive frameworks for training educators on AI tools and data interpretation is essential for ensuring effective implementation. Professional development programs should focus on enhancing educators' digital literacy, including the ability to interpret data insights and integrate AI tools into their teaching practices (Trust et al., 2016). Workshops, online courses, and collaborative learning opportunities can empower educators to embrace AI technologies confidently. Moreover, institutions should establish clear policies to guide the effective adoption of AI in distance education. These policies should encompass ethical guidelines, data governance frameworks, and protocols for evaluating the effectiveness of AI tools. Creating interdisciplinary committees comprising educators, data scientists, and ethicists can facilitate a comprehensive approach to policy development, ensuring that all perspectives are considered (Cohen & Kahn, 2021). In addition, institutions must foster a culture of innovation and experimentation. Encouraging educators to pilot new AI tools and share their experiences can promote a collaborative learning environment where best practices can be identified and disseminated. Providing incentives for faculty engagement in AI-related projects can further enhance the adoption of these technologies in distance education. Finally, ongoing evaluation and feedback mechanisms should be established to assess the effectiveness of AI tools in enhancing learning outcomes. By regularly collecting feedback from students and educators, institutions can make data-informed decisions to refine their approaches and ensure continuous improvement in the integration of AI and learning analytics.

FUTURE RESEARCH DIRECTIONS

As the landscape of distance learning continues to evolve, the integration of AI and learning analytics is expected to expand significantly. This section outlines emerging trends, research gaps, and opportunities for interdisciplinary collaboration that can drive future research in this field.

Emerging Trends in AI and Learning Analytics for Distance Learning

The potential of AI in virtual and augmented reality (VR/AR) learning environments represents a cutting-edge frontier in distance education. VR and AR technologies provide immersive learning experiences that can enhance engagement and retention. For instance, AI can be used to create adaptive VR learning scenarios that respond to individual learner behaviors and preferences, fostering a more personalized educational experience (Jensen & Konradsen, 2018). Future research could explore how these technologies can be effectively integrated into curriculum design, focusing on both pedagogical approaches and the technical infrastructure necessary to support such innovations. Advances in real-time data analytics and predictive modeling also promise to enhance learner support. As AI technologies improve, the ability to analyze data in real-time allows for timely interventions tailored to individual learner needs. This could include instant feedback on assessments, recommendations for additional resources, or alerts to educators when students exhibit signs of disengagement (He et al., 2019). Research could investigate the effectiveness of these predictive models in various educational contexts, including how they can be optimized for different learning environments and diverse student populations. Furthermore, the development of AI-driven analytics platforms that can analyze emotional and social cues in learners such as facial expressions and engagement levels opens new avenues for research. Understanding how these emotional data points correlate with academic performance could lead to significant improvements in learner support strategies (D'Mello & Graesser, 2015). Future studies should focus on the ethical implications of collecting and analyzing such sensitive data while ensuring that learners' privacy and autonomy are respected.

Research Gaps and Unanswered Questions

Despite the advancements in AI and learning analytics, several research gaps remain. One critical area is the long-term impact of AI interventions on learning outcomes. While many studies have demonstrated short-term benefits of AI tools, comprehensive longitudinal studies are needed to assess their effects over time. This includes understanding how sustained engagement with AI tools influences student performance, retention, and overall educational attainment (Wang et al., 2020). Researchers should prioritize designing studies that track students over multiple semesters or years to provide insights into the lasting effects of AI integration. Another pressing area for research is the exploration of ethical AI in education and the transparency of algorithms used in learning analytics. As educational institutions increasingly rely on AI-driven tools, concerns about bias, discrimination, and the lack of accountability in algorithmic decision-making are paramount (O'Neil, 2016). Future studies should focus on developing frameworks for ethical AI use in education, including best practices for ensuring fairness and transparency in algorithmic processes. This research should also examine how educators and students perceive these issues and how they influence trust in AI tools. Moreover, research should investigate the effectiveness of various approaches to educating stakeholders about AI technologies. Understanding how to best inform educators, students, and parents about the capabilities and limitations of AI tools is crucial for fostering a positive acceptance of these technologies. This includes developing guidelines for interpreting data insights generated by AI systems and ensuring that all stakeholders are equipped to engage critically with these tools (Hollands & Tirthali, 2014).

Opportunities for Interdisciplinary Collaboration

Interdisciplinary collaboration will play a vital role in advancing research on AI and learning analytics in distance education. The intersection of education, technology, and policy provides a rich landscape for collaborative efforts. Researchers, educators, technologists, and policymakers can work together to address the complex challenges posed by integrating AI into educational practices. Such collaborations can lead to innovative solutions that are grounded in both theoretical understanding and practical application. For example, partnerships between educational institutions and technology companies can facilitate the development of scalable AI solutions that address specific educational needs. Industry partnerships can provide access to cutting-edge technologies and resources that may not be available within academic settings. Collaborative research initiatives can focus on evaluating the effectiveness of AI tools in diverse educational contexts, ensuring that solutions are adaptable and responsive to varying learner demographics and environments (Schneider et al., 2021). Additionally, cross-disciplinary research can help bridge the gap between theoretical frameworks and practical applications. By involving experts from fields such as cognitive science, data ethics, and instructional design, researchers can develop holistic approaches that prioritize learner outcomes while addressing ethical considerations. This comprehensive perspective is essential for creating AI tools that not only enhance learning experiences but also promote equity and accessibility in education.

Summary of Key Insights

The integration of artificial intelligence (AI) and learning analytics is fundamentally reshaping the landscape of distance learning, providing innovative solutions that enhance educational experiences. Throughout this chapter, we have explored how AI applications, such as adaptive learning platforms, predictive analytics, and personalized learning pathways, enable educators to meet diverse learner needs effectively. By harnessing data from various sources—such as learning management systems and student interactions educators can tailor their instructional approaches to improve student engagement and success. For instance, predictive analytics can identify at-risk students early, allowing timely interventions that foster academic persistence and completion (Murray et al., 2020). However, the implementation of AI in education also presents significant challenges. Concerns regarding data privacy and security have become increasingly pronounced, as educational institutions must navigate the complexities of handling sensitive student information while ensuring compliance with regulations such as FERPA and GDPR (Regan & Jesse, 2021). Additionally, issues of algorithmic bias and the need for transparency in AI systems must be addressed to promote equity and trust among stakeholders. Research indicates that biases in AI algorithms can disproportionately affect marginalized student populations, leading to inequitable educational outcomes (Barocas et al., 2019). These findings underscore the dual nature of AI in education it has the potential to drive significant improvements in learning outcomes while simultaneously posing ethical dilemmas that require careful consideration. Consequently, a balanced approach that prioritizes both innovation and ethical standards is essential for the successful integration of AI in distance learning environments.

Implications for the Future of Distance Learning

Looking ahead, the trajectory of AI in education appears promising, with the potential for transformative impacts on teaching and learning practices. As technology continues to advance, we can expect the development of more sophisticated AI systems capable of providing deeper insights into learner behavior and engagement. This evolution could lead to even more personalized learning experiences, where AI tools not only adapt content but also recommend tailored learning paths that align with individual students' goals, preferences, and learning styles (VanLehn, 2018). Moreover, the incorporation of virtual and augmented reality (VR/AR) into educational contexts presents exciting opportunities for immersive learning experiences that engage students in unprecedented ways. Research indicates that such technologies can enhance student motivation and retention of information, leading to improved educational outcomes (Jensen & Konradsen, 2018). Future research will be crucial in exploring how AI can be effectively integrated into VR/AR environments, as well as understanding the pedagogical implications of these innovations. As AI becomes more prevalent in education, there is also a growing need for interdisciplinary collaboration among educators, technologists, and policymakers. Such partnerships can facilitate the development of scalable AI solutions that address specific educational needs while ensuring that ethical considerations are at the forefront of design and implementation (Schneider et al., 2021). The role of industry partnerships cannot be overlooked; collaboration with technology companies can provide educators with the tools and resources necessary to effectively utilize AI in their teaching practices.

CONCLUSION

The effective implementation of AI and learning analytics in distance learning necessitates a multi-faceted approach that encompasses best practices, ethical considerations, and clear guidelines for educators and institutions. By leveraging successful case studies, addressing challenges related to data privacy and algorithmic bias, and providing comprehensive training for educators, institutions can create enriching learning experiences that significantly enhance student engagement and outcomes. As the educational landscape continues to evolve, the integration of AI and learning analytics will play a pivotal role in shaping the future of distance education. In addition, the future of AI and learning analytics in distance learning presents a wealth of opportunities for research and collaboration. Exploring emerging trends, addressing existing research gaps, and fostering interdisciplinary partnerships will enable scholars to contribute to a more nuanced understanding of how these technologies can enhance educational practices. Continuous inquiry into the ethical implications of AI in education will also be vital for ensuring that these tools are implemented in ways that respect and empower all learners. Moreover, ongoing research and innovation in AI and learning analytics are crucial for creating accessible, inclusive, and effective educational experiences in distance learning environments. As we explore the potential of these technologies, it is essential to maintain a focus on ethical practices that safeguard student privacy and promote equity. A commitment to understanding and addressing the challenges associated with AI implementation will be critical in shaping a future where all learners can benefit from advancements in educational technology. By fostering a culture of continuous improvement and collaboration, educational institutions can harness the power of AI to not only enhance learning outcomes but also create a more inclusive educational landscape. The journey ahead will require dedication from all stakeholders, including researchers, educators, and policymakers, to ensure that the integration of AI in education remains focused on the ultimate goal: empowering learners to achieve their fullest potential.

REFERENCES

Adedoyin, O. B., & Soykan, E. (2020). COVID-19 pandemic and online learning: The challenges and opportunities. *Interactive Learning Environments*, *28*(4), 357–366. DOI: 10.1080/10494820.2020.1813180

Al-Azawei, A., Serenelli, F., & Lundqvist, K. (2020). Developing an accessible e-learning system: An exploration of the relationship between accessibility and user satisfaction. *Journal of Educational Technology & Society*, *23*(1), 88–98.

Arnold, K. E., & Pistilli, M. D. (2012). Course signals at Purdue: Using learning analytics to increase student success. In *Proceedings of the 2nd International Conference on Learning Analytics and Knowledge* (pp. 267–270). DOI: 10.1145/2330601.2330666

Baker, R. S. (2019). Challenges for the future of educational data mining: The Baker learning analytics prerequisites. *Journal of Educational Data Mining*, *11*(1), 1–17.

Baker, R. S., & Siemens, G. (2014). Educational data mining and learning analytics. *Learning Analytics Review*, *1*(3), 33–49.

Baker, R. S. J. D. (2014). Educational data mining: An overview. In *Handbook of learning analytics* (pp. 3–16). Society for Learning Analytics Research., DOI: 10.1007/978-1-4614-3305-7_4

Baker, R. S. J. D., Corbett, A. T., & Koedinger, K. R. (2019). Developing a learning analytics framework. In *Handbook of Learning Analytics* (pp. 59–72). Society for Learning Analytics Research.

Baker, R. S. J. D., & Inventado, P. S. (2014). Educational data mining and learning analytics. In Learning, Education and Data Mining: A Systematic Review (pp. 43-56). Springer.

Barocas, S., Hardt, M., & Narayanan, A. (2019). Fairness and machine learning. https://fairmlbook.org/

Bishop, C. M. (2006). *Pattern recognition and machine learning*. Springer.

Brusilovsky, P., & Millán, E. (2007). User modeling in personalized learning environments. In *User Modeling 2007* (pp. 1–18). Springer., DOI: 10.1007/978-3-540-73078-1_1

Cohen, J., & Kahn, B. (2021). The ethical implications of AI in education: A policy perspective. *International Journal of Educational Technology in Higher Education*, *18*(1), 1–15. DOI: 10.1186/s41239-021-00254-x

Creswell, J. W., & Plano Clark, V. L. (2018). *Designing and conducting mixed methods research* (3rd ed.). SAGE Publications.

Czerkawski, B. C., & Lyman, E. W. (2016). Beyond the LMS: A framework for learning analytics in online courses. *International Journal of Online Pedagogy and Course Design, 6*(2), 27–41. DOI: 10.4018/IJOPCD.2016040103

D'Mello, S. K., & Graesser, A. C. (2015). Feeling, thinking, and computing: The role of affect in learning with technology. In O'Reilly, H. K. E., Zhang, K. W. H. F., & Graesser, A. C. (Eds.), *The Cambridge handbook of the learning sciences* (pp. 305–325). Cambridge University Press., DOI: 10.1017/CBO9781139819085.021

Deci, E. L., & Ryan, R. M. (2000). The "what" and "why" of goal pursuits: Human needs and the self-determination of behavior. *Psychological Inquiry, 11*(4), 227–268. DOI: 10.1207/S15327965PLI1104_01

Delen, E., & Gamage, D. (2013). The role of learning analytics in higher education: A systematic review. *Journal of Educational Technology & Society, 16*(1), 114–125.

Dziuban, C., Graham, C. R., Moskal, P. D., Norberg, A., & Sicilia, N. (2018). Blended learning: The new normal and emerging technologies. *International Journal of Educational Technology in Higher Education, 15*(1), 3. DOI: 10.1186/s41239-017-0087-5

Ferguson, R. (2012). Learning analytics: Drivers, developments, and challenges. *International Journal of Technology Enhanced Learning, 4*(5), 304–317. DOI: 10.1504/IJTEL.2012.051816

Garrison, D. R., & Anderson, T. (2003). E-learning in the 21st century: A community of inquiry framework for building online learning communities. Routledge.

Garrison, D. R., Anderson, T., & Archer, W. (2000). Critical inquiry in a text-based environment: Computer conferencing in higher education. *The Internet and Higher Education, 2*(2), 87–105. DOI: 10.1016/S1096-7516(00)00016-6

Garrison, D. R., & Vaughan, N. D. (2008). *Blended learning in higher education: Framework, principles, and guidelines*. Jossey-Bass.

Gašević, D., Dawson, S., & Siemens, G. (2015). Let's not forget: Learning analytics are about learning. *TechTrends, 59*(1), 64–71. DOI: 10.1007/s11528-014-0822-x

Gilpin, L. H., Zollers, F., & Yalcin, A. (2018). Explaining explanations: An overview of interpretability of machine learning. In 2018 IEEE 5th International Conference on Data Science and Advanced Analytics (DSAA) (pp. 80-89). DOI: 10.1109/DSAA.2018.00018

Goodfellow, I., Bengio, Y., & Courville, A. (2016). *Deep learning*. MIT Press.

Harris, A. J., Hovey, A. L., & Wyman, M. (2020). Protecting student data in educational research: Ethical and legal considerations. *Educational Researcher*, *49*(2), 104–112. DOI: 10.3102/0013189X20914383

Hattie, J., & Timperley, H. (2007). The power of feedback. *Review of Educational Research*, *77*(1), 81–112. DOI: 10.3102/003465430298487

He, Y., Chen, S., & Huang, T. (2019). Real-time learning analytics in a blended learning environment. *Journal of Educational Technology & Society*, *22*(4), 57–70. https://www.jstor.org/stable/26705000

Hollands, F. M., & Tirthali, D. (2014). Online learning and student outcomes: A systematic review of the evidence. *Online Learning : the Official Journal of the Online Learning Consortium*, *18*(3), 115–138. DOI: 10.24059/olj.v18i3.490

Holmes, W., Bialik, M., & Fadel, C. (2019). *Artificial intelligence in education: Promises and implications for teaching and learning*. Center for Curriculum Redesign.

Hsu, C.-C., Chiu, P.-S., & Chang, Y.-S. (2021). Predictive modeling of students' learning behaviors in a MOOC environment. *Interactive Learning Environments*, *29*(5), 753–770. DOI: 10.1080/10494820.2019.1701818

Jannach, D., & Adomavicius, G. (2016). *Recommendation systems: Challenges and research opportunities*. Wiley.

Jensen, L. M., & Konradsen, F. (2018). A review of VR and AR in education: Implications for teacher education. *Journal of Educational Technology & Society*, *21*(1), 36–45. https://www.jstor.org/stable/26388439

Kay, J., & Knaack, L. (2011). Self-regulated learning in technology-enhanced learning environments. In *Handbook of Self-Regulated Learning and Performance* (pp. 61–79). Routledge.

Kerr, K. (2016). Adaptive learning technology: How personalized learning works. *Educational Technology Review*, *24*(2), 12–24.

Knewton. (2018). Adaptive learning: What is it and how does it work? Retrieved from https://www.knewton.com/adaptive-learning/

Long, P., & Siemens, G. (2011). Penetrating the fog: Analytics in learning and education. *EDUCAUSE Review*, *46*(5), 30–32.

Luckin, R., Holmes, W., Griffiths, M., & Forcier, L. B. (2016). *Intelligence unleashed: An argument for AI in education*. Pearson Education.

Margaryan, A., Garcia, M., & Littlejohn, A. (2019). Learning analytics in higher education: A review of the literature. *Educational Research Review*, *25*, 30–42. DOI: 10.1016/j.edurev.2019.01.001

Mikhael, J., Murray, S., & Lang, C. (2022). The effects of AI-driven personalized learning on student performance: A meta-analysis. *Journal of Educational Psychology*, *114*(4), 730–748. DOI: 10.1037/edu0000614

Mishra, P., & Koehler, M. J. (2006). Technological pedagogical content knowledge: A framework for teacher knowledge.

Moore, M. G., Dickson-Deane, C., & Galyen, K. (2011). e-Learning, online learning, and distance learning environments: Are they the same? *The Internet and Higher Education*, *14*(2), 129–135. DOI: 10.1016/j.iheduc.2010.10.001

Murray, C., Alonzo, A., & Kuhlman, K. (2020). Predictive analytics in higher education: Leveraging data to improve student retention. *The Journal of Higher Education Management*, *35*(2), 5–15.

Norvig, P., & Russell, S. (2021). *Artificial intelligence: A modern approach* (4th ed.). Pearson.

O'Neil, C. (2016). *Weapons of math destruction: How big data increases inequality and threatens democracy*. Crown Publishing.

Papamitsiou, Z., & Economides, A. A. (2014). Learning analytics and educational data mining in a nutshell: A systematic literature review. *Journal of Educational Technology & Society*, *17*(4), 49–64.

Pardo, A., Mirriahi, N., & Gašević, D. (2019). Academic performance prediction in blended and online learning: The role of social networks. *Internet and Higher Education*, *42*, 13–21. DOI: 10.1016/j.iheduc.2019.04.002

Regan, P. M., & Jesse, J. (2021). Data privacy in education: An analysis of policies and practices. *Education Policy Analysis Archives*, *29*(1), 1–22. DOI: 10.14507/epaa.29.4794

Rienties, B., Cross, S., & Zdrahal, Z. (2018). Implementing learning analytics in higher education: The role of institutional context. *European Journal of Higher Education*, *8*(3), 257–271. DOI: 10.1080/21568235.2018.1509733

Schneider, E. F., Browne, K., & Daugherty, J. (2021). Industry-academic partnerships in AI education: Strategies for success. *Journal of Business and Educational Leadership*, *8*(1), 45–61.

Sclater, N., Peasgood, A., & Mullan, J. (2016). Learning analytics in higher education. JISC. https://www.jisc.ac.uk/reports/learning-analytics-in-higher-education

Shute, V., & Rahimi, S. (2017). Formative assessment and adaptive learning: A tale of two practices. *Educational Psychologist*, *52*(4), 211–227. DOI: 10.1080/00461520.2017.1363880

Siemens, G. (2013). Learning analytics: The emergence of a discipline. *The American Behavioral Scientist*, *57*(10), 1380–1400.

Siemens, G., & Long, P. (2011). Penetrating the fog: Analytics in learning and education. *EDUCAUSE Review*, *46*(5), 30–32.

Trust, T., & P. A. (2016). Professional development for educators in the age of technology. *TechTrends*, *60*(4), 366–371. DOI: 10.1007/s11528-016-0053-5

VanLehn, K. (2011). The effectiveness of intelligent tutoring systems: A meta-analysis. *Educational Psychologist*, *46*(3), 197–207. DOI: 10.1080/00461520.2011.550993

VanLehn, K. (2018). The relative effectiveness of human tutoring, intelligent tutoring systems, and other tutoring systems. *Educational Psychologist*, *53*(2), 108–138. DOI: 10.1080/00461520.2018.1442494

Wang, X., Wu, Y., & Wang, Y. (2020). The impact of AI on educational outcomes: A review of empirical research. *International Journal of Educational Technology in Higher Education*, *17*(1), 1–24. DOI: 10.1186/s41239-020-00218-6

Winne, P. H., & Baker, R. S. (2013). Analytics in support of self-regulated learning. Handbook of Learning Analytics, 1(1), 105-114.

Zawacki-Richter, O., Marín, V. I., Bond, M., & Gouverneur, A. (2019). Systematic review of research on artificial intelligence applications in higher education—What are the implications for students and educators? *International Journal of Educational Technology in Higher Education*, *16*(39). Advance online publication. DOI: 10.1186/s41239-019-0176-8

Zhang, K., Liu, Y., & Zhao, J. (2018). A survey on deep learning for big data. *Artificial Intelligence Review*, *50*(4), 557–580. DOI: 10.1007/s10462-018-9623-1

Zhang, K., Liu, Y., & Zhao, J. (2020). A survey on deep learning for big data. *Artificial Intelligence Review*, *50*(4), 557–580. DOI: 10.1007/s10462-018-9623-1

KEY TERMS AND DEFINITIONS

Artificial Intelligence (AI): Artificial Intelligence (AI) refers to the simulation of human intelligence processes by computer systems. These processes include learning, reasoning, problem-solving, perception, and language understanding. In educational contexts, AI encompasses a wide range of technologies, such as machine learning, natural language processing, and intelligent tutoring systems, designed to enhance teaching and learning experiences.

Machine Learning (ML): Machine Learning (ML) is a subset of AI that focuses on the development of algorithms that enable computers to learn from and make predictions based on data. ML systems improve their performance over time by analyzing patterns and correlations within large datasets without explicit programming. In education, ML techniques are employed to personalize learning experiences, analyze student behaviors, and inform instructional strategies.

Deep Learning: Deep Learning is a specialized area of ML that utilizes neural networks with multiple layers (deep architectures) to model complex patterns in large datasets. This approach has shown remarkable success in fields such as image and speech recognition and is increasingly being applied in education for tasks such as automated grading, content generation, and analyzing student interactions.

Learning Analytics: Learning Analytics refers to the measurement, collection, analysis, and reporting of data about learners and their contexts to understand and optimize learning. This data-driven approach allows educators to gain insights into student performance, engagement, and learning behaviors, ultimately informing instructional decisions and enhancing educational outcomes.

Distance Learning: Distance Learning is an educational process in which students receive instruction and participate in learning activities remotely, often through digital platforms and technologies. This mode of education allows for flexibility in scheduling and location, making education more accessible to a diverse range of learners. Distance learning can encompass various formats, including online courses, hybrid models, and synchronous or asynchronous learning experiences.

Digital Learning Environments: Digital Learning Environments (DLEs) are virtual spaces that facilitate educational interactions and learning experiences through digital tools and resources. These environments can include learning management systems (LMS), virtual classrooms, and collaborative platforms that support communication and content delivery among learners and educators. DLEs enable the integration of multimedia resources, interactive assessments, and personalized learning pathways.

Adaptive Learning: Adaptive Learning is an instructional approach that tailors educational content and experiences to the individual needs of learners based on their performance, preferences, and learning pace. This dynamic process relies on real-time data analytics to adjust the learning path, ensuring that students receive the appropriate level of challenge and support. Adaptive learning systems aim to enhance learner engagement and improve academic outcomes by providing personalized pathways.

Recommendation Systems: Recommendation Systems are AI-driven tools that suggest relevant content, resources, or learning activities to learners based on their historical interactions and preferences. These systems analyze user data to identify patterns and make personalized recommendations, fostering a more tailored learning experience. In education, recommendation systems can guide students toward relevant readings, assignments, or supplementary materials that align with their learning goals.

Predictive Analytics: Predictive Analytics involves the use of statistical techniques and machine learning algorithms to analyze historical data and make predictions about future outcomes. In education, predictive analytics can identify trends and patterns related to student performance, retention, and engagement, allowing educators to intervene proactively and enhance student success. This data-driven approach provides valuable insights for institutional decision-making and instructional design.

Data Privacy: Data Privacy refers to the protection of personal information and ensuring that individuals have control over how their data is collected, used, and shared. In educational settings, data privacy is a critical consideration as institutions leverage AI and learning analytics to gather and analyze student data. Maintaining data privacy is essential for fostering trust among learners and complying with legal and ethical standards.

Chapter 9
Integrating AI and Learning Analytics in Distance Learning:
Strategies for Educators and Institutions

T. C. Catherin
https://orcid.org/0000-0002-1324-136X
Saveetha Engineering College, India

R. Vettriselvan
https://orcid.org/0000-0002-2469-5893
Academy of Maritime Education and Training, India

Suruchi Mathur
Saraswathi Institute of Medical Sciences, Hapur, India

Jimmy Carter Regins
https://orcid.org/0009-0005-2669-3727
Bishop Heber College, India

Palanivel Rathinasabapathi Rathinasabapathi Velmurugan
https://orcid.org/0000-0002-0395-9060
Berlin School of Business and Innovation, Germany

ABSTRACT

The integration of artificial intelligence (AI) and learning analytics (LA) into distance learning programs, focusing on effective implementation strategies for educators and institutions. As distance education becomes increasingly prevalent,

DOI: 10.4018/979-8-3693-7195-4.ch009

leveraging AI and LA can enhance personalized learning experiences, improve student engagement, and optimize educational outcomes. Key applications of AI, such as adaptive learning systems and intelligent tutoring, alongside the insights gained from learning analytics, enable educators to identify learning gaps and tailor support to individual students. The paper emphasizes the importance of aligning AI and LA tools with institutional goals, providing faculty training, and ensuring data privacy. Additionally, it highlights successful case studies that demonstrate the positive impact of these technologies on student performance and retention. By adopting a systematic approach to integration, educators and institutions can create more effective and responsive distance learning environments that cater to diverse learner needs.

INTRODUCTION

Distance learning has evolved significantly over the past few decades, driven by advancements in technology and changing educational needs. Originally, distance education relied on traditional methods such as correspondence courses, where students received printed materials via mail. However, the rise of the internet and digital technologies has revolutionized this field, enabling real-time interactions, multimedia content, and flexible learning environments. As of 2021, approximately 70% of higher education institutions in the United States reported offering distance education programs, reflecting the increasing acceptance and integration of this mode of learning (U.S. Department of Education, 2021). The COVID-19 pandemic further accelerated this trend, compelling educational institutions worldwide to transition to online learning platforms almost overnight. This rapid shift highlighted both the potential and challenges of distance education, emphasizing the need for effective pedagogical strategies to ensure student engagement and learning outcomes. Artificial Intelligence (AI) and learning analytics have emerged as critical components in enhancing the efficacy of distance education. AI encompasses a range of technologies that enable machines to perform tasks that typically require human intelligence, such as problem-solving, pattern recognition, and decision-making. In the context of education, AI can provide personalized learning experiences by adapting content to meet individual student needs. For instance, intelligent tutoring systems can analyze a learner's performance and suggest tailored resources to support their understanding (Shute & Rahimi, 2020). Similarly, learning analytics involves the systematic collection and analysis of data about learners and their contexts to improve learning experiences. By leveraging learning analytics, educators can identify trends, predict student outcomes, and implement interventions that foster student success (Siemens & Long, 2019). Together, AI and learning analytics offer powerful tools to create more responsive and effective distance learning environments. The purpose of this chapter is to explore the integration of AI and learning analytics in distance learning programs and to provide practical strategies for educators and institutions. As distance education continues to evolve, understanding how these technologies can be utilized to enhance learning experiences is paramount. This chapter will first outline the theoretical frameworks that underpin the application of AI and learning analytics in education, providing a foundation for the discussion. It will then delve into the research methodology employed in the analysis of existing literature, highlighting best practices and case studies that illustrate the successful implementation of these technologies. Finally, the chapter will offer solutions and recommendations for integrating AI and learning analytics into distance learning programs, emphasizing the importance of ethical considerations and data privacy.

By examining the intersection of AI, learning analytics, and distance education, this chapter aims to contribute to the ongoing discourse on educational innovation and transformation. As the landscape of education continues to shift, it is crucial for educators and institutions to stay informed about emerging technologies and their potential to enhance teaching and learning. This exploration will not only highlight the benefits of AI and learning analytics but also address the challenges and considerations that must be navigated to ensure their effective implementation in distance learning contexts.

CONCEPTUAL FRAMEWORK

In the context of distance education, a well-defined conceptual framework is crucial for understanding the interplay between key components such as Artificial Intelligence (AI), learning analytics, and distance learning. This framework provides a foundation for examining how these elements interact to enhance educational outcomes.

Artificial Intelligence (AI) refers to the simulation of human intelligence processes by machines, particularly computer systems. This encompasses a variety of technologies, including machine learning, natural language processing, and expert systems. In education, AI can facilitate personalized learning experiences by analyzing student data to adapt content and pedagogical approaches to individual learner needs (Luckin et al., 2016).

Learning Analytics involves the collection, measurement, analysis, and reporting of data about learners and their contexts, primarily for understanding and optimizing learning outcomes. It aims to provide insights into learning behaviors and trends, allowing educators to make informed decisions regarding instructional strategies

(Siemens, 2013). Learning analytics can also help in predicting student success and identifying those who may require additional support.

Distance Learning is an educational process where students and instructors are separated by time and/or location, utilizing technology to facilitate communication and learning. This approach allows for flexibility in learning and has gained prominence with the advancement of online platforms and digital resources, making education accessible to a broader audience (Moore & Kearsley, 2012).

Interrelationships

The integration of AI and learning analytics within distance learning creates a dynamic ecosystem that enhances the educational experience. AI technologies can process and analyze vast amounts of data generated through learning activities, enabling personalized learning paths that cater to individual student needs. For instance, AI-driven systems can assess a learner's progress in real-time, providing immediate feedback and recommendations for improvement.

Learning analytics complements this by offering insights into overall learning trends and patterns across the student population. By analyzing data collected from various interactions—such as participation in discussions, submission of assignments, and assessment results—educators can identify common challenges and success factors (Ferguson, 2012). This information can inform instructional design, allowing for the continuous improvement of distance learning programs.

Moreover, the collaboration between AI and learning analytics fosters a feedback loop that benefits both students and educators. As AI systems provide personalized recommendations, learning analytics tracks the effectiveness of these interventions, ensuring that instructional strategies remain aligned with student needs. This iterative process ultimately contributes to improved learning outcomes and student satisfaction in distance learning environments.

Framework Diagram

The following diagram visually represents the interrelationships among AI, learning analytics, and distance learning:

Figure 1. Visual representation of the interrelationships among AI, learning analytics, and distance learning

In this diagram, distance learning serves as the overarching context, while learning analytics and AI function as complementary components that enhance the educational experience. This conceptual framework illustrates how these elements interact, providing a foundation for further exploration of their implications for effective distance education.

THEORETICAL FRAMEWORK

The integration of Artificial Intelligence (AI) and learning analytics in distance education is underpinned by various theoretical perspectives that provide a robust foundation for understanding their applications and implications. This theoretical framework explores constructivist learning theory and behaviorism in the context of AI, discusses key theoretical models of learning analytics, and analyzes how these perspectives guide the implementation and effectiveness of AI and learning analytics in educational settings.

Theories Informing AI and Learning Analytics

Constructivist Learning Theory posits that learners actively construct their knowledge through experiences and interactions with their environment. This theory emphasizes the role of social interactions and contextual learning, asserting that knowledge is built collaboratively rather than passively absorbed (Piaget, 1976; Vygotsky, 1978). In the context of AI, constructivist principles can be applied through adaptive learning systems that respond to individual learner needs. For instance, AI-driven platforms can analyze a student's learning style, preferences, and prior knowledge to provide personalized resources and suggestions that facilitate deeper engagement with the material (Luckin et al., 2016). Constructivist learning environments foster critical thinking, problem-solving, and collaboration, all of which are essential for effective distance education. AI technologies can enhance these environments by offering tools that simulate real-world problems, promote peer interaction, and support reflective practices. For example, intelligent tutoring systems can adapt to learners' responses, encouraging exploration and experimentation, which are hallmarks of constructivist learning (VanLehn, 2011).

Behaviorism, on the other hand, focuses on observable behaviors and the external factors that shape them. This theory emphasizes the role of reinforcement and feedback in learning, positing that behavior is shaped by responses to stimuli (Skinner, 1953). In distance education, behaviorist principles can be operationalized through learning analytics that track student engagement and performance, providing immediate feedback to reinforce desired behaviors. For example, learning analytics can identify patterns in student interactions, enabling educators to implement timely interventions for those at risk of underperforming (Ferguson, 2012). The integration of behaviorism with AI allows for the creation of systems that provide personalized feedback based on learners' actions. AI algorithms can analyze data from student interactions, such as quiz scores and participation rates, to identify strengths and weaknesses. This analysis can inform tailored feedback and interventions designed to motivate and guide learners toward their goals (Siemens, 2013).

Theoretical Models of Learning Analytics

Several theoretical models underpin the field of learning analytics, providing frameworks for understanding how data can be utilized to enhance learning outcomes. One prominent framework is the Learning Analytics and Knowledge (LAK) framework, which emphasizes the use of data to improve learning processes and outcomes (Siemens & Long, 2011). This framework outlines key components of learning analytics, including data collection, analysis, and interpretation, and emphasizes the importance of aligning analytics practices with educational goals. The LAK framework is grounded in the idea that effective learning analytics should not only focus on the technical aspects of data analysis but also consider the social and ethical dimensions of data use. For instance, learning analytics should prioritize student privacy and ensure that data is used responsibly to support learning rather than penalize learners. This ethical dimension is critical for fostering trust among students and educators and for promoting a culture of transparency in educational institutions. Another important model is the Activity Theory, which provides a comprehensive lens through which to analyze learning processes. Activity Theory posits that learning is a mediated process involving interactions among individuals, tools, and the community. In the context of learning analytics, this theory highlights the importance of considering the broader context in which learning occurs, including social interactions, cultural norms, and institutional practices (Engeström, 1987). By applying Activity Theory to learning analytics, educators can gain insights into how learners engage with content, collaborate with peers, and utilize available resources, thereby informing instructional design and intervention strategies.

Implications of Theoretical Perspectives

The interplay between these theoretical perspectives has significant implications for the implementation and effectiveness of AI and learning analytics in distance education. Constructivist learning theory encourages the development of AI systems that support personalized and contextualized learning experiences. By leveraging AI to create adaptive learning environments, educators can foster student agency and autonomy, enabling learners to take ownership of their educational journeys. This approach not only enhances student engagement but also promotes deeper learning through exploration and critical thinking. Conversely, behaviorism emphasizes the importance of feedback and reinforcement in shaping learning behaviors. Learning analytics, grounded in behaviorist principles, can provide valuable insights into student engagement and performance. By utilizing data to inform instructional decisions, educators can implement timely interventions that guide learners toward academic success. This data-driven approach can help address issues related to retention and completion rates, which are critical challenges in distance education.

The integration of these theoretical perspectives also highlights the need for a holistic approach to learning analytics. By considering both the individual learner and the broader context in which learning occurs, educators can design more effective interventions that cater to diverse learner needs. For example, using Activity Theory in conjunction with learning analytics can inform the development of collaborative learning opportunities that leverage peer interactions and community resources. The theoretical framework presented in this chapter underscores the importance of understanding the interplay between AI, learning analytics, and distance education. By grounding the integration of these technologies in established educational theories, educators can create more effective and responsive learning environments that promote student success. The insights gained from constructivist learning theory, behaviorism, and learning analytics frameworks not only inform the development of AI-driven educational tools but also guide the ethical and responsible use of data in educational settings.

RESEARCH METHODOLOGY

In this chapter, we present the research methodology used to explore the integration of Artificial Intelligence (AI) and learning analytics in distance education. The focus of the methodology is on a theoretical review approach, which involves systematically examining existing literature to synthesize and analyze key concepts, trends, and implications associated with AI and learning analytics. This methodology is particularly pertinent given the rapidly evolving nature of educational technologies and the need to understand their applications in enhancing distance learning. The theoretical review methodology begins with an overview of the research approach, emphasizing its purpose in developing a comprehensive understanding of the topic. This methodology facilitates a deeper examination of existing theories and frameworks that inform the integration of AI and learning analytics in educational settings. By reviewing and synthesizing theoretical perspectives, we aim to identify gaps in the literature, highlight emerging trends, and propose areas for future research. This approach is grounded in the principles of systematic review methodologies, which emphasize transparency, replicability, and rigor in literature analysis (Kitchenham, 2004).

The next component of our research methodology involves the literature review strategy, which outlines the criteria for selecting sources and types of literature reviewed. To ensure a comprehensive analysis, we focused on peer-reviewed journal articles, conference proceedings, and reputable books published within the last five years. This time frame was chosen to capture the most current advancements and discussions surrounding AI and learning analytics in distance education. Additionally, we prioritized literature that provided empirical evidence, theoretical frameworks, or conceptual analyses relevant to our research focus. To facilitate a balanced and diverse representation of perspectives, we employed a keyword search strategy utilizing terms such as "AI in education," "learning analytics," "distance education," and "educational technology." The selected literature was further screened based on relevance to the research questions and objectives, ensuring that only the most pertinent sources were included in the final analysis.

In conducting the literature review, we also took into consideration the methodologies employed in the studies we reviewed. This consideration provided insights into the research designs, data collection methods, and analysis techniques utilized by other researchers in the field, thereby enhancing the credibility and contextual understanding of our findings. By critically engaging with the existing literature, we were able to identify prevailing themes, contradictions, and areas requiring further exploration, thereby laying a solid foundation for our theoretical analysis. The analysis techniques utilized in this research methodology involve a systematic framework for synthesizing and interpreting existing literature on AI and learning analytics in distance education. We adopted a thematic analysis approach, which allows for the identification of recurring themes and patterns across the selected literature (Braun & Clarke, 2006). This framework involves several stages, including familiarization with the literature, coding, theme development, and interpretation of findings. During the familiarization stage, we immersed ourselves in the literature by reading and annotating key texts, which facilitated a comprehensive understanding of the context and key findings. Following this, we conducted a coding process, wherein we identified significant concepts and statements related to our research questions. This coding process was conducted using qualitative data analysis software, enabling a systematic organization of data and identification of themes across the literature.

Once the coding was completed, we engaged in theme development, which involved grouping related codes into broader themes that encapsulate the key findings and insights derived from the literature. This thematic structure allowed us to synthesize the diverse perspectives and insights found in the literature, providing a cohesive narrative on the integration of AI and learning analytics in distance education. Finally, the interpretation of findings involved critically analyzing the themes in relation to our research questions and objectives. This stage emphasized the practical implications of the literature review, highlighting how AI and learning analytics can enhance distance education through personalized learning, improved student engagement, and data-informed decision-making. Additionally, we discussed the limitations of the current literature, including gaps in empirical studies and the need for further research to validate theoretical claims and models.

The research methodology employed in this study adopts a theoretical review approach that systematically analyzes existing literature on AI and learning analytics in distance education. By utilizing a rigorous literature review strategy and a thematic analysis framework, we aim to synthesize key insights and inform future research directions in this rapidly evolving field. The findings of this review will not only contribute to the academic discourse surrounding AI and learning analytics but also provide practical guidance for educators and institutions seeking to enhance their distance learning programs.

SOLUTIONS AND RECOMMENDATIONS

As distance learning continues to evolve, the integration of Artificial Intelligence (AI) and learning analytics offers significant potential to enhance educational outcomes. However, successful implementation requires thoughtful strategies, comprehensive training, and a strong focus on ethical considerations. This section presents solutions and recommendations that educators and institutions can adopt to effectively harness AI and learning analytics in distance learning environments.

Strategies for Implementing AI in Distance Learning

To maximize the benefits of AI in distance education, educators must adopt best practices for implementation. These practices include selecting appropriate AI tools, aligning technology with pedagogical goals, and engaging students in meaningful ways.

One effective strategy is to adopt AI-powered learning platforms that offer personalized learning experiences. Tools such as Knewton **and** Squirrel AI provide adaptive learning solutions that tailor content delivery to individual student needs based on real-time analytics. For example, Knewton analyzes students' interactions with learning materials to offer personalized recommendations, helping them progress at their own pace (Knewton, 2022).

Another key practice is the integration of AI-driven chatbots and virtual assistants to enhance student engagement and support. Tools like IBM Watson Assistant and ChatGPT can answer students' questions, provide instant feedback, and assist with administrative tasks, thus reducing the workload on instructors while improving the learning experience (Feng et al., 2023). Educators should also ensure that these tools are user-friendly and accessible to all students to foster inclusivity. Moreover, incorporating AI analytics into course design can lead to more informed decision-making. Educators can analyze data on student performance, engagement levels, and learning behaviors to adjust instructional strategies accordingly. For instance, platforms such as Blackboard and Canvas now feature built-in analytics dashboards that enable educators to monitor student progress and intervene when necessary (Blackboard, 2023). Lastly, it is essential for institutions to establish clear guidelines for integrating AI tools into the curriculum. This includes developing policies around technology use, data security, and academic integrity, which can guide educators in making informed choices about AI applications in their teaching practices.

Leveraging Learning Analytics for Improvement

Learning analytics can significantly enhance distance learning by informing instructional design and providing insights into student performance. To effectively leverage learning analytics, institutions should adopt comprehensive data collection and analysis techniques.

One approach is to implement Learning Management Systems (LMS) that offer robust analytics features. These systems can track various data points, such as student engagement, assessment scores, and course completion rates. Educators can utilize this data to identify trends and patterns that inform curriculum development. For instance, analytics can reveal common areas of struggle among students, enabling instructors to modify course content or provide additional resources to support learning (Siemens & Long, 2011). Furthermore, data visualization tools can help educators interpret complex datasets more effectively. Tools like Tableau and Google Data Studio can transform raw data into intuitive visualizations, allowing educators to quickly identify key insights and areas needing attention. By presenting data in a visually engaging manner, educators can facilitate discussions about instructional strategies and foster a collaborative approach to improving learning outcomes (Baker & Inventado, 2014). Institutions should also consider establishing data-sharing agreements between departments to facilitate a holistic view of student progress. This collaborative approach allows for more comprehensive insights and encourages a culture of data-driven decision-making across the institution (Ifenthaler & Yau, 2020). Additionally, regular assessment and reflection on the impact of learning analytics on student performance is crucial. Educators should engage in ongoing discussions about how data informs their teaching practices and seek feedback from students regarding the effectiveness of instructional changes. This continuous feedback loop can lead to iterative improvements and a more responsive learning environment.

Faculty Training and Support

Professional development and support structures for educators are vital for the successful integration of AI and learning analytics in distance learning. Institutions must prioritize faculty training to ensure that educators are equipped with the knowledge and skills necessary to effectively use these technologies. One effective strategy is to implement comprehensive training programs that cover both technical skills and pedagogical strategies. Workshops and webinars focusing on the use of AI tools and analytics can empower educators to explore innovative teaching methods and enhance their instructional practices. Institutions may also consider offering mentoring programs where experienced faculty members support their peers in implementing AI and learning analytics in their courses (Wang et al., 2021). Furthermore, creating a community of practice among educators can foster collaboration and knowledge sharing. Regular meetings or online forums where faculty can discuss challenges, share best practices, and exchange ideas can help build a supportive network for educators as they navigate the integration of AI and analytics into their teaching. By establishing such communities, institutions can create an environment conducive to continuous professional growth. Additionally, institutions should provide ongoing technical support for educators. This includes access to IT resources, troubleshooting assistance, and responsive helpdesk services. Providing readily available support can alleviate the technological barriers educators face and encourage the exploration of new tools and methodologies (Benson & Torkzadeh, 2021).

Ethical Considerations and Data Privacy

As AI and learning analytics become more integrated into distance education, addressing ethical considerations and data privacy is paramount. Institutions must develop policies and practices that protect student data and ensure ethical usage of AI technologies. First, it is essential to adhere to data protection regulations, such as the General Data Protection Regulation (GDPR) and the Family Educational Rights and Privacy Act (FERPA). These regulations establish guidelines for the collection, storage, and use of personal data, emphasizing the need for informed consent and transparency in data practices (European Union, 2016; U.S. Department of Education, 2020). Moreover, institutions should implement robust data governance frameworks that outline the ethical use of AI and learning analytics. This includes defining the purposes for data collection, establishing protocols for data access, and ensuring data anonymization to protect student identities. Institutions should also regularly audit their data practices to ensure compliance with established policies and identify areas for improvement (Lathrop & Lathrop, 2018). Finally, fostering a culture of ethical awareness among educators and students is crucial. Institutions should provide training on ethical considerations related to AI and data usage, encouraging open discussions about the implications of technology in education. By promoting a shared understanding of ethical responsibilities, institutions can ensure that AI and learning analytics are used to enhance learning without compromising student privacy and trust. Integrating AI and learning analytics into distance learning presents an opportunity to enhance educational outcomes and foster student engagement. By adopting effective strategies for implementation, leveraging analytics for improvement, prioritizing faculty training and support, and addressing ethical considerations, educators and institutions can create a more responsive and effective distance learning environment. As technology continues to evolve, ongoing reflection and adaptation will be essential to harness the full potential of AI and learning analytics in education.

FUTURE RESEARCH DIRECTIONS

The integration of Artificial Intelligence (AI) and learning analytics in distance education represents a dynamic and evolving field, characterized by rapid advancements and emerging trends. As institutions increasingly adopt these technologies to enhance learning outcomes, it is essential to explore future research directions that can contribute to the ongoing development of this area. This section discusses emerging trends, identifies potential areas for further study, and analyzes the impact of technological innovations on distance education.

Emerging Trends in AI and Learning Analytics

One of the most significant emerging trends in AI and learning analytics is the shift towards more personalized and adaptive learning experiences. Future advancements are expected to enhance the capability of AI systems to analyze vast amounts of data and provide tailored educational interventions that align with individual student needs. The use of AI algorithms that can predict student performance and engagement based on historical data will allow educators to proactively address learning challenges and enhance the overall educational experience (Baker, 2023). Another trend is the increasing focus on learner autonomy and self-regulated learning. As learning analytics tools become more sophisticated, they are likely to empower students to take greater ownership of their learning processes. By providing real-time feedback and insights into their learning behaviors, analytics can help students develop metacognitive skills and make informed decisions about their study habits (Hattie & Donoghue, 2016). Future research could explore the efficacy of various analytics tools in fostering self-regulated learning and how they impact student motivation and success. Furthermore, the rise of machine learning and natural language processing (NLP) in education is set to revolutionize content delivery and student interaction. Tools leveraging these technologies, such as intelligent tutoring systems and chatbots, will continue to evolve, providing personalized support and feedback to learners in real time (Tschofen & Dawley, 2013). Research could investigate the effectiveness of these tools in enhancing student engagement, retention, and academic performance across diverse learning contexts.

Potential Areas for Further Study

Despite the progress made in integrating AI and learning analytics into distance education, there remain several gaps in the current literature that warrant further investigation. One critical area is the examination of ethical implications surrounding data collection and usage in AI-driven learning environments. As educational institutions increasingly rely on data analytics, understanding the ethical considerations, including privacy concerns and data security, is paramount (Slade & Prinsloo, 2013). Future research could explore best practices for ensuring ethical compliance and building student trust in the use of learning analytics.

Another potential area for study is the impact of AI and learning analytics on diverse learner populations. Most existing research focuses on general student populations, often overlooking the needs of underrepresented or marginalized groups. Investigating how AI tools can be tailored to support diverse learning needs such as those of students with disabilities, non-native speakers, or learners from low socio-economic backgrounds can contribute to more equitable education practices (Baker et al., 2022). Additionally, there is a need for longitudinal studies that track the long-term impact of AI and learning analytics on educational outcomes. Much of the current research is cross-sectional, which limits the understanding of how these technologies affect student performance over time. By employing longitudinal methodologies, researchers can gain insights into the sustained effects of AI and analytics on learner engagement, retention, and academic success (Ifenthaler & Yau, 2020).

The Impact of Technological Innovations

As technological innovations continue to reshape distance education, understanding their potential impact is crucial for educators and institutions. Emerging technologies, such as augmented reality (AR), virtual reality (VR), and the Internet of Things (IoT), have the potential to create immersive and interactive learning environments that enhance student engagement and motivation (Baker, 2023). Future research should explore how these technologies can be integrated with AI and learning analytics to create holistic learning experiences that cater to different learning styles and preferences. Moreover, the rise of blockchain technology in education could revolutionize credentialing and data management. Blockchain offers a secure and transparent method for storing and sharing educational records, potentially transforming how institutions verify student achievements and credentials (Sharples & Domingue, 2016). Research on the implications of blockchain for learning analytics and student data privacy will be essential as institutions consider adopting this technology. Finally, the COVID-19 pandemic has accelerated the adoption of online learning and highlighted the need for resilient and adaptive educational models. Future research should examine how AI and learning analytics can support educational continuity in the face of disruptions and contribute to the development of flexible learning pathways that accommodate varying circumstances (Keis & Steed, 2020). Understanding the role of technology in fostering educational resilience will be crucial for preparing institutions for future challenges. The integration of AI and learning analytics in distance education is a rapidly evolving field with significant potential for enhancing educational outcomes. Emerging trends, potential areas for further study, and the impact of technological innovations will shape the future of this area. As researchers, educators, and institutions continue to explore these dimensions, the insights gained will contribute to the development of more effective, equitable, and resilient distance learning environments.

SUMMARY OF KEY FINDINGS

AI and learning analytics have demonstrated significant advancements in enhancing distance education. AI technologies, such as adaptive learning systems, intelligent tutoring, and chatbots, have been shown to provide personalized support tailored to individual student needs, thereby increasing engagement and motivation (Baker, 2023). Learning analytics plays a crucial role in this process by analyzing data from diverse learning activities, enabling educators to identify patterns and trends in student performance and engagement. This data-driven approach allows for timely interventions, fostering a more supportive learning environment (Ifenthaler & Yau,

2020). Moreover, the integration of these technologies has been linked to improved educational outcomes. Studies indicate that institutions utilizing AI-driven analytics can better identify at-risk students, predict their future performance, and implement targeted strategies to enhance their learning experience (Hattie & Donoghue, 2016). By facilitating a deeper understanding of learner behaviors, institutions can create more responsive and adaptive learning environments, ultimately leading to higher retention rates and academic success (Baker et al., 2022).

Implications for Educators and Institutions

The implications of integrating AI and learning analytics into distance education are profound. For educators, these tools provide opportunities to enhance instructional design and adapt pedagogical strategies based on real-time data insights. By utilizing analytics to monitor student engagement and performance, educators can make informed decisions about curriculum adjustments, identify areas for improvement, and develop tailored support mechanisms for diverse learners (Tschofen & Dawley, 2013). Institutions, on the other hand, can leverage AI and learning analytics to foster a culture of continuous improvement and innovation. The data generated from learning analytics can inform institutional policies and practices, guiding resource allocation, curriculum development, and student support services (Slade & Prinsloo, 2013). By embracing a data-informed approach, institutions can enhance their operational efficiency and effectiveness, ultimately leading to improved student outcomes and satisfaction. Additionally, the ethical implications of using AI and learning analytics in education cannot be overlooked. As institutions collect and analyze large amounts of student data, they must prioritize data privacy and security. Ensuring compliance with regulations and maintaining transparency in data usage will be critical for building trust with students and stakeholders (Baker, 2023). Future research should focus on establishing best practices for ethical data use, ensuring that educational institutions can harness the benefits of AI and analytics while respecting learners' rights and privacy.

CONCLUSION

The integration of AI and learning analytics in distance education represents a transformative shift in how educational institutions deliver learning experiences. As this chapter has illustrated, the potential benefits of these technologies are substantial, with the ability to enhance personalization, improve engagement, and drive positive educational outcomes. However, the journey is not without challenges. As the field continues to evolve, ongoing research and adaptation will be essential for realizing the full potential of AI and learning analytics in education. The rapid pace of technological advancements necessitates a commitment from educators and institutions to stay informed and engaged with emerging trends and best practices. Collaborative efforts between researchers, educators, and technology developers will be crucial for fostering innovation and ensuring that AI and analytics tools are effectively integrated into educational practices. Furthermore, continuous evaluation of the impact of these technologies on learning outcomes will be necessary to refine approaches and address any unintended consequences. The integration of Artificial Intelligence (AI) and learning analytics into distance education has emerged as a pivotal force in transforming teaching and learning methodologies. As highlighted throughout this chapter, AI and learning analytics hold immense potential to enhance educational experiences, personalize learning pathways, and improve student engagement and success. This conclusion synthesizes the key findings, explores implications for educators and institutions, and emphasizes the necessity for ongoing research and adaptation in this rapidly evolving field. Ultimately, the successful implementation of AI and learning analytics in distance education requires a holistic approach that prioritizes ethical considerations, data privacy, and learner agency. By fostering a culture of innovation, collaboration, and reflection, educational institutions can harness the power of these technologies to create more equitable, engaging, and effective learning environments for all students.

REFERENCES

Baker, R. K. (2023). Leveraging AI and learning analytics in education. *International Journal of Educational Technology in Higher Education, 20*(1), 10–29. PMID: 36811132

Baker, R. K., D'Mello, S., & Inventado, P. (2022). Exploring the role of AI in fostering inclusive education. *Journal of Learning Analytics, 9*(2), 25–37.

Baker, R. K., & Inventado, P. S. (2014). Educational data mining and learning analytics. In Learning, Design, and Technology (pp. 1-24). Springer.

Benson, V., & Torkzadeh, G. (2021). E-learning and distance education technologies: Future directions. *Journal of Management Information Systems, 38*(1), 43–62.

Black, A. (2023). *Analytics: Data-informed decision-making for educators*. Blackboard Learn. Retrieved from Blackboard.

Braun, V., & Clarke, V. (2006). Using thematic analysis in psychology. *Qualitative Research in Psychology, 3*(2), 77–101. DOI: 10.1191/1478088706qp063oa

Engeström, Y. (1987). *Learning by Expanding: An Activity-Theoretical Approach to Developmental Research*. Orienta-Konsultit.

European Union. (2016). General Data Protection Regulation (GDPR). Retrieved from GDPR.

Feng, S., Wang, T., & Lin, H. (2023). The role of AI in education: Transforming learning through technology. *International Journal of Educational Technology in Higher Education, 20*(1), 12–28. PMID: 36883192

Ferguson, R. (2012). Learning analytics: Drivers, developments and challenges. *International Journal of Technology Enhanced Learning, 4*(5), 304–317. DOI: 10.1504/IJTEL.2012.051314

Hattie, J., & Donoghue, G. (2016). Learning strategies: A synthesis and meta-analysis. *Educational Psychologist, 51*(3), 247–265.

Ifenthaler, D., & Yau, J. Y.-K. (2020). Utilizing learning analytics to support student engagement: A case study. *Education and Information Technologies, 25*(4), 3191–3208.

Keis, O., & Steed, B. (2020). The role of technology in supporting resilient educational practices. *International Review of Education, 66*(4), 439–458.

Kitchenham, B. (2004). Procedures for performing systematic reviews. Keele University. https://www.cs.stir.ac.uk/~kitchenham/ systematic_review_process.pdf

Knewton. (2022). Adaptive learning technology. Retrieved from Knewton.

Lathrop, A., & Lathrop, L. (2018). Data governance and privacy: Creating a data management framework. *Educational Research Review*, *26*, 145–158.

Luckin, R., Holmes, W., Griffiths, M., & Forcier, L. B. (2016). Intelligence Unleashed: An Argument for AI in Education. Pearson Education. https://www.pearson.com/uk/learners/learn-about-ai-in-education.html

Moore, M. G., & Kearsley, G. (2012). *Distance Education: A Systems View of Online Learning*. Wadsworth Cengage Learning.

Piaget, J. (1976). *The Child and Reality: Problems of Genetic Psychology*. Viking Press.

Sharples, M., & Domingue, J. (2016). The blockchain and education. *Proceedings of the 15th European Conference on e-Learning*, 25-32.

Shute, V., & Rahimi, S. (2020). Intelligent Tutoring Systems: A Review of Research and Practice. *Educational Psychology Review*, *32*(4), 827–855. DOI: 10.1007/s10648-020-09517-2

Siemens, G. (2013). Learning analytics: The emergence of a new educational technology. In *Education and Information Technologies* (pp. 1–11). Springer., DOI: 10.1007/s10639-012-9256-2

Siemens, G., & Long, P. (2011). Penetrating the fog: Analytics in learning and education. *EDUCAUSE Review*, *46*(5), 30–32.

Siemens, G., & Long, P. (2011). Penetrating the Fog: Analytics in Learning and Education. *EDUCAUSE Review*, *46*(5), 30–32. https://er.educause.edu/articles/2011/11/penetrating-the-fog-analytics-in-learning-and-education

Skinner, B. F. (1953). *Science and Human Behavior*. Simon and Schuster.

Slade, S., & Prinsloo, P. (2013). Learning analytics: The challenges of the ethical use of data. *Proceedings of the 3rd International Conference on Learning Analytics and Knowledge*, 114-118.

Tschofen, C., & Dawley, L. (2013). Connectivism and learner autonomy in MOOCs. *International Review of Research in Open and Distance Learning*, *14*(4), 87–103.

U.S. Department of Education. (2020). *Family Educational Rights and Privacy Act (FERPA)*. Retrieved from FERPA.

U.S. Department of Education. (2021). Distance Education Enrollment Report. https://nces.ed.gov/programs/digest/d21/tables/dt21_301.10.asp

VanLehn, K. (2011). The Relative Effectiveness of Human Tutoring, Intelligent Tutoring Systems, and Other Tutoring Systems. *Educational Psychologist*, *46*(4), 197–221. DOI: 10.1080/00461520.2011.610732

Wang, Q., Li, X., & Yang, Y. (2021). Professional development for teachers: Using learning analytics to improve instruction. *Journal of Computer Assisted Learning*, *37*(5), 1426–1438.

KEY TERMS AND DEFINITIONS

Artificial Intelligence (AI): AI refers to the simulation of human intelligence processes by machines, particularly computer systems. These processes include learning, reasoning, and self-correction. In education, AI encompasses various applications, including adaptive learning systems and intelligent tutoring, enhancing personalized learning experiences.

Learning Analytics: Learning analytics is the measurement, collection, analysis, and reporting of data about learners and their contexts. Its goal is to understand and optimize learning outcomes by leveraging data generated during the learning process to identify patterns and inform instructional strategies.

Distance Learning: Distance learning refers to educational practices that provide instruction to students who are not physically present in a traditional classroom setting. This method can include online courses, blended learning environments, and other forms of remote education that utilize technology.

Adaptive Learning: Adaptive learning is an educational method that uses technology to tailor learning experiences to the individual needs of each student. By analyzing data on student performance, adaptive learning systems adjust content, pace, and delivery to optimize learning outcomes.

Personalized Learning: Personalized learning customizes educational experiences to meet the unique needs, interests, and abilities of each learner. This approach often incorporates learning analytics and AI to facilitate individualized instruction and feedback, promoting greater student engagement and success.

Data Privacy: Data privacy refers to the protection of personal information collected during the educational process. It encompasses regulations and practices designed to safeguard student data from unauthorized access and misuse.

Learning Management System (LMS): An LMS is a software application used for the administration, documentation, tracking, and delivery of educational courses or training programs. It provides a centralized platform for educators to manage course content, track student progress, and facilitate communication.

Predictive Analytics: Predictive analytics involves using statistical algorithms and machine learning techniques to analyze historical data and predict future outcomes. In education, predictive analytics can help identify at-risk students and inform interventions that enhance retention and academic performance.

Intelligent Tutoring System (ITS): An ITS is a computer system that provides personalized instruction and feedback to students, often utilizing AI technologies. These systems simulate one-on-one tutoring by adapting to a learner's needs and progress, providing tailored support.

Engagement Analytics: Engagement analytics measures and analyzes student interactions with educational content and platforms to assess levels of engagement. This data helps educators identify areas for improvement and tailor instructional strategies to foster greater involvement.

Gamification: Gamification applies game design elements and principles in non-game contexts, such as education. By incorporating elements like points, badges, and leaderboards, gamification aims to enhance motivation and engagement in learning activities.

Blended Learning: Blended learning is an educational approach that combines traditional face-to-face instruction with online learning components. This model leverages the strengths of both methods to create a more flexible and personalized learning experience.

AI: Artificial Intelligence - The simulation of human intelligence processes by machines.

LMS: Learning Management System - A software platform for managing educational courses and training programs.

LA: Learning Analytics - The collection and analysis of data about learners to enhance learning outcomes.

ITS: Intelligent Tutoring System - A computer system that provides personalized instruction to students.

MOOC: Massive Open Online Course - An online course aimed at unlimited participation and open access via the web.

K-12: Refers to the range of education from kindergarten through 12th grade, encompassing primary and secondary education.

RPA: Robotic Process Automation - The use of software robots to automate repetitive tasks, often employed to enhance operational efficiency.

NLP: Natural Language Processing - A field of AI focused on the interaction between computers and human language.

SLO: Student Learning Outcomes - Specific objectives that students are expected to achieve by the end of an educational program or course.

CBE: Competency-Based Education - An educational approach where students progress based on their ability to demonstrate competency in a subject area.

Chapter 10

From Data to Action: How AI and Learning Analytics Are Shaping the Future of Distance Education

João Tiago Dias
https://orcid.org/0000-0002-0686-7540
Universidade Aberta, Portugal

Arnaldo Santos
https://orcid.org/0000-0001-5139-6728
INESC TEC, Universidade Aberta, Portugal

Henrique São Mamede
https://orcid.org/0000-0002-5383-9884
INESC TEC, Universidade Aberta, Portugal

ABSTRACT

This chapter examines how Artificial Intelligence (AI) and Learning Analytics (LA) are transforming distance education, accelerated by the COVID-19 shift to e-learning. By using data from Learning Management Systems (LMS), these technologies can personalize learning, improve student retention, and automate tasks. AI, particularly machine learning, enables dynamic adaptation to student needs, while LA provides valuable insights for informed instructional decisions. However, ethical concerns, including data privacy and algorithmic bias, must be addressed to ensure equitable access and fair learning outcomes. The future of distance learning lies in responsible integration of AI and LA, creating immersive and inclusive educational experiences.

DOI: 10.4018/979-8-3693-7195-4.ch010

1. INTRODUCTION

The digital revolution has significantly reshaped the educational landscape, pushing distance learning from a complementary educational option to a primary mode of instruction in many settings. This shift, particularly intensified by the COVID-19 pandemic, has underscored the importance of innovative educational technologies such as Artificial Intelligence (AI) and Learning Analytics (LA) in addressing the needs of remote learners and creating adaptive, flexible learning environments. These technologies have the potential to transform how students interact with educational content, instructors, and each other, thereby redefining the learning experience in ways that traditional models cannot achieve.

AI and LA have emerged as critical components in building an efficient, scalable, and personalized educational system. AI's capabilities, including machine learning, natural language processing, and computer vision, allow for real-time, data-driven interactions with students, automating tasks that range from providing individualized feedback to grading assignments (Chen et al., 2020). LA, on the other hand, focuses on collecting and analyzing data generated from student interactions, providing valuable insights into learning behaviors, performance trends, and engagement patterns (Dias & Santos, 2022; Ye, 2022). Together, AI and LA provide a powerful framework for creating customized learning experiences that meet individual students' needs, an essential consideration in distance education where direct, face-to-face interaction is limited.

The historical development of LA reflects the broader evolution of educational data usage, moving from simple record-keeping to sophisticated analytics that inform personalized instruction (Ye, 2022). LA has its roots in educational data mining (EDM), which emerged as a response to the growing need for quantitative data in instructional design. Initially, behaviorist philosophies influenced EDM, focusing on observable and measurable learning objectives that could be tracked and analyzed (Ye, 2022). This foundational approach laid the groundwork for the development of LA, as it emphasized the importance of using data to understand and optimize learning outcomes. Unlike EDM, which primarily uses data to uncover patterns, LA leverages this data in real-time to directly inform and adapt instructional strategies, making it a particularly valuable tool in distance education, where the flexibility to adapt to students' changing needs is paramount (Christopoulos et al., 2020; Brown, 2012).

The COVID-19 pandemic served as a catalyst for digital transformation in education, accelerating the adoption of AI and LA as institutions worldwide grappled with the challenges of maintaining instructional quality in a remote setting. This shift revealed both the possibilities and limitations of existing distance learning systems, emphasizing the need for technologies that can enhance engagement, provide immediate feedback, and support diverse learning paths. AI enables personalized learning experiences that are responsive to each student's progress, preferences, and challenges. By analyzing student data, AI algorithms can adjust the difficulty of tasks, recommend supplementary resources, or offer targeted feedback, creating a more tailored and effective learning environment than one-size-fits-all approaches (Ahmed, 2020; Limna et al., 2022).

Learning Analytics complements AI by offering insights into student behavior and engagement, which educators can use to make data-informed decisions about curriculum design, instructional methods, and intervention strategies. For example, LA can track metrics such as login frequency, forum participation, and quiz completion rates to identify students who may be at risk of disengagement or underperformance (Shurygin et al., 2021). Such real-time insights enable educators to provide timely support, fostering student retention and success. Moreover, LA helps institutions understand broader trends in student engagement and learning outcomes, allowing for ongoing refinement of educational practices (Dias & Santos, 2022; Ye, 2022).

In the context of Learning Management Systems (LMS) like Moodle and Blackboard, AI and LA integrate seamlessly to provide a cohesive, data-informed learning experience. LMS platforms facilitate the collection of large amounts of data related to student activities, assessments, and interactions. This data, when processed by AI and analyzed through LA, becomes a valuable resource for customizing learning paths and identifying areas where students may need additional support. According to Limna et al. (Limna et al., 2022), AI-driven LMS platforms can deliver content that aligns with students' learning progress and adapt as they advance, creating a dynamic and personalized learning environment.

Despite these advantages, the adoption of AI and LA in distance education is not without challenges. Technical issues, such as integrating these technologies with existing LMS platforms and ensuring interoperability, can limit their effectiveness. Additionally, the quality of the data available for LA can significantly impact the insights generated, underscoring the importance of accurate and comprehensive data collection (Chen et al., 2020). Another significant challenge is the ethical considerations associated with using AI and LA in education. The extensive data collection required for LA raises concerns about student privacy and data security, particularly considering regulations such as the General Data Protection Regulation (GDPR) in Europe (Marler & Boudreau, 2017). There is also the risk of bias in AI algorithms, which could lead to inequitable learning experiences if not carefully managed (Blackmon & Moore, 2020). Educators and institutions must, therefore, adopt responsible data practices that prioritize transparency, consent, and inclusivity to ensure that AI and LA benefit all students.

The theoretical frameworks supporting AI and LA emphasize their role in creating adaptable learning environments that meet the needs of diverse learners. According to Greller and Drachsler (Greller & Drachsler, 2012), as cited in Ye (Ye, 2022), LA can be understood as part of a broader ecosystem that combines data from multiple sources to create a comprehensive view of student learning. This perspective aligns with Mamede & Santos (Mamede & Santos, 2024) view on digital transformation, which advocates for integrating AI and LA within an organizational learning framework that promotes continuous improvement and responsiveness to change. By embedding these technologies in the educational infrastructure, institutions can develop a resilient system that evolves with technological advancements and educational needs.

Looking to the future, the potential of AI and LA in distance education extends beyond personalization and data analysis. Emerging technologies such as augmented reality (AR) and virtual reality (VR) hold promise for creating immersive learning environments that engage students in new and meaningful ways. When combined with AI and LA, these technologies could offer experiences that go beyond traditional instructional methods, providing opportunities for hands-on, experiential learning that adapts in real-time to students' progress and feedback. As Ye (Ye, 2022) suggests, the integration of AI with these advanced technologies could create a symbiotic relationship where human expertise and artificial intelligence work in tandem to optimize learning outcomes.

In conclusion, AI and LA represent a paradigm shift in the design and delivery of distance education, offering tools that enhance engagement, personalization, and adaptability. However, realizing the full potential of these technologies requires careful consideration of the ethical, technical, and organizational challenges involved. As educational institutions continue to integrate AI and LA, they must also adopt best practices that ensure equity, transparency, and inclusivity, paving the way for a future where digital learning is accessible, effective, and responsive to the needs of all learners.

2. FOUNDATIONS OF ARTIFICIAL INTELLIGENCE AND LEARNING ANALYTICS

The application of Artificial Intelligence (AI) and Learning Analytics (LA) in education builds upon a foundation of technological and theoretical advancements aimed at optimizing the learning process, particularly in distance education. Both AI and LA are instrumental in creating adaptive, personalized learning environments, with AI contributing through data-driven interactions and LA focusing on the systematic collection and analysis of learner data.

Developing a robust framework for Learning Analytics (LA) requires a deep understanding of existing models, tools, and best practices for implementation. As pinpointed by Dias´ (Dias & Santos, 2022) research, to support this framework, a Systematic Literature Review (SLR) was conducted, focusing on Learning Analytics practices within training environments. This process allowed for the identification of key challenges, benefits, enablers, and inhibitors associated with LA frameworks as extensively documented in the literature. Additionally, a survey was administered to specific individuals who use use Learning Management Systems (LMS) to validate findings and better understand the impact of Learning Analytics on learner retention, engagement, and outcomes.

These technologies work synergistically to address individual learners' needs, ensuring a responsive and flexible approach that significantly enhances the quality of education (Chen et al., 2020; Dias & Santos, 2022).

Learning Analytics in Education

Learning Analytics (LA) is crucial for understanding, assessing, and optimizing distance education by using student data to gain insights into learning processes, engagement patterns, and academic performance. LA involves the systematic collection and analysis of data on students' interactions with learning materials, enabling educators to understand behaviours and predict outcomes in real-time. This data-driven approach is particularly significant for distance learning environments where face-to-face interaction is limited, as it empowers educators to implement tailored interventions based on students' unique needs and progress (Dias & Santos, 2022).

The role of LA in education extends beyond basic tracking; it creates actionable insights that allow educators to address students' needs promptly, thereby enhancing student success. LA applications are supported by Learning Management Systems (LMS), such as Moodle and Blackboard, which collect vast amounts of data on student interactions. LMS platforms gather data on variables like login frequency, discussion forum activity, quiz performance, and assessment completions. This granular data provides educators with a holistic understanding of student engagement and allows institutions to identify students at risk of academic struggles, enabling pre-emptive interventions to support their learning journey (Bradley, 2021).

One key advantage of LA is its capacity for adaptive learning, where the educational content and instructional pace are adjusted according to individual student needs and behaviours. As highlighted in the dissertation, adaptive learning is facilitated by continuously analyzing data on each learner's strengths, weaknesses, and learning progress. This data enables the design of personalized learning pathways, ensuring that students receive content aligned with their unique learning styles and academic requirements (Kleimola & Leppisaari, 2022). Personalized recommendations can be generated from student data, leading to enhanced learning outcomes by guiding learners through a curriculum optimized to their specific needs (Dias & Santos, 2022).

The implementation of Learning Analytics frameworks in organizational or educational settings provides significant benefits, such as supporting data-driven decision-making and personalizing content for learners. However, field studies in this research revealed critical challenges, including the difficulty of integrating advanced and personalized methods that accommodate diverse user learning styles, limited technical support in some LMS platforms, and the need for an adaptive, intuitive instructional design that enhances learner engagement. Additionally, the lack of frequent feedback and continuous oversight can negatively impact the learning experience, emphasizing the need for more dynamic tools to ensure analyzed data leads to effective interventions (Dias & Santos, 2022). One example of a LA framework is suggested by Dias et al. (Dias & Santos, 2022) and it is shown below:

Figure 1. Proposed LA framework by Dias et al. (Dias & Santos, 2022)

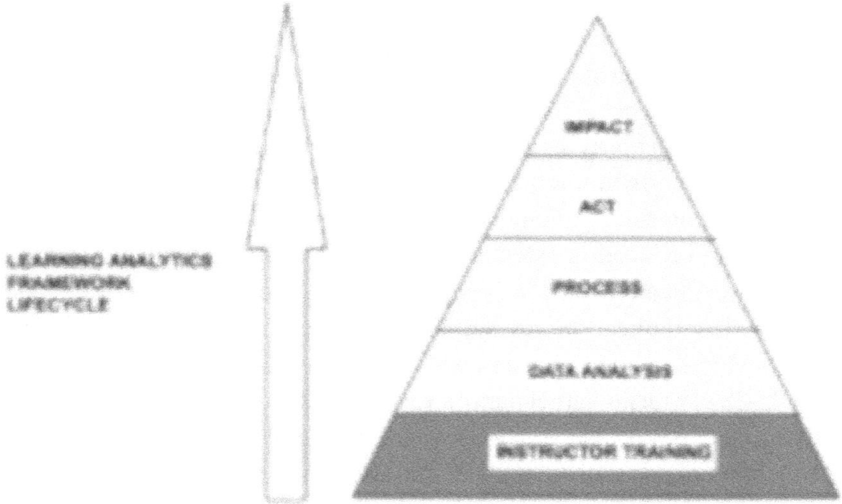

In a broader sense, LA serves as a powerful tool for evidence-based decision-making in educational institutions. By examining aggregated student data, institutions can identify patterns and trends that guide resource allocation, curriculum development, and instructional strategies. The data-driven insights derived from

LA foster continuous improvement within learning organizations, allowing educational institutions to refine and optimize instructional methods based on empirical evidence (Greller & Drachsler, 2012). This evidence-based approach benefits not only students but also educators, as it provides instructors with feedback on the effectiveness of their teaching methods, helping them to adjust and innovate their strategies in response to real-world data (Lodge et al., 2018).

LA also bridges formative and summative assessment by offering continuous data to monitor and improve learning outcomes. Formative assessment, focused on monitoring learning progress, and summative assessment, which evaluates cumulative learning achievements, can both be enhanced through LA by tracking students' performance and engagement over time. Such continuous feedback enables educators to assess whether learning objectives are being met and to adjust instructional methods as necessary, ensuring that both short-term understanding and long-term learning goals are achieved (Ifenthaler & Yau, 2020).

Moreover, the implementation of LA supports early warning systems and intervention strategies, crucial for improving student retention and reducing dropout rates. The predictive power of LA helps institutions identify students who may be at risk of disengagement or failure, allowing educators to intervene proactively. By analyzing behavioural patterns, LA systems can forecast academic difficulties, thereby allowing institutions to provide additional resources or adjust course content to better support students' learning journeys (Dias & Santos, 2022).

In distance learning, where students often study in isolation, LA has a unique role in fostering a sense of connection and support. LA insights enable educators to maintain student engagement by identifying when learners may need encouragement or additional assistance. For instance, students who consistently miss deadlines or have low engagement rates may receive automated reminders, encouragement, or even personalized messages from instructors, helping to maintain a supportive learning environment despite the physical separation inherent in distance education (Macfadyen, 2022; Mamede & Santos, 2024).

From an organizational perspective, LA is instrumental in creating learning organizations that adapt continuously to the evolving educational needs of students and faculty. According to some authors (Dias & Santos, 2022; Mamede & Santos, 2024), integrating LA into institutional frameworks fosters a culture of ongoing improvement, where educational decisions are informed by reliable data rather than anecdotal evidence or outdated practices. This transformative approach promotes an environment where both teaching effectiveness and student satisfaction are prioritized, and where educational policies are constantly refined to meet modern demands (Tsai et al., 2021).

To realize its full potential, however, LA must be implemented thoughtfully, with a strong emphasis on data quality, ethical use, and alignment with institutional goals. Effective LA frameworks require careful consideration of the types of data collected, the analytical methods applied, and the technical infrastructure available. Additionally, addressing ethical concerns related to student privacy, data security, and transparency is critical to maintaining trust in LA systems. The importance of responsible data practices, including anonymization and adherence to privacy regulations like the General Data Protection Regulation (GDPR), is paramount, as highlighted by (Marler & Boudreau, 2017).

LA has become an indispensable component of distance education, enabling personalized learning and fostering data-informed decision-making at both the individual and institutional levels. Through its ability to provide continuous feedback, support personalized interventions, and offer insights into learning behaviours, LA enhances educational outcomes and promotes a more effective, adaptive, and responsive learning experience. As educational institutions continue to evolve, LA will play an increasingly central role in shaping distance education, making it possible to create learning environments that are as effective, engaging, and supportive as traditional classroom settings.

Artificial Intelligence in Education

The integration of Artificial Intelligence (AI) in education has initiated transformative changes, enhanced the teaching and learning experience by enabling adaptive, data-driven approaches. AI leverages machine learning, natural language processing (NLP), and computer vision to create systems that respond dynamically to student needs, fostering interactive and personalized learning environments (Chen et al., 2020). This adaptability is especially beneficial in distance education, where AI-based tools offer support that simulates one-on-one tutoring through customized feedback and engagement strategies.

A key application of AI in educational contexts is through Intelligent Tutoring Systems (ITS), which provide individualized learning experiences by adjusting content and feedback based on real-time data analysis. ITS are particularly effective in supporting students in distance education, where traditional face-to-face support is limited. These systems collect data on students' responses, learning styles, and engagement, then use machine learning algorithms to modify instructional materials accordingly (Ahmed, 2020). Chen et al. (Chen et al., 2020) emphasizes that ITS help in promoting self-regulated learning, encouraging students to interact with content aligned with their skill level and progress.

Moreover, chatbots and virtual assistants, increasingly used within Learning Management Systems (LMS) such as Moodle, are AI applications that enhance student engagement by providing direct interaction. These tools leverage NLP to communicate effectively with students, answering questions in real-time and offering guidance throughout the course. Such AI-driven support is particularly valuable for maintaining student motivation and engagement in remote learning contexts, where access to educators is limited. Some authors underscore the role of AI-powered chatbots in extending educational support beyond standard classroom hours, providing students with round-the-clock assistance and alleviating instructors' workloads by handling routine queries (Dias & Santos, 2022; Mamede & Santos, 2024).

AI also plays a transformative role in assessment and feedback. Automated grading systems, driven by machine learning and NLP, facilitate timely feedback, enhancing formative assessment processes crucial for student development. These systems can evaluate assignments, quizzes, and even short written responses with high accuracy, ensuring that students receive immediate feedback. Limna et al. (Limna et al., 2022) note that such automation allows educators to focus more on personalized instruction and higher order teaching tasks, optimizing the use of instructional time while maintaining high standards of feedback.

Adaptive learning platforms are another essential application of AI in education. By continuously collecting and analyzing data on individual learner progress, these platforms tailor instructional content to better meet each student's needs. Adaptive learning addresses the limitations of the traditional "one-size-fits-all" model by creating a dynamic educational environment that adjusts content and pacing based on a learner's unique requirements and progress (Hasanov et al., 2019). Hasanov et al. (Hasanov et al., 2019) discuss the efficacy of these platforms in large-scale online courses, where diverse learner backgrounds and varying levels of preparedness are common. Such systems help promote student retention by fostering a personalized and engaging learning experience that resonates with everyone's academic profile.

As referred by Tapalova et al. (Tapalova & Zhiyenbayeva, 2022), Educational Technologies, combined with innovative teaching methods, enable personalized learning, making it key to achieving learning goals effectively. The figure shown below presents the possibilities of AIEd technologies for personalised approaches in education.

Figure 2. AIEd technologies in personalised approaches to learning (Tapalova & Zhiyenbayeva, 2022)

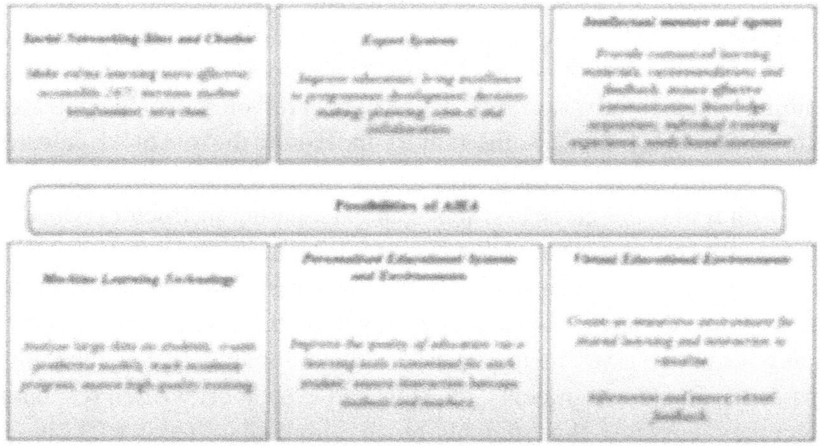

Despite the benefits, the application of AI in education raises challenges that require careful consideration. One significant concern involves data privacy and security, as AI-driven systems require substantial data collection, as outlined previously. This data dependency raises concerns over the handling and storage of student information, especially considering regulations like the General Data Protection Regulation (GDPR). Marler & Boudreau (Marler & Boudreau, 2017) emphasize the importance of implementing robust data management and security practices to mitigate these risks and ensure compliance with privacy standards. Additionally, the potential for algorithmic bias in AI systems could lead to unintended inequities in educational outcomes, a concern that underscores the need for transparent and ethical AI design and deployment (Boikanyo, 2024; Cascio, 2019).

AI integration into education has enabled considerable advancements in personalized learning, efficient feedback, and interactive support systems. ITS, chatbots, and adaptive learning platforms exemplify how AI can bridge the gap between traditional and digital learning environments, particularly in remote education where personalized support is often limited.

However, the ethical and technical challenges associated with AI in education call for responsible implementation practices. With ongoing research and commitment to ethical standards, AI has the potential to transform educational experiences, providing a more inclusive, engaging, and effective learning environment for students across diverse educational settings.

The Synergy Between AI and Learning Analytics

The combination of Artificial Intelligence (AI) and Learning Analytics (LA) has led to significant advancements in creating adaptive, personalized learning environments. While AI provides the computational power and data-processing capabilities to enable real-time, tailored interventions, LA offers the frameworks and insights necessary to understand learner behaviours, identify trends, and inform instructional adjustments. This synergy enables educational platforms to continuously refine learning experiences to match each student's needs and optimize outcomes in distance and digital learning (Chen et al., 2020; Dias & Santos, 2022).

AI plays a vital role in processing vast datasets that originate from student interactions within Learning Management Systems (LMS), allowing educational systems to predict and respond dynamically to individual learning trajectories. For instance, machine learning algorithms analyze engagement patterns and predict potential risks, such as a student's likelihood of disengagement or academic struggle. This predictive capability is enhanced by LA, which gathers extensive data on student performance and engagement, providing the context that allows AI to personalize educational content accurately. As Chen et al. (Chen et al., 2020) highlight, LA's role is essential in refining AI-driven systems by providing detailed, structured data, which AI then processes to generate tailored learning interventions.

As already mentioned, one of the primary applications of this synergy is in Intelligent Tutoring Systems (ITS), which utilize AI's analytical power combined with LA insights to adjust content difficulty, provide customized feedback, and suggest additional resources based on each student's progress (Hasanov et al., 2019). According to Ahmed (Ahmed, 2020), ITS can offer personalized instruction at a scale, identifying knowledge gaps and dynamically adjusting to address these areas, particularly beneficial in distance learning where direct educator support may be limited.

Moreover, LA's continuous tracking capabilities play a crucial role in adaptive learning platforms by allowing AI algorithms to make real-time adjustments based on student data, thus maintaining engagement and promoting effective learning. Lim et al. (Lim et al., 2024) describe how adaptive platforms adjust content pacing and complexity using LA data, ensuring students are neither overwhelmed nor disengaged. This adaptability is particularly useful in large-scale online courses, where diverse learner backgrounds require a nuanced approach to maintaining student retention and engagement (Dias & Santos, 2022; Hasanov et al., 2019).

The feedback loop created by AI and LA is another critical aspect of their synergy. LA analyzes student behaviours and performance, providing educators with insights on areas that may require additional support or modification. AI then automates responses to these insights, offering personalized recommendations or adapting content as needed, which reinforces learning paths and supports self-regulated learning (Rodrigues et al., 2018). For example, in formative assessments, LA data can reveal patterns in student errors, while AI algorithms suggest targeted resources or review modules, directly addressing knowledge gaps in a timely manner (Limna et al., 2022).

However, implementing AI and LA in education is not without challenges. Significant concerns around data privacy, security, and ethical use of student information persist, especially as these systems require extensive data collection to function effectively. Ensuring data protection while maintaining the integrity of personalized recommendations is essential. Marler and Boudreau (Marler & Boudreau, 2017) stress the importance of ethical standards in AI applications to safeguard student privacy and prevent biases in educational recommendations. Addressing these concerns is necessary to establish student trust and ensure fair, inclusive learning experiences across AI-driven educational platforms (Dias & Santos, 2022).

In conclusion, the synergy between AI and LA fosters a highly responsive, adaptable educational environment that supports individual learning journeys. By merging LA's capacity for collecting and interpreting educational data with AI's predictive and adaptive capabilities, educational institutions can deliver tailored learning experiences at scale, improving both engagement and retention rates. This synergy provides a powerful tool for addressing the diverse needs of learners, particularly in large-scale online settings, creating a promising path forward in the evolution of digital and distance education.

2. THE RELEVANCE OF LEARNING ANALYTICS IN DISTANCE EDUCATION

Learning Analytics (LA) plays a crucial role in the effectiveness of distance education by providing real-time insights into student behaviours, engagement levels, and academic progress. In distance learning environments, where direct face-to-face interaction is limited, LA's data-driven insights help bridge the gap by allowing educators to monitor and support students remotely. By collecting and analyzing data such as login frequency, interaction patterns, quiz performance, and assignment completion, LA enables institutions to identify at-risk students and proactively intervene to support their academic success (Bradley, 2021; Dias & Santos, 2022).

LA's integration into Learning Management Systems (LMS) like Moodle and Blackboard facilitates continuous tracking and assessment of student engagement, providing educators with a comprehensive view of individual learning paths. As noted by Ye (Ye, 2022), this capability allows institutions to offer personalized support based on patterns in student engagement and performance. By providing detailed, actionable insights, LA assists educators in adjusting course content, delivery methods, and support strategies to enhance student retention and success, which is particularly important in online courses where students may feel isolated from the broader learning community (Chen et al., 2020).

One of the most significant contributions of LA in distance education is its ability to promote adaptive learning. Adaptive learning platforms use LA to continuously adjust content and instructional pacing to meet individual students' needs, ensuring that each learner receives personalized support throughout their educational journey. According to Greller & Drachsler (2012, as cited in Ye (Ye, 2022)), adaptive learning aligns instructional material with students' unique learning preferences and current progress levels. This adaptability is particularly valuable in distance education, where standardized instruction may not address the diverse backgrounds and skill levels of students. Additionally, the continuous feedback loop created by LA allows for formative assessments, where educators can identify knowledge gaps and adjust their teaching strategies to meet students' evolving needs (Hasanov et al., 2019; Upadhyay & Khandelwal, 2019).

Beyond its impact on individual student outcomes, LA also provides valuable insights at the institutional level, supporting evidence-based decision-making processes. By aggregating data from multiple students across courses and departments, institutions can identify trends in student engagement, monitor the effectiveness of instructional methods, and make informed adjustments to curricula and resources. This approach, as discussed by Lim et al. (Lim et al., 2024), fosters a culture of continuous improvement in educational institutions, where data-driven decisions enhance learning outcomes and promote a high-quality educational experience. LA thereby supports both the immediate needs of learners and the long-term strategic goals of institutions (Mamede & Santos, 2024).

Ethical considerations are central to the application of LA in distance education. The collection and use of student data must be handled responsibly, with strict adherence to data privacy regulations such as the General Data Protection Regulation (GDPR). Ensuring transparency and maintaining student trust is essential, as inappropriate use of data can lead to a loss of confidence in LA tools. Responsible data practices, as emphasized by Marler & Boudreau (Marler & Boudreau, 2017), are critical in establishing an ethical framework for LA in educational settings. With careful management of these ethical concerns, LA can continue to provide a powerful foundation for supporting personalized, effective, and engaging distance education.

3. APPLICATIONS OF AI AND LEARNING ANALYTICS IN DISTANCE LEARNING ENVIRONMENTS

The integration of Artificial Intelligence (AI) and Learning Analytics (LA) in distance education has led to diverse applications that enhance personalized learning, automate processes, and provide real-time support for both students and educators. By combining the predictive power of AI with LA's data-driven insights, distance learning platforms can create tailored learning experiences that address each student's unique needs and improve overall educational outcomes.

One of the most notable applications of AI and LA in distance learning is through Intelligent Tutoring Systems (ITS). These systems analyze student interactions with course content and use machine learning algorithms to provide personalized feedback, recommend additional resources, and adjust the difficulty level of materials based on each student's progress. According to Hasanov et al. (Hasanov et al., 2019), ITS are particularly valuable in distance education, where they simulate the support provided by a human tutor and offer students a sense of guided instruction even in an online setting. ITS is highlighted as a critical component in distance learning environments, where tailored support can significantly improve engagement and retention (Dias & Santos, 2022).

Chatbots and virtual assistants are also essential AI applications in distance learning, especially within Learning Management Systems (LMS). These tools provide instant support to students by answering questions, guiding them through course content, and sending reminders about deadlines. As noted by Chen et al. (Chen et al., 2020), chatbots powered by natural language processing (NLP) allow students to interact with course materials autonomously, providing an added layer of engagement that can enhance the distance learning experience. It is emphasized that AI-powered chatbots reduce the workload for educators by managing routine queries, enabling instructors to focus on more complex educational tasks and one-on-one student support (Chen et al., 2020).

Another important application is adaptive learning platforms, which use AI and LA to modify instructional content in real-time, responding to each student's learning pace and performance. These platforms rely on LA to continuously assess students' strengths and weaknesses, enabling AI algorithms to adjust content delivery to better suit individual needs. This level of personalization is critical in large-scale online courses, where students come from diverse educational backgrounds and may require different levels of support. Lim et al. (Lim et al., 2024) discuss the effectiveness of adaptive learning in promoting student retention and ensuring a positive learning experience by creating an individualized pathway that resonates with each learner's profile (Hasanov et al., 2019).

AI-driven automation in grading and assessment is another application that has significantly impacted distance education. Automated grading systems, often based on machine learning and NLP, provide immediate feedback on quizzes, assignments, and written responses. This automation reduces the time spent on grading tasks and ensures that students receive prompt, constructive feedback that supports their learning. Limna et al. (Limna et al., 2022) observe that automated grading allows educators to focus on instructional and developmental tasks, making it possible to deliver personalized attention and higher-order feedback in distance learning environments.

While the benefits of AI and LA in distance education are substantial, challenges related to data privacy, security, and ethical use remain prominent. The extensive data required to fuel AI and LA systems raises concerns about student privacy, especially with regulations like the GDPR. As Marler & Boudreau (Marler & Boudreau, 2017) stress, educational institutions must ensure that AI and LA applications adhere to ethical standards that protect student information and avoid potential biases in personalized recommendations. Addressing these concerns is essential for building trust and ensuring that AI and LA applications create equitable, effective learning environments.

In conclusion, the combination of AI and LA has brought forward diverse applications that transform distance learning, making it more personalized, efficient, and responsive to students' needs. From ITS and chatbots to adaptive learning platforms and automated grading, AI and LA provide the tools necessary to support high-quality, data-informed education. By addressing the ethical and technical challenges associated with these technologies, educational institutions can harness AI and LA to deliver impactful, accessible, and inclusive distance learning experiences.

4. CHALLENGES AND ETHICAL CONSIDERATIONS

While the integration of Artificial Intelligence (AI) and Learning Analytics (LA) offers transformative potential for education, it also presents significant challenges that need to be carefully addressed. The successful and ethical implementation of these technologies requires overcoming technical limitations, protecting student privacy, ensuring data security, and maintaining transparency and inclusivity.

Technical Challenges

One of the foremost technical challenges in adopting AI and LA in educational settings is the need for seamless integration with existing Learning Management Systems (LMS) such as Moodle and Blackboard, for example. Many LMS were not initially designed to accommodate sophisticated AI and LA algorithms, creating interoperability and scalability issues (Chen et al., 2020). AI and LA systems also rely heavily on large, high-quality datasets to provide accurate insights and predictions.

However, the availability and quality of data vary across institutions, which can impact the reliability and effectiveness of AI and LA applications. Furthermore, institutions may face significant financial and technical resource constraints in implementing and maintaining these technologies at scale (Dias & Santos, 2022; Mamede & Santos, 2024).

Data Privacy and Security Concerns

AI and LA systems require the collection and analysis of extensive data on student interactions, engagement, and performance, raising concerns about data privacy and security. The General Data Protection Regulation (GDPR) in Europe and similar regulations worldwide have set strict guidelines on how student data must be collected, stored, and used, imposing accountability on institutions to protect student information (Marler & Boudreau, 2017). Ensuring compliance with these regulations requires institutions to invest in secure data storage and processing solutions, which may not always be feasible, especially for smaller educational institutions.

Additionally, data security risks such as unauthorized access or data breaches pose significant threats to student privacy. If AI and LA systems are not secured properly, sensitive data could be exposed, leading to potential misuse and loss of student trust in educational technologies. Implementing encryption, access control, and secure data storage are essential steps to safeguard against these risks and to establish a robust ethical framework for using AI and LA in education (Ahmed, 2020).

Algorithmic Bias and Fairness

AI algorithms are not immune to biases, which can result in unintended, inequitable outcomes. Since AI systems often learn from historical data, any existing biases within these datasets may be perpetuated in AI-driven educational decisions. For instance, certain groups of students might receive disproportionately different recommendations or be inaccurately identified as "at-risk" based on biased historical patterns. As noted by Boikanyo (Boikanyo, 2024), the risk of algorithmic bias necessitates careful evaluation of the datasets used and consistent monitoring to ensure AI applications promote equitable learning opportunities across diverse student populations.

Ensuring fairness requires that educational institutions adopt transparent practices in the development and deployment of AI systems. According to Cascio (Cascio, 2019), transparency in AI algorithms is critical for building trust among users, allowing both students and educators to understand how decisions are made and to challenge them if needed. Regular audits and algorithm reviews are essential to identify and mitigate biases that may exist within AI-driven educational tools, fostering an inclusive learning environment.

Ethical Use of Student Data

The ethical use of data is foundational in AI and LA applications in education. Institutions must balance the benefits of personalized, data-driven instruction with the need to protect students' rights to privacy and autonomy. The extensive data collection inherent in LA raises questions about the appropriate limits of data use, consent, and the ownership of student information. Marler & Boudreau (Marler & Boudreau, 2017) emphasize that educational institutions should clearly communicate how student data will be used, obtain informed consent, and ensure that data is used solely for purposes that benefit student learning and engagement.

Furthermore, ethical considerations extend to the transparency and accountability of AI-driven recommendations. For instance, when AI systems suggest interventions or modifications to a student's learning path, it is essential that educators are involved in interpreting and implementing these recommendations, as the consequences of AI-driven decisions directly impact students' educational experiences (Lim et al., 2024). Maintaining human oversight ensures that decisions reflect educational values and ethical standards rather than relying solely on automated processes.

Balancing Automation and Human Interaction

While AI and LA offer powerful tools for automating feedback, assessment, and administrative tasks, there is an ongoing concern about over-reliance on automation, potentially diminishing valuable human interactions in the learning process. Chatbots and automated grading systems can be highly effective in managing routine tasks and providing timely feedback. However, these technologies cannot replace the nuanced understanding and empathy that educators bring to student interactions (Chen et al., 2020). As noted by Hasanov et al. (Hasanov et al., 2019), maintaining a balance between automated and human interaction is essential to preserving the quality of the educational experience and ensuring that students receive the support and guidance they need.

Institutions should strive to use AI and LA to complement, rather than replace, the role of educators. By automating repetitive tasks, AI and LA allow educators to dedicate more time to personalized interactions, mentorship, and complex problem-solving with students. This balanced approach leverages the strengths of

AI while retaining the irreplaceable value of human engagement in education (Dias & Santos, 2022).

Addressing the challenges and ethical considerations associated with AI and LA in education is critical to their successful and responsible implementation. Ensuring technical interoperability, protecting student privacy, preventing algorithmic bias, and upholding ethical data practices are essential to building trustworthy, equitable AI and LA systems. As educational institutions continue to integrate these technologies, a commitment to transparency, fairness, and accountability will be necessary to foster a supportive and inclusive learning environment.

With responsible practices in place, AI and LA have the potential to enhance educational experiences and expand access to personalized, high-quality learning in ways that respect and support every student's unique educational journey.

5. CONCLUSIONS AND FUTURE IMPLEMENTATION WITH AI

The integration of Artificial Intelligence (AI) and Learning Analytics (LA) in education marks a paradigm shift, enabling personalized, efficient, and adaptive learning experiences that are especially critical in distance learning. By combining AI's predictive capabilities with LA's data-driven insights, educational institutions can better meet individual student needs, promote engagement, and improve academic outcomes. However, the successful implementation of AI and LA in educational settings depends on addressing key technical, ethical, and organizational challenges, ensuring that these technologies are used responsibly and inclusively.

Research pinpoints efforts to create adaptive learning environments using AI and LA have already yielded promising results, particularly in personalizing instructional content to suit diverse student backgrounds and learning preferences. AI-powered systems, including Intelligent Tutoring Systems (ITS) and adaptive learning platforms, dynamically adjust content based on real-time data, helping students learn at their own pace and offering targeted interventions when needed (Dias & Santos, 2022). This work, emphasized by several ongoing research, is foundational for creating AI-enhanced educational ecosystems where the learning experience continuously adapts to each student's progress, thereby promoting retention and improving student outcomes in distance education.

Looking forward, future implementations of AI in education may expand further with emerging technologies like augmented reality (AR) and virtual reality (VR), for example. These immersive technologies can be integrated with AI and LA to create highly engaging, interactive environments that transcend the limitations of traditional classroom and distance learning formats. By simulating real-world scenarios, AR and VR could allow students to engage in hands-on, experiential learning while receiving real-time feedback from AI-driven systems. According to Hasanov et al. (Hasanov et al., 2019), combining these immersive technologies with AI enables institutions to deliver learning experiences that are not only more engaging but also aligned with industry demands, preparing students for careers in complex, skill-intensive fields.

Furthermore, the use of AI and LA to support predictive analytics is poised to play an increasingly significant role in education. By analyzing historical data and learning patterns, AI systems can anticipate student needs, enabling early intervention for those at risk of academic challenges or disengagement. As outlined in this chapter, predictive analytics allows institutions to proactively address issues like dropout rates, which are particularly high in distance learning environments. With early warning systems in place, educational institutions can provide targeted support and resources to students in need, fostering a more inclusive and supportive learning environment (Ahmed, 2020; Dias & Santos, 2022).

AI and LA are also reshaping the roles of educators. By automating administrative tasks, grading, and certain types of feedback, AI allows educators to focus more on mentoring, facilitating, and providing complex guidance. This shift positions educators as mentors and guides who support students in developing critical thinking, creativity, and problem-solving skills that go beyond routine assessments (Chen et al., 2020). As AI-driven tools continue to evolve, they will offer more sophisticated insights and recommendations, allowing educators to make data-informed decisions that enhance the quality of education. Current research emphasizes that AI and LA should be used to complement, rather than replace, the role of educators, ensuring that human interaction remains a core element of the learning process (Marler & Boudreau, 2017).

As AI and LA become more prevalent in educational settings, addressing ethical considerations around data privacy and algorithmic fairness will be essential to ensuring equitable access for all students. Responsible data practices, including transparency, consent, and data security, are foundational for building student trust in AI systems. With regulations like the General Data Protection Regulation (GDPR) in place, institutions must establish stringent protocols to protect student information and prevent misuse (Marler & Boudreau, 2017). Current research also highlights the importance of ongoing research into the ethical implications of AI in education, as well as the need for institutions to adopt fair and transparent practices to mitigate potential biases and uphold ethical standards (Boikanyo, 2024).

As an example, Dias´ research (Dias & Santos, 2022) proposes a Learning Analytics framework designed to optimize the use of Learning Management Systems in organizational or educational contexts. However, expanding LA framework functionalities will require exploration of data analysis models that integrate emerging technologies, such as augmented reality and advanced artificial intelligence, as well as promoting digital competency development among educators and LMS administrators. Furthermore, the importance of ethical data management practices remains significant, as student data privacy and security are ongoing concerns. Future research should consider cultural and technical adaptations for LA frameworks' success across varied organizational contexts.

In conclusion, the future of AI and LA in education offers a promising path toward creating dynamic, personalized, and inclusive learning environments. Building on the foundational work outlined previously, educational institutions can leverage AI and LA to address diverse student needs, reduce dropout rates, and foster a more adaptable educational ecosystem. However, to realize this potential, institutions must commit to ethical, transparent, and responsible use of these technologies. By focusing on inclusivity, data security, and student-centred approaches, AI and LA can reshape education, making it more responsive, effective, and accessible for all learners in an increasingly digital world.

REFERENCES

Ahmed, O. (2020). *Artificial Intelligence in Human Resources*. OSF. https://doi.org/DOI: 10.31221/osf.io/cfwvm

Blackmon, S. J., & Moore, R. L. (2020). A Framework to Support Interdisciplinary Engagement with Learning Analytics. In Ifenthaler, D., & Gibson, D. (Eds.), *Adoption of Data Analytics in Higher Education Learning and Teaching* (pp. 39–52). Springer International Publishing., DOI: 10.1007/978-3-030-47392-1_3

Boikanyo, D. H. (2024). Utilization of 4ir technologies to enhance strategic intelligence and dynamic capabilities for a sustainable competitive advantage. *Business Excellence & Management*, *14*(1), 5–24.

Bradley, V. M. (2021). Learning Management System (LMS) Use with Online Instruction. *International Journal of Technology in Education*, *4*(1), 68–92.

Brown, M. (2012). *Learning Analytics: Moving from Concept to Practice | EDUCAUSE Library*. https://library.educause.edu/resources/2012/7/learning-analytics-moving-from-concept-to-practice

Cascio, W. F. (2019). Training trends: Macro, micro, and policy issues. *Human Resource Management Review*, *29*(2), 284–297. DOI: 10.1016/j.hrmr.2017.11.001

Chen, L., Chen, P., & Lin, Z. (2020). Artificial Intelligence in Education: A Review. *IEEE Access*, *8*, 75264–75278. IEEE Access. DOI: 10.1109/ACCESS.2020.2988510

Christopoulos, A., Pellas, N., & Laakso, M.-J. (2020). A learning analytics theoretical framework for stem education virtual reality applications. *Education Sciences*, *10*(11), 1–15. *Scopus*. Advance online publication. DOI: 10.3390/educsci10110317

Dias, J., & Santos, A. (2022). Learning Analytics Framework Applied to Training Context. In Reis, A., Barroso, J., Martins, P., Jimoyiannis, A., Huang, R. Y.-M., & Henriques, R. (Eds.), *Technology and Innovation in Learning, Teaching and Education* (pp. 110–130). Springer Nature Switzerland., DOI: 10.1007/978-3-031-22918-3_9

Dias, J., & Santos, A. (2022). *Learning Analytics Framework Applied to Training Context* [Master Thesis, Instituto Superior Técnico]. https://fenix.tecnico.ulisboa.pt/cursos/mise/dissertacao/1972678479055490

Greller, W., & Drachsler, H. (2012). Translating Learning into Numbers: A Generic Framework for Learning Analytics. *Journal of Educational Technology & Society*, *15*(3), 42–57.

Hasanov, A., Laine, T. H., & Chung, T.-S. (2019). A survey of adaptive context-aware learning environments. *Journal of Ambient Intelligence and Smart Environments*, *11*(5), 403–428.

Ifenthaler, D., & Yau, J. Y.-K. (2020). Utilising learning analytics to support study success in higher education: A systematic review. *Educational Technology Research and Development*, *68*(4), 1961–1990. DOI: 10.1007/s11423-020-09788-z

Kleimola, R., & Leppisaari, I. (2022). Learning analytics to develop future competences in higher education: A case study. *International Journal of Educational Technology in Higher Education*, *19*(1), 17. DOI: 10.1186/s41239-022-00318-w

Lim, Z. Y., Yap, J. H., Lai, J. W., Mokhtar, I. A., Yeo, D. J., & Cheong, K. H. (2024). Advancing Lifelong Learning in the Digital Age: A Narrative Review of Singapore's SkillsFuture Programme. *Social Sciences (2076-0760)*, *13*(2), 73.

Limna, P., Jakwatanatham, S., Siripipattanakul, S., Kaewpuang, P., & Sriboonruang, P. (2022). *A Review of Artificial Intelligence (AI) in Education during the Digital Era* (SSRN Scholarly Paper No. 4160798). Social Science Research Network. https://papers.ssrn.com/abstract=4160798

Lodge, J. M., Horvath, J. C., & Corrin, L. (2018). *Learning Analytics in the Classroom: Translating Learning Analytics Research for Teachers*. Routledge.

Macfadyen, L. P. (2022). Institutional Analytics. Em C. Lang, G. Siemens, & A. F. Wise (Eds.), *The Handbook of Learning Analytics* (2.ª ed., pp. 173–186). SOLAR. DOI: 10.18608/hla22.017

Mamede, H. S., & Santos, A. (2024). Creating Learning Organizations Through Digital Transformation. Em Https://services.igi-global.com/resolvedoi/resolve.aspx?doi=10.4018/979-8-3693-0556-0. IGI Global. https://www.igi-global.com/book/creating-learning-organizations-through-digital/www.igi-global.com/book/creating-learning-organizations-through-digital/323358

Marler, J. H., & Boudreau, J. W. (2017). An evidence-based review of HR Analytics. *International Journal of Human Resource Management*, *28*(1), 3–26. DOI: 10.1080/09585192.2016.1244699

Rodrigues, M. W., Isotani, S., & Zárate, L. E. (2018). Educational Data Mining: A review of evaluation process in the e-learning. *Telematics and Informatics*, *35*(6), 1701–1717. DOI: 10.1016/j.tele.2018.04.015

Shurygin, V., Berestova, A., Litvinova, T., Kolpak, E., & Nureyeva, A. (2021). Universal Models and Platforms in E-Learning. [Education Source.]. *International Journal of Emerging Technologies in Learning*, *16*(9), 63–75.

Tapalova, O., & Zhiyenbayeva, N. (2022). Artificial Intelligence in Education: AIEd for Personalised Learning Pathways. *Electronic Journal of E-Learning, 20*(5). *Electronic Journal of e-Learning*, *5*(5), 639–653. Advance online publication. DOI: 10.34190/ejel.20.5.2597

Tsai, Y.-S., Whitelock-Wainwright, A., & Gašević, D. (2021). More Than Figures on Your Laptop: (Dis)trustful Implementation of Learning Analytics. *Journal of Learning Analytics, 8*(3). *Journal of Learning Analytics*, *3*(3), 81–100. Advance online publication. DOI: 10.18608/jla.2021.7379

Upadhyay, A. K., & Khandelwal, K. (2019). Artificial intelligence-based training learning from application. *Development and Learning in Organizations*, *33*(2), 20–23. DOI: 10.1108/DLO-05-2018-0058

Ye, D. (2022). The History and Development of Learning Analytics in Learning, Design, & Technology Field. *TechTrends*, *66*(4), 607–615. DOI: 10.1007/s11528-022-00720-1

Compilation of References

Adedoyin, O. B., & Soykan, E. (2020). COVID-19 pandemic and online learning: The challenges and opportunities. *Interactive Learning Environments*, *28*(4), 357–366. DOI: 10.1080/10494820.2020.1813180

Agarwal, M. B., & Lahoti, Y. (2023). Transforming education: The impact and potential of artificial intelligence in personalized learning environments. *Journal for ReAttach Therapy and Developmental Diversities*, *6*(1), 1754–1761.

Ahmed, O. (2020). *Artificial Intelligence in Human Resources*. OSF. https://doi.org/DOI: 10.31221/osf.io/cfwvm

Al-Azawei, A., Serenelli, F., & Lundqvist, K. (2020). Developing an accessible e-learning system: An exploration of the relationship between accessibility and user satisfaction. *Journal of Educational Technology & Society*, *23*(1), 88–98.

Alenezi, A. (2023). Teacher perspectives on AI-driven gamification: Impact on student motivation, engagement, and learning outcomes.

Aljawarneh, Nader Mohammad. "Effect of User Satisfaction between Cloud Learning Applications & University Education Agility." (2024).

Allen, I. E., & Seaman, J. (2013). *Changing Course: Ten Years of Tracking Online Education in the United States*. Babson Survey Research Group. Retrieved from https://www.babson.edu

Allen, I. E., & Seaman, J. (2017). *Digital learning compass: Distance education enrollment report 2017*. Babson Survey Research Group. https://www.onlinelearningsurvey.com/reports/digtiallearningcompass.pdf

Allen, I. E., & Seaman, J. (2017). *Digital Learning Compass: Distance Education Enrollment Report 2017*. Babson Survey Research Group. Retrieved from https://www.babson.edu

Almarashdeh, I., & Alzahrani, A. (2021). The impact of artificial intelligence on higher education: A review of the literature. *Journal of Education and Learning, 10*(4), 61–73. DOI: 10.5539/jel.v10n4p61

Almulla, M., Alanazi, H., & Alshammari, S. (2022). The impact of artificial intelligence on education: A systematic review. *Educational Technology Research and Development, 70*(4), 757–778. DOI: 10.1007/s11423-022-10140-1

Almusaed, A., Almssad, A., Yitmen, I., & Homod, R. Z. (2023). Enhancing student engagement: Harnessing "AIED"'s power in hybrid education—A review analysis. *Education Sciences, 13*(7), 632.78.

Alpaydin, E. (2020). Introduction to Machine Learning (4th ed.). MIT Press.Mitchell, T. M. (1997). *Machine Learning*. McGraw-Hill.Jurafsky, D., & Martin, J. H. (2020). *Speech and Language Processing* (3rd ed.). Pearson.Chen, M., & Zhu, Q. (2019). "Applications of Natural Language Processing in Education: A Review." *Education and Information Technologies*, 24(3), 1695-1716.

Anderson, T., & Dron, J. (2011). Three generations of distance education pedagogy. *International Review of Research in Open and Distance Learning, 12*(3), 80–97. DOI: 10.19173/irrodl.v12i3.890

Arnold, K. E., & Pistilli, M. D. (2012). Course signals at Purdue: Using learning analytics to increase student success. In *Proceedings of the 2nd International Conference on Learning Analytics and Knowledge* (pp. 267–270). DOI: 10.1145/2330601.2330666

Ayeni, O. O., Al Hamad, N. M., Chisom, O. N., Osawaru, B., & Adewusi, O. E. (2024). AI in education: A review of personalized learning and educational technology. *GSC Advanced Research and Reviews, 18*(2), 261–271.

Baba, K., Faddouli, E., & Cheimanoff, N. (2024). Mobile-optimized AI-driven personalized learning: A case study at Mohammed VI Polytechnic University. *International Journal of Interactive Mobile Technologies, 18*(4).

Baker, R. K., & Inventado, P. S. (2014). Educational data mining and learning analytics. In Learning, Design, and Technology (pp. 1-24). Springer.

Baker, R. S. J. D., & Inventado, P. S. (2014). Educational data mining and learning analytics. In Learning, Education and Data Mining: A Systematic Review (pp. 43-56). Springer.

Baker, R. K. (2023). Leveraging AI and learning analytics in education. *International Journal of Educational Technology in Higher Education, 20*(1), 10–29. PMID: 36811132

Baker, R. K., D'Mello, S., & Inventado, P. (2022). Exploring the role of AI in fostering inclusive education. *Journal of Learning Analytics*, *9*(2), 25–37.

Baker, R. S. (2016). Stupid Tutoring Systems: The Current State of Educational Technology. *International Journal of Artificial Intelligence in Education*, *26*(4), 148–164.

Baker, R. S. (2019). Challenges for the future of educational data mining: The Baker learning analytics prerequisites. *Journal of Educational Data Mining*, *11*(1), 1–17.

Baker, R. S. J. D. (2014). Educational data mining: An overview. In *Handbook of learning analytics* (pp. 3–16). Society for Learning Analytics Research., DOI: 10.1007/978-1-4614-3305-7_4

Baker, R. S. J. D., Corbett, A. T., & Koedinger, K. R. (2019). Developing a learning analytics framework. In *Handbook of Learning Analytics* (pp. 59–72). Society for Learning Analytics Research.

Baker, R. S., & Siemens, G. (2014). Educational data mining and learning analytics. *Learning Analytics Review*, *1*(3), 33–49.

Barocas, S., Hardt, M., & Narayanan, A. (2019). Fairness and machine learning. https://fairmlbook.org/

Barrera Castro, G. P., Chiappe, A., Becerra Rodríguez, D. F., & Gonzalo Sepulveda, F. (2024). Harnessing AI for education 4.0: Drivers of personalized learning. *Electronic Journal of e-Learning*, *22*(5), 01–14. DOI: 10.34190/ejel.22.5.3467

Benson, V., & Torkzadeh, G. (2021). E-learning and distance education technologies: Future directions. *Journal of Management Information Systems*, *38*(1), 43–62.

Bin Salem, I. (2024). Integrating artificial intelligence in personalized learning: A future-oriented approach to enhance student engagement and achievement. *International Journal of Post Axial: Futuristic Teaching and Learning*, 111-119.

Binns, R. (2018). "Fairness in Machine Learning: Lessons from Political Philosophy." *Proceedings of the 2018 Conference on Fairness, Accountability, and Transparency*.

Bishop, C. M. (2006). *Pattern recognition and machine learning*. Springer.

Biswas, R. A., & Molla, A. (2024). Impact of artificial intelligence on personalized learning. In *Artificial intelligence in education* (p. 302).

Black, A. (2023). *Analytics: Data-informed decision-making for educators*. Blackboard Learn. Retrieved from Blackboard.

Blackmon, S. J., & Moore, R. L. (2020). A Framework to Support Interdisciplinary Engagement with Learning Analytics. In Ifenthaler, D., & Gibson, D. (Eds.), *Adoption of Data Analytics in Higher Education Learning and Teaching* (pp. 39–52). Springer International Publishing., DOI: 10.1007/978-3-030-47392-1_3

Bloom, B. S. (1956). *Taxonomy of educational objectives: The classification of educational goals*. Longman.

Bobadilla, J., Ortega, F., Serradilla, F., & Hernando, A. (2013). Collaborative Filtering and Recommendation Systems: A Review. *ACM Computing Surveys*, *45*(3), 19.

Boikanyo, D. H. (2024). Utilization of 4ir technologies to enhance strategic intelligence and dynamic capabilities for a sustainable competitive advantage. *Business Excellence & Management*, *14*(1), 5–24.

Bradley, V. M. (2021). Learning Management System (LMS) Use with Online Instruction. *International Journal of Technology in Education*, *4*(1), 68–92.

Braun, V., & Clarke, V. (2006). Using thematic analysis in psychology. *Qualitative Research in Psychology*, *3*(2), 77–101. DOI: 10.1191/1478088706qp063oa

Brown, M. (2012). *Learning Analytics: Moving from Concept to Practice | EDUCAUSE Library*. https://library.educause.edu/resources/2012/7/learning-analytics-moving-from-concept-to-practice

Brusilovsky, P., & Millán, E. (2007). User modeling in personalized learning environments. In *User Modeling 2007* (pp. 1–18). Springer., DOI: 10.1007/978-3-540-73078-1_1

Brynjolfsson, E., & McAfee, A. (2014). *The second machine age: Work, progress, and prosperity in a time of brilliant technologies*. W. W. Norton & Company.

Calvo, R. A., & D'Mello, S. K. (2010). Affect detection: An interdisciplinary review of the literature. *IEEE Transactions on Affective Computing*, *1*(1), 18–37. DOI: 10.1109/T-AFFC.2010.1

Cascio, W. F. (2019). Training trends: Macro, micro, and policy issues. *Human Resource Management Review*, *29*(2), 284–297. DOI: 10.1016/j.hrmr.2017.11.001

Castro, G. P. B., Chiappe, A., Rodríguez, D. F. B., & Sepulveda, F. G. (2024). Harnessing AI for education 4.0: Drivers of personalized learning. *Electronic Journal of e-Learning, 22*(5), 01-14.

Chen, C. M., & Hwang, G. J. (2018). "Personalized Learning Environments in Distance Education: A Systematic Review." *Computers & Education*, 126, 1-14.Dziuban, C., Hartman, J., & Moskal, P. (2004). "Blended Learning." *Educause Center for Applied Research.*

Chen, L., Chen, P., & Lin, Z. (2020). Artificial Intelligence in Education: A Review. *IEEE Access, 8*, 75264–75278. IEEE Access. DOI: 10.1109/ACCESS.2020.2988510

Chen, L., Xie, H., & Zhu, X. (2020). Personalized learning in higher education: An artificial intelligence perspective. *International Journal of Educational Technology in Higher Education*, *17*(1), 1–19. DOI: 10.1186/s41239-020-00217-5

Christopoulos, A., Pellas, N., & Laakso, M.-J. (2020). A learning analytics theoretical framework for stem education virtual reality applications. *Education Sciences*, *10*(11), 1–15. *Scopus*. Advance online publication. DOI: 10.3390/educsci10110317

Cohen, J., & Kahn, B. (2021). The ethical implications of AI in education: A policy perspective. *International Journal of Educational Technology in Higher Education*, *18*(1), 1–15. DOI: 10.1186/s41239-021-00254-x

Construction and Innovative Exploration of Personalized Learning Systems in the Context of Educational Data Mining. (•••).. . *International Journal of Information and Communication Technology Education*, *20*(1), 1–14. DOI: 10.4018/ijicte.2014010107

Creswell, J. W., & Creswell, J. D. (2018). *Research design: Qualitative, quantitative, and mixed methods approaches* (5th ed.). SAGE Publications.

Creswell, J. W., & Plano Clark, V. L. (2018). *Designing and conducting mixed methods research* (3rd ed.). SAGE Publications.

Czerkawski, B. C., & Lyman, E. W. (2016). Beyond the "one size fits all": Differentiating instruction using artificial intelligence in online learning environments. *International Journal of Educational Technology in Higher Education*, *13*(1), 1–10. DOI: 10.1186/s41239-016-0004-5

Czerkawski, B. C., & Lyman, E. W. (2016). Beyond the LMS: A framework for learning analytics in online courses. *International Journal of Online Pedagogy and Course Design*, *6*(2), 27–41. DOI: 10.4018/IJOPCD.2016040103

D'Mello, S. K., & Graesser, A. C. (2015). Feeling, thinking, and computing: A review of the affective computing literature. *International Journal of Artificial Intelligence in Education*, *25*(1), 1–13. DOI: 10.1007/s40593-014-0028-0

D'Mello, S. K., & Graesser, A. C. (2015). Feeling, thinking, and computing: The role of affect in learning with technology. In O'Reilly, H. K. E., Zhang, K. W. H. F., & Graesser, A. C. (Eds.), *The Cambridge handbook of the learning sciences* (pp. 305–325). Cambridge University Press., DOI: 10.1017/CBO9781139819085.021

Dandachi, I. E. (2024). AI-powered personalized learning: Toward sustainable education. In *Navigating the intersection of business, sustainability and technology* (pp. 109–118). Springer Nature Singapore.

Dawson, S., & Siemens, G. (2014). Analytics to literacies: The development of a learning analytics framework for multiliteracies assessment. *International Review of Research in Open and Distance Learning*, *15*(4). Advance online publication. DOI: 10.19173/irrodl.v15i4.1878

Deci, E. L., & Ryan, R. M. (2000). The "what" and "why" of goal pursuits: Human needs and the self-determination of behavior. *Psychological Inquiry*, *11*(4), 227–268. DOI: 10.1207/S15327965PLI1104_01

Delen, E., & Gamage, D. (2013). The role of learning analytics in higher education: A systematic review. *Journal of Educational Technology & Society*, *16*(1), 114–125.

Deterding, S., Dixon, D., Khaled, R., & Nacke, L. (2011). From game design elements to gamefulness: defining" gamification." In Proceedings of the 15th international academic MindTrek conference: Envisioning future media environments (pp. 9-15). DOI: 10.1145/2181037.2181040

Dias, J., & Santos, A. (2022). *Learning Analytics Framework Applied to Training Context* [Master Thesis, Instituto Superior Técnico]. https://fenix.tecnico.ulisboa.pt/cursos/mise/dissertacao/1972678479055490

Dias, J., & Santos, A. (2022). Learning Analytics Framework Applied to Training Context. In Reis, A., Barroso, J., Martins, P., Jimoyiannis, A., Huang, R. Y.-M., & Henriques, R. (Eds.), *Technology and Innovation in Learning, Teaching and Education* (pp. 110–130). Springer Nature Switzerland., DOI: 10.1007/978-3-031-22918-3_9

Dignum, V. (2019). Responsible Artificial Intelligence: Designing AI for Human Values. *Computer*, *52*(8), 28–36.

Djaouti, D., Alvarez, J., & Jessel, J.-P. (2011). Classifying Serious Games: The G/P/S Model. In Handbook of Research on Improving Learning and Motivation through Educational Games: Multidisciplinary Approaches (pp. 118–136). IGI Global. DOI: 10.4018/978-1-60960-495-0.ch006

DreamBox Learning. (2021). "The Impact of DreamBox Learning on K-12 Student Achievement." McKinsey & Company. (2019). "Georgia State University: Transforming Student Outcomes through Predictive Analytics."

Dziuban, C., Graham, C. R., Moskal, P. D., Norberg, A., & Sicilia, N. (2018). Blended learning: The new normal and emerging technologies. *International Journal of Educational Technology in Higher Education*, *15*(1), 3. DOI: 10.1186/s41239-017-0087-5

Ellikkal, A., & Rajamohan, S. (2024). *AI-enabled personalized learning: Empowering management students for improving engagement and academic performance*. Vilakshan-XIMB Journal of Management.

Engeström, Y. (1987). *Learning by Expanding: An Activity-Theoretical Approach to Developmental Research*. Orienta-Konsultit.

European Commission. (2018). "General Data Protection Regulation (GDPR)." Retrieved from https://ec.europa.eu/info/law/law-topic/data-protection_enO'Neil, C. (2016). *Weapons of Math Destruction: How Big Data Increases Inequality and Threatens Democracy*. Crown Publishing Group.

European Union. (2016). General Data Protection Regulation (GDPR). Retrieved from GDPR.

Experience, A. P. I. (xAPI) Standard. (n.d.). ADL Initiative. Retrieved July 15, 2024, from https://adlnet.gov/projects/xapi/

Feng, S., Wang, T., & Lin, H. (2023). The role of AI in education: Transforming learning through technology. *International Journal of Educational Technology in Higher Education*, *20*(1), 12–28. PMID: 36883192

Ferguson, R. (2012). Learning analytics: Drivers, developments and challenges. *International Journal of Technology Enhanced Learning*, *4*(5), 304–317. DOI: 10.1504/IJTEL.2012.051314

Ferguson, R. (2012). Learning analytics: Drivers, developments, and challenges. *International Journal of Technology Enhanced Learning*, *4*(5), 304–317. DOI: 10.1504/IJTEL.2012.051816

Ferguson, R., Shum, S. B., & McAndrew, P. (2016). Learning analytics to identify exploratory dialogue within synchronous text chat. *Learning Analytics Review*, *6*, 1–21. DOI: 10.18608/jla.2016.32

Fredricks, J. A., Blumenfeld, P. C., & Paris, A. H. (2004). "School Engagement: Potential of the Concept, State of the Evidence." *Review of Educational Research*, 74(1), 59-109. Deterding, S. (2011). "Gamification: Designing for Motivation." *Interactions*, 18(4), 14-17. LinkKapp, K. M. (2012). *Gamification in Training and Education: What, Why, and How.*

García, I., Ayllón, F., & López, C. (2020). The ethical and social implications of AI in education: A systematic review. *Education and Information Technologies*, *25*(4), 3135–3156. DOI: 10.1007/s10639-020-10332-8

García-Peñalvo, F. J., Cruz-Benito, J., & Rodríguez-Conde, M. J. (2020). Educational innovation and learning analytics. *Journal of Universal Computer Science*, *26*(4), 476–486. DOI: 10.3217/jucs-026-04-0476

Garrison, D. R., & Anderson, T. (2003). E-learning in the 21st century: A community of inquiry framework for building online learning communities. Routledge.

Garrison, D. R., Anderson, T., & Archer, W. (2000). Critical inquiry in a text-based environment: Computer conferencing in higher education. *The Internet and Higher Education*, *2*(2), 87–105. DOI: 10.1016/S1096-7516(00)00016-6

Garrison, D. R., & Vaughan, N. D. (2008). *Blended learning in higher education: Framework, principles, and guidelines*. Jossey-Bass.

Gašević, D., Dawson, S., & Siemens, G. (2015). Let's not forget: Learning analytics are about learning. *TechTrends*, *59*(1), 64–71. DOI: 10.1007/s11528-014-0822-x

Gilpin, L. H., Zollers, F., & Yalcin, A. (2018). Explaining explanations: An overview of interpretability of machine learning. In 2018 IEEE 5th International Conference on Data Science and Advanced Analytics (DSAA) (pp. 80-89). DOI: 10.1109/DSAA.2018.00018

Gonzalez, A. I., Caballero, R., & Nunez, A. (2021). AI and student engagement: A case study in higher education. *Journal of Computer Assisted Learning*, *37*(1), 23–32. DOI: 10.1111/jcal.12475

Goodfellow, I., Bengio, Y., & Courville, A. (2016). *Deep learning*. MIT Press.

Gordon, R., Vang, C., & O'Neill, R. (2021). The power of social and behavioral analytics in education. *Journal of Learning Analytics*, *8*(2), 19–31. DOI: 10.18608/jla.2021.82.3

Grau-Valldosera, J., & Minguillón, J. (2014). Rethinking dropout in online higher education: The case of the Universitat Oberta de Catalunya. *International Review of Research in Open and Distance Learning*, *15*(1), 290–308. DOI: 10.19173/irrodl.v15i1.1628

Greller, W., & Drachsler, H. (2012). Translating Learning into Numbers: A Generic Framework for Learning Analytics. *Journal of Educational Technology & Society*, *15*(3), 42–57.

Harris, A. J., Hovey, A. L., & Wyman, M. (2020). Protecting student data in educational research: Ethical and legal considerations. *Educational Researcher*, *49*(2), 104–112. DOI: 10.3102/0013189X20914383

Hasanov, A., Laine, T. H., & Chung, T.-S. (2019). A survey of adaptive context-aware learning environments. *Journal of Ambient Intelligence and Smart Environments*, *11*(5), 403–428.

Hattie, J., & Donoghue, G. (2016). Learning strategies: A synthesis and meta-analysis. *Educational Psychologist*, *51*(3), 247–265.

Hattie, J., & Timperley, H. (2007). The power of feedback. *Review of Educational Research*, *77*(1), 81–112. DOI: 10.3102/003465430298487

Henrie, C. R., Halverson, L. R., & Graham, C. R. (2015). Measuring student engagement in technology-mediated learning: A review. *Computers & Education*, *90*, 36–53. DOI: 10.1016/j.compedu.2015.09.005

He, Y., Chen, S., & Huang, T. (2019). Real-time learning analytics in a blended learning environment. *Journal of Educational Technology & Society*, *22*(4), 57–70. https://www.jstor.org/stable/26705000

Hodges, C., Moore, S., Lockee, B., Trust, T., & Bond, A. (2020). The difference between emergency remote teaching and online learning. *EDUCAUSE Review*, *27*(2). https://er.educause.edu/articles/2020/3/the-difference-between-emergency-remote-teaching-and-online-learning

Hollands, F. M., & Tirthali, D. (2014). Online learning and student outcomes: A systematic review of the evidence. *Online Learning : the Official Journal of the Online Learning Consortium*, *18*(3), 115–138. DOI: 10.24059/olj.v18i3.490

Holmes et al. (2019) Zawacki-Richter et al.,(2019), (Luckin et al., 2016), (Zawacki-Richter et al., 2019), (Zawacki-Richter et al., 2019).

Holmes, W., Bialik, M., & Fadel, C. (2021). Artificial Intelligence in Education: Promises and Implications for Teaching and Learning. Center for Curriculum Redesign. https://curriculumredesign.org/wp-content/uploads/AI-in-Education-Report-2021.pdf

Holmes, W., Bialik, M., & Fadel, C. (2019). *Artificial intelligence in education: Promises and implications for teaching and learning*. Center for Curriculum Redesign.

Holmes, W., Bialik, M., & Fadel, C. (2019). *Artificial Intelligence in Education: Promises and Implications for Teaching and Learning*. Center for Curriculum Redesign.

Holstein, K., Wortman, J., Daumé, H.III, & Dudik, M. (2019). Improving fairness in machine learning systems: A survey. *SIGKDD Explorations*, *21*(2), 18–20. DOI: 10.1145/3361689.3361691

Hsu, C.-C., Chiu, P.-S., & Chang, Y.-S. (2021). Predictive modeling of students' learning behaviors in a MOOC environment. *Interactive Learning Environments*, *29*(5), 753–770. DOI: 10.1080/10494820.2019.1701818

Huang, R. H., & Liaw, S. S. (2021). Artificial intelligence in education: A review. *Journal of Educational Technology & Society*, *24*(1), 10–22. https://www.jstor.org/stable/26996858

Huang, Y., Xu, H., & Ma, X. (2020). Data privacy and security in learning analytics: A systematic review. *Educational Technology Research and Development*, *68*(3), 1643–1669. DOI: 10.1007/s11423-020-09706-3

Huynh-Kim-Bang, B., Wisdom, J., & Labat, J.-M. (2010). Design patterns in Serious Games: A blue print for combining fun and learning. Project SE-SG, 1–18. https://seriousgames.lip6.fr/DesignPatterns/designPatternsForSeriousGames.pdf

Hwang, G. J., Wu, P. H., & Chen, C. H. (2021). AI-based personalized learning: A systematic review and meta-analysis. *Computers & Education*, *175*, 104356. DOI: 10.1016/j.compedu.2021.104356

Ifenthaler, D., & Yau, J. Y. (2020). Utilising learning analytics to support study success in higher education: A systematic review. *Educational Technology Research and Development*, *68*(4), 1829–1851. DOI: 10.1007/s11423-020-09788-z

Ifenthaler, D., & Yau, J. Y.-K. (2020). Utilizing learning analytics to support student engagement: A case study. *Education and Information Technologies*, *25*(4), 3191–3208.

Jannach, D., & Adomavicius, G. (2016). *Recommendation systems: Challenges and research opportunities*. Wiley.

Jensen, L. M., & Konradsen, F. (2018). A review of VR and AR in education: Implications for teacher education. *Journal of Educational Technology & Society, 21*(1), 36–45. https://www.jstor.org/stable/26388439

Jobin, A., Ienca, M., & Andorno, R. (2019). Artificial Intelligence: The Global Landscape of Ethics Guidelines. *Nature Machine Intelligence, 1*(9), 389–399. DOI: 10.1038/s42256-019-0088-2

Kanchon, M. K. H., Sadman, M., Nabila, K. F., Tarannum, R., & Khan, R. (2024). Enhancing personalized learning: AI-driven identification of learning styles and content modification strategies. *International Journal of Cognitive Computing in Engineering, 5*, 269–276. DOI: 10.1016/j.ijcce.2024.06.002

Kapp, K. M. (2012). *Gamification in Training and Education: What*. Why, and How.

Kara, N. (2021). A Systematic Review of the Use of Serious Games in Science Education. *Contemporary Educational Technology, 13*(2), ep295. https://www.cedtech.net/article/asystematic-review-of-the-use-of-serious-games-in-science-education-9608

Katiyar, N., Awasthi, M. V. K., Pratap, R., Mishra, M. K., Shukla, M. N., & Tiwari, M. (2024). AI-driven personalized learning systems: Enhancing educational effectiveness. *Educational Administration: Theory and Practice, 30*(5), 11514–11524.

Kaur, S., Budhraja, K., Pahuja, A., Nayyar, V., & Saluja, S. (2024). Leveraging Artificial Intelligence in Education: Enhancing Learning Experience. In *Ethical AI and Data Management Strategies in Marketing* (pp. 125-140). IGI Global. DOI: DOI: 10.4018/979-8-3693-6660-8

Kay, J., & Knaack, L. (2011). Self-regulated learning in technology-enhanced learning environments. In *Handbook of Self-Regulated Learning and Performance* (pp. 61–79). Routledge.

Keis, O., & Steed, B. (2020). The role of technology in supporting resilient educational practices. *International Review of Education, 66*(4), 439–458.

Kerr, D., & McCormick, R. (2019). Adaptive learning technologies in distance education: A review of the literature. *Educational Technology Research and Development, 67*(6), 1237–1265. DOI: 10.1007/s11423-019-09680-4

Kerr, K. (2016). Adaptive learning technology: How personalized learning works. *Educational Technology Review, 24*(2), 12–24.

Khalil, M., Prinsloo, P., & Slade, S. (2022). A Comparison of Learning Analytics Frameworks: a Systematic Review. *LAK22: 12th International Learning Analytics and Knowledge Conference*, 152–163. DOI: 10.1145/3506860.3506878

Khasawneh, N. A. S., Khasawneh, A. J., Khasawneh, D. M. A. S., & Khasawneh, D. Y. (2024). Improving Arabic Content Delivery on Cloud Computing Platforms for Jordanian E-learning Environments. *Migration Letters : An International Journal of Migration Studies*, *21*(S1), 575–585. DOI: 10.59670/ml.v21iS1.6181

Kim, K. J., & Park, J. H. (2021). The role of artificial intelligence in promoting student engagement in online learning environments. *Computers & Education*, *162*, 104059. DOI: 10.1016/j.compedu.2020.104059

Kitchenham, B. (2004). Procedures for performing systematic reviews. Keele University. https://www.cs.stir.ac.uk/~kitchenham/ systematic_review_process.pdf

Kizilcec, R. F., & Schneider, E. F. (2015). Siemens, G. (2013). "Learning Analytics: The Emergence of a New Learning Discipline." *Journal of Educational Technology & Society*, 16(2), 14-20 114 (17) 4348-4353 https://doi.org/DOI: 10.1073/ pnas.1611898114

Kleimola, R., & Leppisaari, I. (2022). Learning analytics to develop future competences in higher education: A case study. *International Journal of Educational Technology in Higher Education*, *19*(1), 17. DOI: 10.1186/s41239-022-00318-w

Knewton. (2018). Adaptive learning: What is it and how does it work? Retrieved from https://www.knewton.com/adaptive-learning/

Knewton. (2022). Adaptive learning technology. Retrieved from Knewton.

Kukulska-Hulme, A. (2020). Will student learning be different in the future? *Distance Education*, *41*(3), 285–293. DOI: 10.1080/01587919.2020.1776633

Kumar, A., Bala, P. K., Chakraborty, S., & Behera, R. K. (2024). Exploring antecedents impacting user satisfaction with voice assistant app: A text mining-based analysis on Alexa services. *Journal of Retailing and Consumer Services*, *76*, 103586. DOI: 10.1016/j.jretconser.2023.103586

Kumar, K. L., & Sharma, S. (2021). Personalized learning: The potential of AI to drive engagement and success in online education. *Journal of Educational Technology & Society*, *24*(3), 23–35.

Kumar, V., Das, S., & Choudhary, A. (2021). The role of AI in enhancing student engagement in online learning environments. *Journal of Educational Computing Research*, *59*(1), 45–60. DOI: 10.1177/0735633120944516

Lamborn, S., Newmann, F., & Wehlage, G. (1992). The significance and sources of student engagement. *Student engagement and achievement in American secondary schools*, 11-39.

Lathrop, A., & Lathrop, L. (2018). Data governance and privacy: Creating a data management framework. *Educational Research Review*, *25*, 145–158.

Le, D. N., Hoang, V. Q., & Hwang, G. J. (2020). Effects of virtual patient simulation on learning outcomes in nursing education: A systematic review and meta-analysis. *Nurse Education Today*, *90*, 104465. DOI: 10.1016/j.nedt.2020.104465

Lim, Z. Y., Yap, J. H., Lai, J. W., Mokhtar, I. A., Yeo, D. J., & Cheong, K. H. (2024). Advancing Lifelong Learning in the Digital Age: A Narrative Review of Singapore's SkillsFuture Programme. *Social Sciences (2076-0760), 13*(2), 73.

Limna, P., Jakwatanatham, S., Siripipattanakul, S., Kaewpuang, P., & Sriboonruang, P. (2022). *A Review of Artificial Intelligence (AI) in Education during the Digital Era* (SSRN Scholarly Paper No. 4160798). Social Science Research Network. https://papers.ssrn.com/abstract=4160798

List of Cited Literature

Liu, H., Zhao, J., Zhou, L., Yang, J., & Liang, K. (2024). Intelligent performance evaluation of e-commerce express services using machine learning: A case study with quantitative analysis. *Expert Systems with Applications*, *240*, 122511. DOI: 10.1016/j.eswa.2023.122511

Lodge, J. M., Horvath, J. C., & Corrin, L. (2018). *Learning Analytics in the Classroom: Translating Learning Analytics Research for Teachers*. Routledge.

Long, P., & Siemens, G. (2011). Penetrating the fog: Analytics in learning and education. *EDUCAUSE Review*, *46*(5), 30–32.

Lopes, R., & Bidarra, R. (2011). Adaptivity Challenges in Games and Simulations: A Survey. *IEEE Transactions on Computational Intelligence and AI in Games*, *3*(2), 85–99. DOI: 10.1109/TCIAIG.2011.2152841

Luckin, R. (2017). *Enhancing Learning and Teaching with Technology: What the Research Says*. UCL Institute of Education Press.Kober, N. (2015). *Reaching Students: What Research Says About Effective Instruction in Undergraduate Science and Engineering*. National Academies Press.

Luckin, R., Holmes, W., Griffiths, M., & Forcier, L. B. (2016). Intelligence Unleashed: An Argument for AI in Education. Pearson Education. https://www.pearson.com/uk/learners/learn-about-ai-in-education.html

Luckin, R., Holmes, W., Griffiths, M., & Forcier, L. B. (2016). Intelligence unleashed: An argument for AI in education. *Pearson.*https://www.pearson.com/content/dam/one-dot-com/one-dot-com/pedagogical-services/Intelligence-Unleashed-Paper.pdf

Luckin, R., Holmes, W., Griffiths, M., & Forcier, L. B. (2016). *Intelligence unleashed: An argument for AI in education*. Pearson.

Macfadyen, L. P. (2022). Institutional Analytics. Em C. Lang, G. Siemens, & A. F. Wise (Eds.), *The Handbook of Learning Analytics* (2.ª ed., pp. 173–186). SOLAR. DOI: 10.18608/hla22.017

Maghsudi, S., Lan, A., Xu, J., & van Der Schaar, M. (2021). Personalized education in the artificial intelligence era: What to expect next. *IEEE Signal Processing Magazine*, *38*(3), 37–50. DOI: 10.1109/MSP.2021.3055032

Mahmoud, C. F., & Sørensen, J. T. (2024). Artificial intelligence in personalized learning with a focus on current developments and future prospects. *Research and Advances in Education*, *3*(8), 25–31. DOI: 10.56397/RAE.2024.08.04

Mamede, H. S., & Santos, A. (2024). Creating Learning Organizations Through Digital Transformation. Em Https://services.igi-global.com/resolvedoi/resolve.aspx?doi=10.4018/979-8-3693-0556-0. IGI Global. https://www.igi-global.com/book/creating-learning-organizations-through-digital/www.igi-global.com/book/creating-learning-organizations-through-digital/323358

Margaryan, A., Garcia, M., & Littlejohn, A. (2019). Learning analytics in higher education: A review of the literature. *Educational Research Review*, *25*, 30–42. DOI: 10.1016/j.edurev.2019.01.001

Marler, J. H., & Boudreau, J. W. (2017). An evidence-based review of HR Analytics. *International Journal of Human Resource Management*, *28*(1), 3–26. DOI: 10.1080/09585192.2016.1244699

Mayer, R. E. (2014). Computer games for learning: An evidence-based approach. MIT Press. https://www.google.com/books?hl=pt-BR&lr=&id=VckIBAAAQBAJ&oi=fnd&pg=PR7&dq=Mayer+2014+game+review&ots=5xIU86Tf9F&sig=5dQmaQfr4NlEcBWIl8YNHmJgnHc

McFarlane, A., & Sakai, K. (2018). The challenges of artificial intelligence in education: A critical perspective. *AI & Society*, *33*(4), 503–515. DOI: 10.1007/s00146-018-0852-4

Mikhael, J., Murray, S., & Lang, C. (2022). The effects of AI-driven personalized learning on student performance: A meta-analysis. *Journal of Educational Psychology*, *114*(4), 730–748. DOI: 10.1037/edu0000614

Mishra, P., & Koehler, M. J. (2006). Technological pedagogical content knowledge: A framework for teacher knowledge.

Moore, M. G., Dickson-Deane, C., & Galyen, K. (2011). e-Learning, online learning, and distance learning environments: Are they the same? *The Internet and Higher Education*, *14*(2), 129–135. DOI: 10.1016/j.iheduc.2010.10.001

Moore, M. G., & Kearsley, G. (2012). *Distance education: A systems view of online learning* (3rd ed.). Wadsworth Publishing.

Moore, M. G., & Kearsley, G. (2012). *Distance Education: A Systems View of Online Learning*. Wadsworth Cengage Learning.

Muilenburg, L. Y., & Berge, Z. L. (2005). Student Barriers to Online Learning: A Factor Analytic Study. *The Distance Education Report*, *9*(4), 7–8.

Mukul, E., & Büyüközkan, G. (2023). Digital transformation in education: A systematic review of education 4.0. *Technological Forecasting and Social Change*, *194*, 122664. DOI: 10.1016/j.techfore.2023.122664

Murray, C., Alonzo, A., & Kuhlman, K. (2020). Predictive analytics in higher education: Leveraging data to improve student retention. *The Journal of Higher Education Management*, *35*(2), 5–15.

Nissenbaum, H. (2010). *Privacy in Context: Technology, Policy, and the Integrity of Social Life*. Stanford University Press.Binns, R. (2018). "Fairness in Machine Learning: Lessons from Political Philosophy." *Proceedings of the 2018 Conference on Fairness, Accountability, and Transparency*.

Nursalim, A., Judijanto, L., & Asfahani, A. (2022). Educational revolution through the application of AI in the digital era. *Journal of Artificial Intelligence and Development*, *1*(1), 31–40.

O'Brien, H. L., & Toms, E. G. (2008). What is user engagement? A conceptual framework for defining user engagement with technology. Journal of the American Society for Information Science. *Journal of the American Society for Information Science and Technology*, *59*(6), 938–955. DOI: 10.1002/asi.20801

O'Neil, C. (2016). *Weapons of math destruction: How big data increases inequality and threatens democracy*. Crown Publishing Group.

O'Neil, C. (2016). *Weapons of Math Destruction: How Big Data Increases Inequality and Threatens Democracy*. Crown Publishing Group.

Omar, Z. F., Mior Harun, M. H., Mohd Ishar, N. I., Mustapha, N. A., & Ismail, Z. (2024). Enhancing professional development and training through AI for personalized learning: A framework to engaging learners. *International Journal of e-Learning and Higher Education (IJELHE), 19*(3), 115-138.

Ouyang, F., & Zhang, L. (2024). AI-driven learning analytics applications and tools in computer-supported collaborative learning: A systematic review. *Educational Research Review, 44*, 100616. DOI: 10.1016/j.edurev.2024.100616

Papamitsiou, Z., & Economides, A. A. (2014). Learning analytics and educational data mining in a nutshell: A systematic literature review. *Journal of Educational Technology & Society, 17*(4), 49–64.

Pappano, L. (2020). The learning future: 5 ways AI can help students. *The New York Times*. Retrieved from https://www.nytimes.com/2020/03/05/education/learning-future-ai.html

Pardo, A., Mirriahi, N., & Gašević, D. (2019). Academic performance prediction in blended and online learning: The role of social networks. *Internet and Higher Education, 42*, 13–21. DOI: 10.1016/j.iheduc.2019.04.002

Pardo, A., & Siemens, G. (2014). Ethical and privacy considerations in learning analytics. *Proceedings of the Fourth International Conference on Learning Analytics and Knowledge*, 1-5. DOI: 10.1145/2567574.2567585

Pazzani, M. J., & Billsus, D. (2007). "Content-Based Recommendation Systems." In *The Adaptive Web* (pp. 325-341). Springer. DOI: 10.1007/978-3-540-72079-9_10

Pérez, F. J., Pérez, P. A., & García, J. E. (2021). AI-driven assessment: A new approach for complex cognitive skills. *Computers & Education, 167*, 104179. DOI: 10.1016/j.compedu.2021.104179

Piaget, J. (1971). *The construction of reality in the child*. Ballantine Books.

Piaget, J. (1976). *The Child and Reality: Problems of Genetic Psychology*. Viking Press.

Picciano, A. G. (2017). Theories and frameworks for online education: Seeking an integrated model. *Online Learning: the Official Journal of the Online Learning Consortium, 21*(3), 166–190. DOI: 10.24059/olj.v21i3.1225

Pistono, A. M. A. de A. (2023). Influence of adaptability of Serious Games on learning outcomes and the application of knowledge and skills in professional training. https://hdl.handle.net/10348/12187

Pistono, A. M. A. de A., dos Santos, A. M. P., Baptista, R. J. V., & Mamede, H. S. (2024). Framework for adaptive serious games. Computer Applications in Engineering Education, n/a(n/a), e22731. DOI: 10.1002/cae.22731

Pistono, A. M. A. A., Santos, A. M. P., & Baptista, R. J. V. (2021). A Review of Adaptable Serious Games Applied to Professional Training. *Journal of Digital Media & Interaction*, *4*(11), 60–85. DOI: 10.34624/jdmi.v4i11.26419

Popenici, S. A. D., & Kerr, S. (2017). Exploring the impact of artificial intelligence on teaching and learning in higher education. *Research and Practice in Technology Enhanced Learning*, *12*(1), 22. DOI: 10.1186/s41039-017-0062-8 PMID: 30595727

Praveen, J. V. S. (2024). Understanding the potential impact of AI-powered classroom management on student engagement, and overall learning outcomes. *Global Journal of Business and Integral Security*, *1*(2).

Rasheed, Z., Ghwanmeh, S., & Abualkishik, A. Z. (2023). Harnessing artificial intelligence for personalized learning: A systematic review. *Data and Metadata*, *2*, 146–146. DOI: 10.56294/dm2023146

Regan, P. M., & Jesse, J. (2021). Data privacy in education: An analysis of policies and practices. *Education Policy Analysis Archives*, *29*(1), 1–22. DOI: 10.14507/epaa.29.4794

Rekha, K., Gopal, K., Satheeskumar, D., Anand, U. A., Doss, D. S. S., & Elayaperumal, S. (2024, May). AI-powered personalized learning system design: Student engagement and performance tracking system. In *2024 4th International Conference on Advance Computing and Innovative Technologies in Engineering (ICACITE)* (pp. 1125-1130). IEEE.

Rienties, B., Cross, S., & Zdrahal, Z. (2018). Implementing learning analytics in higher education: The role of institutional context. *European Journal of Higher Education*, *8*(3), 257–271. DOI: 10.1080/21568235.2018.1509733

Rivers, C., & Holland, A. (2022). Management education and artificial intelligence: Toward personalized learning. In *The future of management education* (pp. 184–204). Routledge.

Rizvi, S. (2023). Revolutionizing student engagement: Artificial intelligence's impact on specialized learning motivation. *International Journal of Advanced Engineering Research and Science*, *10*(09), 27–31. DOI: 10.22161/ijaers.109.4

Rodrigues, M. W., Isotani, S., & Zárate, L. E. (2018). Educational Data Mining: A review of evaluation process in the e-learning. *Telematics and Informatics*, *35*(6), 1701–1717. DOI: 10.1016/j.tele.2018.04.015

Rovai, A. P. (2002). Building Sense of Community at a Distance. *International Review of Research in Open and Distance Learning*, *3*(1). https://www.irrodl.org/index.php/irrodl/article/view/79

Ruksana, T. P. (2024). AI-driven pedagogy: Unveiling ChatGPT's influence in education. *Journal of Applied Science, Engineering, Technology and Management, 2*(01), 09-14.

Russell, S., & Norvig, P. (2020). *Artificial intelligence: A modern approach* (4th ed.). Pearson.

Saaida, M. B. (2023). AI-driven transformations in higher education: Opportunities and challenges. *International Journal of Educational Research and Studies*, *5*(1), 29–36.

Schneider, E. F., Browne, K., & Daugherty, J. (2021). Industry-academic partnerships in AI education: Strategies for success. *Journal of Business and Educational Leadership*, *8*(1), 45–61.

Sclater, N. (2017). Learning analytics: The current state of play in higher education. Jisc Report. https://www.jisc.ac.uk/reports/learning-analytics-the-current-state-of-play-in-higher-education

Sclater, N., Peasgood, A., & Mullan, J. (2016). Learning analytics in higher education. JISC. https://www.jisc.ac.uk/reports/learning-analytics-in-higher-education

SCORM vs xAPI. (2012, July 24). xAPI.com. https://xapi.com/scorm-vs-the-experience-api-xapi/

SCORM®. (n.d.). ADL Initiative. Retrieved May 2, 2020, from https://www.adlnet.gov/projects/scorm/

Serrano-Laguna, Á., Martínez-Ortiz, I., Haag, J., Regan, D., Johnson, A., & Fernández-Manjón, B. (2017). Applying standards to systematize learning analytics in serious games. *Computer Standards & Interfaces*, *50*, 116–123. DOI: 10.1016/j.csi.2016.09.014

Shadiev, R., & Liu, M. (2020). The role of artificial intelligence in distance education: A review. *Computers & Education*, *150*, 103835. DOI: 10.1016/j.compedu.2020.103835

Sharples, M., & Domingue, J. (2016). The blockchain and education. *Proceedings of the 15th European Conference on e-Learning*, 25-32.

Shurygin, V., Berestova, A., Litvinova, T., Kolpak, E., & Nureyeva, A. (2021). Universal Models and Platforms in E-Learning. [Education Source.]. *International Journal of Emerging Technologies in Learning*, *16*(9), 63–75.

Shute, V., & Rahimi, S. (2017). Formative assessment and adaptive learning: A tale of two practices. *Educational Psychologist*, *52*(4), 211–227. DOI: 10.1080/00461520.2017.1363880

Shute, V., & Rahimi, S. (2020). Intelligent Tutoring Systems: A Review of Research and Practice. *Educational Psychology Review*, *32*(4), 827–855. DOI: 10.1007/s10648-020-09517-2

Siemens, G. (2014). Learning analytics: The emerging role of artificial intelligence in education. *Educational Technology Magazine*, 54(6), 24-28. https://www.learntechlib.org/p/147905/

Siemens, G. (2005). Connectivism: A learning theory for the digital age. *International Journal of Instructional Technology and Distance Learning*, *2*(1), 3–10.

Siemens, G. (2013). "Learning Analytics: The Emergence of a New Learning Discipline." *Journal of Educational Technology & Society*, 16(2), 14-20. Wang, F., & Wang, Q. (2019). "The Impact of Learning Analytics on Personalized Learning: A Systematic Review. *Journal of Educational Computing Research*, *57*(4), 962–994.

Siemens, G. (2013). Learning analytics: The emergence of a discipline. *The American Behavioral Scientist*, *57*(10), 1409–1410. DOI: 10.1177/0002764213498851

Siemens, G. (2013). Learning analytics: The emergence of a new educational technology. In *Education and Information Technologies* (pp. 1–11). Springer., DOI: 10.1007/s10639-012-9256-2

Siemens, G., & Long, P. (2011). Penetrating the Fog: Analytics in Learning and Education. *EDUCAUSE Review*, *46*(5), 30–32. https://er.educause.edu/articles/2011/11/penetrating-the-fog-analytics-in-learning-and-education

Skinner, B. F. (1953). *Science and human behavior*. Macmillan.

Skinner, B. F. (1953). *Science and Human Behavior*. Simon and Schuster.

Slade, S., & Prinsloo, P. (2013). Learning analytics: The challenges of the ethical use of data. *Proceedings of the 3rd International Conference on Learning Analytics and Knowledge*, 114-118.

Smith, D. M., & McKinnon, D. H. (2021). Faculty development in online education: A systematic review of the literature. *International Journal of Online Pedagogy and Course Design*, *11*(4), 1–24. DOI: 10.4018/IJOPCD.20211001.oa4

Streicher, A., & Smeddinck, J. D. (2016). Personalized and Adaptive Serious Games. In R. Dörner, S. Göbel, M. Kickmeier-Rust, M. Masuch, & K. Zweig (Eds.), Entertainment Computing and Serious Games: International GI-Dagstuhl Seminar 15283, Dagstuhl Castle, Germany, July 5-10, 2015, Revised Selected Papers (pp. 332-377). Springer International Publishing. DOI: 10.1007/978-3-319-46152-6_14

Suresh Babu, C. V., Anniyappa, C. S., & Sastha, B. D. (2024). Unraveling the Inner Workings of Massive Language Models: Architecture, Training, and Linguistic Capacities. In B. Gupta (Ed.), Challenges in Large Language Model Development and AI Ethics (pp. 239-279). IGI Global. DOI: 10.4018/979-8-3693-3860-5.ch008

Suresh Babu, C. V., & Adhithya, S. (2023). ChatGPT and Other Generative AI Tools in Education: Transformative Potential and Ethical Considerations. In Keengwe, J. (Ed.), *Creative AI Tools and Ethical Implications in Teaching and Learning* (pp. 135–152). IGI Global., DOI: 10.4018/979-8-3693-0205-7.ch007

Suresh Babu, C. V., & Auroshaa, A. (2024). Influence of Data Analysis Tools in Teaching and Learning Economics. In Scott, B., & Fox, M. E. (Eds.), *Cases on Economics Education and Tools for Educators* (pp. 229–248). IGI Global., DOI: 10.4018/978-1-6684-7583-6.ch010

Suresh Babu, C. V., & Rohan, B. (2023). Evaluation and Quality Assurance for Rapid E-Learning and Development of Digital Learning Resources. In Santally, M., Rajabalee, Y., & Rajputh, R. (Eds.), *Implementing Rapid E-Learning Through Interactive Materials Development* (pp. 139–170). IGI Global., DOI: 10.4018/978-1-6684-4940-0.ch008

Swargiary, K. (2024). *The impact of AI-driven personalized learning on mathematics achievement and student engagement in rural vs. urban schools in Karnataka*. Google.

Talent Development Glossary Terms. (n.d.). Retrieved July 15, 2024, from https://www.td.org/talent-development-glossary-terms

Tapalova, O., & Zhiyenbayeva, N. (2022). Artificial Intelligence in Education: AIEd for Personalised Learning Pathways. *Electronic Journal of E-Learning, 20*(5). *Electronic Journal of e-Learning*, *5*(5), 639–653. Advance online publication. DOI: 10.34190/ejel.20.5.2597

Topping, K. J., & Ehly, S. W. (1998). *Peer-assisted learning: A guide for teachers*. Routledge.McTighe, J., & O'Connor, K. (2005). *Understanding by Design*. ASCD. https://doi.org/DOI: 10.1111/tct.12583

Trust, T., & P. A. (2016). Professional development for educators in the age of technology. *TechTrends*, *60*(4), 366–371. DOI: 10.1007/s11528-016-0053-5

Tsai, Y.-S., Whitelock-Wainwright, A., & Gašević, D. (2021). More Than Figures on Your Laptop: (Dis)trustful Implementation of Learning Analytics. *Journal of Learning Analytics, 8*(3). *Journal of Learning Analytics*, *3*(3), 81–100. Advance online publication. DOI: 10.18608/jla.2021.7379

Tschofen, C., & Dawley, L. (2013). Connectivism and learner autonomy in MOOCs. *International Review of Research in Open and Distance Learning*, *14*(4), 87–103.

U.S. Department of Education. (2020). *Family Educational Rights and Privacy Act (FERPA)*. Retrieved from FERPA.

U.S. Department of Education. (2021). Distance Education Enrollment Report. https://nces.ed.gov/programs/digest/d21/tables/dt21_301.10.asp

Upadhyay, A. K., & Khandelwal, K. (2019). Artificial intelligence-based training learning from application. *Development and Learning in Organizations*, *33*(2), 20–23. DOI: 10.1108/DLO-05-2018-0058

VanLehn, K. (2011). “Educational Software.” *Handbook of Human-Computer Interaction*, 3, 978-1008.Kay, J., & Kummerfeld, B. (2016). “Adaptive Learning Technologies: A Review of the Literature.” *Journal of Educational Technology & Society*, 19(1), 10-21.Knewton. (2015). “The Rise of Adaptive Learning: How Technology is Personalizing Education.” Knewton Report.

VanLehn, K. (2011). The effectiveness of intelligent tutoring systems: A meta-analysis. *Educational Psychologist*, *46*(3), 197–207. DOI: 10.1080/00461520.2011.550993

VanLehn, K. (2011). The Relative Effectiveness of Human Tutoring, Intelligent Tutoring Systems, and Other Tutoring Systems. *Educational Psychologist*, *46*(4), 197–221. DOI: 10.1080/00461520.2011.610732

VanLehn, K. (2018). The relative effectiveness of human tutoring, intelligent tutoring systems, and other tutoring systems. *Educational Psychologist*, *53*(2), 108–138. DOI: 10.1080/00461520.2018.1442494

Vashishth, T. K., Sharma, V., Sharma, K. K., Kumar, B., Panwar, R., & Chaudhary, S. (2024). AI-driven learning analytics for personalized feedback and assessment in higher education. In *Using traditional design methods to enhance AI-driven decision making* (pp. 206–230). IGI Global. DOI: 10.4018/979-8-3693-0639-0.ch009

Vygotsky, L. S. (1978). *Mind in society: The development of higher psychological processes*. Harvard University Press.

Wang, F., & Wang, Q. (2019). The Impact of Learning Analytics on Personalized Learning: A Systematic Review. *Journal of Educational Computing Research, 57*(4), 962–994.

Wang, Q., Li, X., & Yang, Y. (2021). Professional development for teachers: Using learning analytics to improve instruction. *Journal of Computer Assisted Learning, 37*(5), 1426–1438.

Wang, X., Wu, Y., & Wang, Y. (2020). The impact of AI on educational outcomes: A review of empirical research. *International Journal of Educational Technology in Higher Education, 17*(1), 1–24. DOI: 10.1186/s41239-020-00218-6

Wang, Y., Wang, Y., & Wang, Y. (2020). Predictive analytics in education: A systematic review. *International Journal of Educational Technology in Higher Education, 17*(1), 1–24. DOI: 10.1186/s41239-020-00219-x

What is Artificial Intelligence (AI)? (2023, August 25). https://www.ibm.com/topics/artificial-intelligence

Widono, S., Saddhono, K., Nurhasanah, F., Nugraheni, A. S. C., & Legowo, B. (2024, May). A strategic design of personalized based learning system for improving the experience of outcome based education. In *2024 4th International Conference on Advance Computing and Innovative Technologies in Engineering (ICACITE)* (pp. 1149-1154). IEEE. DOI: 10.1109/ICACITE60783.2024.10616811

Williamson, B., & Piattoeva, N. (2021). Education governance and datafication: The challenges of data privacy. *International Journal of Education Policy and Leadership, 16*(1), 1–15. DOI: 10.22230/ijepl.2021v16n1a404

Winne, P. H., & Baker, R. S. (2013). Analytics in support of self-regulated learning. Handbook of Learning Analytics, 1(1), 105-114.

Woolf, B. P. (2010). *Building Intelligent Interactive Tutors: Student-Centered Strategies for Revolutionizing E-learning*. Morgan Kaufmann.Smith, R. (2013)

World Economic Forum. (2020). The COVID-19 pandemic has changed education forever. This is how. https://www.weforum.org

Wouters, P., van der Spek, E. D., & van Oostendorp, H. (2009). Current Practices in Serious Game Research: A Review from a Learning Outcomes Perspective. In Games-Based Learning Advancements for Multi-Sensory Human-Computer Interfaces: Techniques and Effective Practices (pp. 232–250). IGI Global. DOI: 10.4018/978-1-60566-360-9.ch014 xAPI officially Becomes a Published IEEE Standard. (n.d.). ADL Initiative. Retrieved July 9, 2024, from https://adlnet.gov/news/2023/11/22/xAPI-Officially-Becomes-a-Published-IEEE-Standard/

xAPI Serious Games profile: A Serious Games Profile for the Experience API (xAPI). (n.d.). Retrieved December 12, 2021, from https://adlnet.gov/news/2016/12/09/a-serious-games-profile-for-xapi/

xAPI-Spec: The xAPI Specification describes communication about learner activity and experiences between technologies. (n.d.). Github. Retrieved November 25, 2022, from https://github.com/adlnet/xAPI-Spec

Xu, Z. (2024). AI in education: Enhancing learning experiences and student outcomes. *Appl. Comput. Eng*, *51*(1), 104–111. DOI: 10.54254/2755-2721/51/20241187

Ye, D. (2022). The History and Development of Learning Analytics in Learning, Design, & Technology Field. *TechTrends*, *66*(4), 607–615. DOI: 10.1007/s11528-022-00720-1

Yekollu, R. K., Bhimraj Ghuge, T., Sunil Biradar, S., Haldikar, S. V., & Farook Mohideen Abdul Kader, O. (2024, February). AI-driven personalized learning paths: Enhancing education through adaptive systems. In *International Conference on Smart Data Intelligence* (pp. 507-517). Springer Nature Singapore. DOI: 10.1007/978-981-97-3191-6_38

Zawacki-Richter, O., Marinsky, V., & Dhanjal, K. (2019). The role of AI in lifelong learning. *International Journal of Educational Technology in Higher Education*, *16*(1), 1–15. DOI: 10.1186/s41239-019-0171-7

Zawacki-Richter, O., Marín, V. I., Bond, M., & Gouverneur, A. (2019). Systematic review of research on artificial intelligence applications in higher education – Where are we now and where are we going? *International Journal of Educational Technology in Higher Education*, *16*(1), 1–20. DOI: 10.1186/s41239-019-0171-0

Zawacki-Richter, O., Marín, V. I., Bond, M., & Gouverneur, A. (2019). Systematic review of research on artificial intelligence applications in higher education—What are the implications for students and educators? *International Journal of Educational Technology in Higher Education*, *16*(39). Advance online publication. DOI: 10.1186/s41239-019-0176-8

Zhang, K., Liu, Y., & Zhao, J. (2018). A survey on deep learning for big data. *Artificial Intelligence Review*, *50*(4), 557–580. DOI: 10.1007/s10462-018-9623-1

Zhao, Y., & Watter, M. (2020). Artificial intelligence in education: Trends and challenges. *International Journal of Artificial Intelligence in Education*, *30*(3), 366–387. DOI: 10.1007/s40593-020-00210-3

About the Contributors

Henrique S. Mamede is an Associate Professor with Habilitation at the Department of Sciences and Technology of Portuguese Open University. Invited Professor at the Information Management School of New University of Lisbon. He is a senior researcher at INESC TEC and at the HumanISE centre, having published over 100 scientific articles in conferences and journals. He holds a Ph.D. in Information Systems and Technologies, a M.Sc. in Informatics, and a B.Sc. in Computer Science and Engineering. He is a specialist in the digital transformation of organizations and information systems. He has more than 30 years of experience in academia and as a consultant, having worked in management in the corporate sector.

Arnaldo Santos is an Assistant Professor at the Department of Sciences and Technologies of Portugal Open University. Invited Professor at the Department of Communication and Art of the University of Aveiro. He is a vice director of the doctorate program in web sciences and technology. He completed his PhD studies at the University of Aveiro, where he obtained degrees in Communication Sciences and Technology. He has participated as author and coauthor in 4 books and more than 100 papers published in international conferences and journals, as well as in several research projects. His current research interests are Learning Organizations, Digital Transformation, Learning Systems and Knowledge Management. He has more than 25 years of experience in management in the Corporate Sector, where he was the Communication and Learning Director.

***

Alvaro Marcos Antonio de Araujo Pistono is a recognized expert in Educational Technology, known for his extensive academic and professional career. He currently serves as the Chief Learning and Innovation Officer (CLIO) at playNwhere, a spinoff of Fábrica de Cursos EdTech, a company he co-founded in

1998. In this role, he drives innovation in the Brazilian e-learning market, significantly contributing to the advancement of education through technology. Alvaro holds a PhD in Web Science and Technology from UTAD/Open University. He strengthened his expertise in Distance Education by specializing in the Planning, Implementation, and Management of Distance Education at Fluminense Federal University. He also holds a degree in Mechanical and Automotive Engineering from the Military Institute of Engineering, where he completed his Master's in Science. This solid academic background has provided him with a strong technical foundation for his subsequent work in Educational Technology.

Swadhi R. Research Scholar, Department of Physics, have rich experience in the the field of Nano materials, interdisciplinary research published more than 15 research articles and book chapters with reputed publishers.

R. Vettriselvan is an Associate Professor, AMET University, specialised in HRM and Marketing. He is acting as Mentor, Saraswathi Institute of Medical Sciences, Hapur. He served as Review Board member, National Council for Higher Education, Malawi, Head of the Department, School of Commerce and Management Studies, St. Eugene University, Zambia, and Director, Research and Publication, St. John the Baptist University, Malawi. He has published 28 books and 95 articles in peer reviewed journals and edited book chapters. Under his guidance two have completed and five are pursuing their PhD.

Palanivel Rathinasabapathi Velmurugan is associated with BSBI, Berlin, as a professor in the Human Resource Management and Finance Stream. Prior to joining BSBI, he held the designation "Head" Faculty of Management at Sharda University, Uzbekistan, Central Asia, and "Dean of Arts" assignments at DMI St. John the Baptist University, Malawi, Central Africa. Also, he has been associated earlier with DMI St. Eugene University in Zambia, MAM Business School and various Engineering Colleges in India. He has a Ph.D. in Management from Mannonmanium Sundaranar University in India. Besides this, he holds an MBA Degree from SRM University in India and a BE Chemical Engineering degree from Annamalai University in India. Also, he completed six NPTEL Certificate Programs conducted by various IITs in India. He brings with him 15 years of rich working experience in teaching and research. Furthermore, he has a keen interest in the Case Method of teaching and research. He is an academic out of passion. Not only that, but he also takes a keen interest in guiding Ph.D. students. He has supervised three Ph.D. research scholars under his supervision at DMI St. Eugene University in Zambia.

Jimmy Carter Regins is a dedicated Assistant Professor of Business Administration at Bishop Heber College, Trichy, Tamil Nadu, India, who brings a wealth of knowledge and practical expertise to the classroom, shaped by his prior experience in the corporate sector. With a strong academic foundation and hands-on exposure to real-world business dynamics, he specializes in areas such as strategic management, organizational behavior, and entrepreneurial development. His teaching philosophy emphasizes bridging the gap between theory and practice, ensuring students are well-prepared to tackle modern business challenges. Known for his innovative teaching techniques and commitment to student growth, Mr.Jimmy fosters critical thinking and leadership skills among his students. In addition to his teaching responsibilities, he actively engages in research, academic collaborations and professional development initiatives, contributing significantly to the field of business education and inspiring the next generation of business leaders.

C.V. Suresh Babu is a pioneer in content development. A true entrepreneur, he founded Anniyappa Publications, a company that is highly active in publishing books related to Computer Science and Management. Dr. C.V. Suresh Babu has also ventured into SB Institute, a center for knowledge transfer. He holds a Ph.D. in Engineering Education from the National Institute of Technical Teachers Training & Research in Chennai, along with seven master's degrees in various disciplines such as Engineering, Computer Applications, Management, Commerce, Economics, Psychology, Law, and Education. Additionally, he has UGC-NET/SET qualifications in the fields of Computer Science, Management, Commerce, and Education. Currently, Dr. C.V. Suresh Babu is a Professor in the Department of Information Technology at the School of Computing Science, Hindustan Institute of Technology and Science (Hindustan University) in Padur, Chennai, Tamil Nadu, India.

Catherin T. C. is an Associate Professor, AMET Business School, AMET University, specialised in HRM and Marketing. He is acting as Mentor, Saraswathi Institute of Medical Sciences, Hapur. He served as Review Board member, National Council for Higher Education, Malawi, Head of the Department, School of Commerce and Management Studies, St. Eugene University, Zambia, and Director, Research and Publication, St. John the Baptist University, Malawi. He has published 20 books and 75 articles in peer reviewed journals and edited book chapters. Under his guidance two have completed and five are pursuing their PhD.

Muhammad Usman Tariq has more than 16+ year's experience in industry and academia. He has authored more than 200+ research articles, 110+ case studies, 85+ book chapters and several books other than 4 patents. He is founder and CEO of The Case HQ, a unique repository for courses, narrative and video case studies. He has been working as a consultant and trainer for industries representing six sigma, quality, health and safety, environmental systems, project management, and information security standards. His work has encompassed sectors in aviation, manufacturing, food, hospitality, education, finance, research, software and transportation. He has diverse and significant experience working with accreditation agencies of ABET, ACBSP, AACSB, WASC, CAA, EFQM and NCEAC. Additionally, Dr. Tariq has operational experience in incubators, research labs, government research projects, private sector startups, program creation and management at various industrial and academic levels. He is Certified Higher Education Teacher from Harvard University, USA, Certified Online Educator from HMBSU, Certified Six Sigma Master Black Belt and has been awarded PFHEA, SMIEEE, and CMBE.

Index

A

C

D

E

F

G

I

L

M

O

P

R

S

T

U

V

X

www.ingramcontent.com/pod-product-compliance
Lightning Source LLC
LaVergne TN
LVHW081328300926
849161LV00008B/1914
* 9 7 9 8 3 6 9 3 7 1 9 5 4 *